Study Guide

for use with

Adolescence

Eighth Edition

John W. Santrock
University of Texas at Dallas

Prepared by
Elaine Cassel
Marymount College

Boston Burr Ridge, IL Dubuque, IA Madison, WI New York San Francisco St. Louis
Bangkok Bogotá Caracas Lisbon London Madrid
Mexico City Milan New Delhi Seoul Singapore Sydney Taipei Toronto

McGraw-Hill Higher Education

A Division of The McGraw-Hill Companies

Study Guide for use with
ADOLESCENCE, EIGHTH EDITION
JOHN W. SANTROCK

Published by McGraw-Hill Higher Education, an imprint of The McGraw-Hill Companies, Inc.,
1221 Avenue of the Americas, New York, NY 10020. Copyright © The McGraw-Hill Companies,
Inc., 2001, 1998. All rights reserved.

This book is printed on acid-free paper.

2 3 4 5 6 7 8 9 0 QPD/QPD 0 3 2 1 0

ISBN 0-07-232350-7

www.mhhe.com

Contents

Preface

How to Use the Study Guide

You are about to undertake the challenging and exciting task of learning about biological, cognitive, and sociocultural influences on adolescents. This *Study Guide* will assist you as you read *Adolescence* by John W. Santrock. It will help you learn and test your understanding of key terms and key persons as well as facts and theories covered in the text. Do remember, however, that its use should supplement rather than substitute for a careful and thorough reading of the text. Each chapter of this *Study Guide* contains several features designed to help you master the content of the chapter in *Adolescence:*

- Learning Objectives with Key Terms in Boldface
- Key Terms
- Key People
- Section Guided Reviews
- Section Reviews
- Explorations in Adolescent Development
- Adventures for the Mind
- Adolescence in Research
- Comprehensive Review
- Adolescence in Books
- Adolescence in Movies
- Answer Key
- Cognitive Maps Exercise

Each chapter of the *Study Guide* presents a detailed set of learning objectives in which key terms designated by the author appear in boldface. I have organized these objectives by major chapter headings, and subheadings, and numbered them accordingly. For example, the first section after the Preview and Images of Adolescents in each chapter is numbered 1.0, and the associated objectives are numbered 1.1, 1.2, and so forth. These objectives cover all material in the chapter, including the Explorations in Adolescent Development and Adventures for the Mind features. The learning objectives indicate as specifically as possible what you should be able to do after you have read and mastered the material in a chapter.

I recommend that you make extensive use of the learning objectives. For example, it is a good idea to review the key terms before and after you read each section, or subsection, of a chapter. In addition, you should review the learning objectives before you do the guided and section reviews. Consistent and extensive review of the learning objectives will help you better learn and remember the chapter content, and that in turn, will help you do your best on the examinations.

Key Terms

Devise your own definitions for these key terms based on your understanding of the text's definitions or on how you use the key terms in a sentence. This is important because you will not know whether you really understand a term until you can define it and use it in your own way.

Key People

This feature asks you to match the key person involved in adolescent research (related to the chapter's content) to the idea or concept with which they are associated. Some of these people will be featured in the margins of the main text with quotations about their theories and research. In all cases, the individual's research will have been discussed in the chapter.

Guided Review

Each chapter heading has its own Guided Review, a fill-in-the-blank activity that helps you review and study the material in the chapter. To benefit most from the Guided Review:

1. Review the Learning Objectives for the section of the chapter.
2. Reread the corresponding section, or subsection, of the chapter.
3. Complete the Guided Review for the section.
4. Check your answers in the Answer Key.
5. Review the learning objectives and textbook for questions that were difficult to answer.

Section Review

Most sections have their own Section Review consisting of a variety of exercises that help you review and study particularly important concepts and material in the chapter. The activities include matching, classifying, completing tables, and short-answer questions.

Explorations in Adolescent Development

Each chapter has one or more features about current research or programs related to adolescent development. The activity generally asks you to respond with short answers to general questions about the feature.

Adventures for the Mind

Each chapter has two or more exercises that ask you to think about specific concepts and principles and apply them to your own life and respond from your personal experience and opinion. For these activities there are generally no answers provided, since they will be unique to each student.

Adolescence in Research

We have chosen research discussed in the chapter and ask you to analyze the research hypothesis, methods, and conclusions and suggest the relevance of the findings for adolescent development.

Comprehensive Review

Each chapter contains a selection of multiple-choice questions that cover the main content of the chapter. They help prepare you to take a multiple-choice exam, as well as reviewing the entire chapters' content one last time.

Adolescence in Books and Movies

After the comprehensive review you will find suggestions for books and movies that explore or depict some facet of the chapter material.

Answer Key

At the end of each Study Guide chapter is the Answer Key. Keep in mind that the answers given for short-answer questions are merely as guide, as individual responses will vary. If you have any questions about whether your answer is accurate after referring to the answer given, always refer to the text for conformation and clarification.

Cognitive Map Exercises

This feature is to reinforce what you have learned in the earlier Key Terms and Key People exercises. You are asked to fill-in the blanks. Answers are provided at the end.

Some Final Thoughts . . .

This *Study Guide* contains activities that will enhance your ability to learn and remember knowledge about *Adolescence*. However, effective studying involves more than the specific things you do to learn the material; it includes developing good general study habits, plans, and strategies.. . . *about active learning*: The learning activities in the *Study Guide* are designed to encourage you to be an active learner. Research has shown that study activities not really help unless you use them in a very active way (e.g., working through the guided review and study on your own, and checking the material you could not remember). If you agree with us, I hope that all of the activities in this *Study Guide* will be useful both as ready-made suggestions for study and as models for activities that you invent on your own to help you achieve your own course goals and objectives.

Okay, so that's the structure of the chapters in the Study Guide. Now, let's talk about effective ways to study. As I mentioned earlier, you may already know some of these ideas, but oftentimes they can bear repeating because you say to yourself, "Oh, yeah, I knew that. I tried it before and it worked, but then for some reason I stopped. I think I'll try it again." Other ideas may be new to you, so you may want to give them a try. Remember that we are all unique, so some strategies work better for some people than for others--try out a suggestion for a fair period of time (only you can decide what "fair" is), and if it works, great--if it doesn't try something else. Read the next section, written by Anita Rosenfield of DeVry Institute of Technology, Southern California, for some more in-depth tips and suggestions on how to succeed in this and other courses.

Happy Learning!

Elaine Cassel

Being An Excellent Student

by Anita Rosenfield DeVry Institute of Technology, Southern California

Most students who are in college want to be good students, and most students have some particular goal in mind, which is probably why they chose the particular college or university they are attending. As you chose your college or university, and perhaps even an area of major interest or concentration, you had certain goals in mind, which likely included doing well in school, earning good grades, and graduating.

Unfortunately, many students do not do as well in college as they had hoped and expected. Let's examine some of the reasons for this disappointing outcome to see how to avoid them and to learn, instead, how to be a good student and guide your behavior to improve your chances of achieving your goals.

A common definition of education is that it is "how people learn stuff." For most of our history, educators have focused on the "stuff." Teachers were required to be masters of their respective academic fields. Even today, some states have requirements that speak only to the need to be qualified in the subject matter one teaches, not in the teaching methods themselves.

In the 1960s, we became more interested in the "people" part of the definition, which was evidenced by moving to strategies like open classrooms and free universities. The idea was that, given the opportunity to do so, people will naturally learn. Although these experiments were dismal failures, they taught us something.

The key to the definition of education is the word *how*. Today, thanks to a wealth of research on the principles that guide the phenomenon of learning, and on the nature of learning and memory, we know much more about how learning occurs and how we can make it better. By using these principles, we can become better students.

Formulating the Plan

Anything worth having is worth planning for. Whether you hope to learn to teach, to fly, to write for profit, or to change diapers correctly, you have in mind a goal. An everyday question from the first days in elementary school is, "What do you want to be when you grow up?" The answer to this question is one way of formulating a goal. Now that you are a college student, many people will expect you to know what you want to do for a profession or career. Yet you may not have the foggiest notion, or you might have an idea that is still slightly foggy. That is OK. What is clear, however, is that you want to succeed in your college courses. This is a relatively long-range goal, and as such can serve a purpose in keeping you on track.

But our day-to-day behavior is often hard to connect to our long-range goals. We need short-term goals to keep us organized and to be sure that the flow of our activities is in the direction we want to be going. To accomplish our long-range goals, we need to focus on three types of short-term goals. First, we need goals for the day; second, we need goals for the week; and third, we need goals for the semester or term. Let's look at each of these separately.

Goals for Today

It is helpful to keep a daily checklist, diary, or schedule as a reminder of what must be done each day. Check off the things as you accomplish them. A pocket calendar is particularly helpful for this task.

Goals for the Week

Students who are successful in college also schedule their time weekly. Sometime during the course of registration, you made up a schedule showing your classes for the whole week. If you have a job, you must allow time for that, too. Also, many college or university students have family obligations that need to be considered as well. Finally, everyone needs some time for relaxing, eating, sleeping, and playing (even in graduate school we were advised that we needed to find some time to have fun in order to keep our balance). With all these things in mind, it is no wonder many students find little time to study.

But good students do all these things, too, yet they study. Do they have more time? No, we all have the same amount of time. But successful students schedule their time carefully. So, make up a weekly schedule and block off time for all these necessary events: classes, work, relaxation, eating, sleeping, playing, family, and studying. Students who actually schedule their time and keep to their schedules are amazed at how much time they find they have!

As you make up your weekly schedule, you may find your study time in a large block. If this is true, please remember to take a short break every twenty to thirty minutes. This is called distributed practice and is far more efficient than studying for hours on end. After the first twenty or thirty minutes, most of us become much less efficient anyway. When you take that break, reward yourself somehow; then get back to your studying. Something I always tell my students is never to try to read a whole chapter in one sitting. In fact, when I am preparing for a new class, or have changed texts in a class I have been teaching, I take that advice myself!

Goals for the Semester

At the beginning of each semester, we find ourselves immersed in many new courses. Often, you will be confronted by several new professors with whom you have never worked before. It is difficult to sort out the expectations and demands of these several courses. However, it is important to organize the information that will be needed for completing all of the course requirements in order to be successful in the courses.

If you can, obtain a large wall calendar, and mark on it all the dates of tests, exams, and term paper due dates, being sure to write on the calendar the course for which each date applies. Now, estimate how long it will take you to make final preparations for those exams, and mark those dates as warning or alert dates. Look over the dates on which papers are due, and see if they are bunched together. If your college is typical, they will probably be close. You can help yourself to avoid the last-minute all-nighters if you simply determine a spread of due dates for yourself, and mark those on the calendar too. As you do this step, please be sure to avoid any days that have personal significance for you, such as birthdays, anniversaries, and so on. This calendar gives you an overview of major dates in your semester.

If you have followed this carefully, you now have a large semester calendar plastered on your wall, a weekly schedule of major life events, classes, and study times taped over your desk, and a daily checklist of must-do items in your pocket or purse. **So, your scheduling is on its way. Let's look now at other important strategies.**

Attending Classes

Many students believe that, since they are in college, they can decide whether to go to class at all. This is true. Some students also believe that attendance in class is not important to their grade. This is not true!

Some colleges or universities have attendance requirements, so that if students miss a given number of classes it will either lower their grade a full letter grade, or the instructor may drop the student from the course; some instructors have in-class activities that count toward students' grades, so if students are not in class, they do not get credit for participating. Even without such strategies, students who do not attend class sessions almost always do more poorly on the tests and exams. Perhaps they were absent when a crucial item was discussed, or when the instructor lectured over the material this examination requires. Remember, that more often than not, instructors will include information in their lectures that is not in your textbook, and that information (whether from class lecture, videos shown in class, guest lectures, and so on) is fair game for tests. Moreover, if you are not there, the instructor cannot get to know you, and therefore cannot give you the benefit of the doubt on your answers. It should come as no surprise that in study after research study, the data clearly show that those students who attend class regularly receive the highest grades and actually learn more, too! So, the first rule of being an effective student is to attend classes. Besides, how else can you get your money's worth?

But okay, now that you've determined you will go to every class, what will you do?

Benefiting from Lectures

Sometimes students think that if they come to class and "pay attention," they will remember what the instructor talked about; they think that if they take notes, they will miss much of what the instructor says. But sitting and paying attention is difficult. For one thing, most people can think much faster than they can speak. While the instructor lectures at 80 words per minute, the student thinks at about 350 words per minute! If the student is using this extra "thinking capacity" to focus on what the instructor is saying, it is fine. This rarely lasts more than five minutes at a time, however. Most of the time, this extra "thinking capacity" is used in daydreaming!

Daydreaming can be helpful in resolving our emotional problems, planning the course of our lives, and avoiding work. Often, it is motivated by the desire to avoid work. For whatever motive, however, daydreaming is not compatible with attending a lecture. Human beings simply cannot attend to more than one stimulus at one time. And you have to admit, your daydreams can be ever so much more interesting than your professor's lectures.

Attending lectures is best done while. Use plenty of paper, and leave blank lines at regular intervals, or leave wide side margins. You will use these spaces later (they are not wasted!). If the instructor permits it, be brave and interrupt with questions if you do not understand what is being said. One thing I try to stress to my students is that I may know what I am talking about, but it may be unclear to them--and if it's unclear to one student, it may well be unclear to other students. So, for the sake of the other students who didn't understand what I was talking about, each student should take on the responsibility of asking me to clarify what I said, or to expand in a way that will help them understand. Remember that lectures have a way of progressing and building on earlier information. It is important to understand each point, or later points will be lost. (But please, DO NOT ask the person sitting next to you what the professor said--it disrupts the class, disturbs your neighbor, and you are likely NOT to get an accurate response!)

When you take notes, write out the major points, and try to just make simple notes on the supporting minor points. If you miss something, and you cannot ask a question about it, approach the instructor immediately afterward, when it is likely to still be fresh in both your minds. DO NOT try to write down every word, and DO try to use abbreviations or symbols, or, you could do what I did--learn shorthand! (Or, make up your own.)

Often my students will ask if they may tape record my lectures. Personally, I have no objection to having students do this. In fact, I did this my first term back in college but found it was terribly tedious trying to transcribe the lecture. The students for whom this may be particularly helpful are those who have visual, auditory, or motor impairments. However, do not ever tape record a lecture without first asking for and obtaining the professor's permission.

Within one or two hours after the lecture, on the same day, go back over your notes, and do two things. First, fill in the rest of the minor points. This often amounts to completing the sentence or other element. Second, write brief summaries and any questions that you now have in the blank spaces (lines or margins) you left earlier (clever of you to leave those spaces!). These few minutes spent reviewing and organizing your notes will pay off in greatly improved memory. The questions you have you can ask in class, or during the instructor's office hours, and reap two benefits. First, you will get the answers. Second, you will demonstrate that you are a serious student, and that will impress your instructor.

One other thing about going to class. While this is not always true, I have found that typically my best students sit in front. And most students seem to have a need to have "their seat," while a few students have a need to move around, sitting in one seat one day and a different seat the next. It wasn't until my graduate school days that I realized why I needed "my seat"--as a student, we are being overwhelmed with new information, a stressful experience; we need some structure we can count on to reduce that stress. So, if you are one of those who likes to wander, be considerate of your classmates' needs for stress reduction.

By the way, to get the most out of the lectures, do complete the assigned reading BEFORE the class begins so you are familiar with the material. This will help you keep up with what the instructor is talking about, will reduce the amount of information you do not understand, but may also bring up important questions for you to ask in class if the instructor does not talk about them.

Reading For Learning

We all know how to read. You are proving it by reading these words. Hopefully, you are also realizing some ideas as a result of reading. If you are only reading words, please WAKE UP! STOP DAYDREAMING!

We can read a variety of things: newspapers, movie reviews, novels, magazines, and textbooks. Textbooks are unlike all the others, and must be read with a strategy all their own.

There are many reading and studying strategies, and all of them work to an extent. Perhaps you learned one or more in the course of going to high school. Perhaps you even took a how-to-study course when you entered college. If so, you probably learned one or two of these systems. If you have one you like, that works for you, keep it. If you are interested in learning a new one, read on.

The PQ4R Method

One of the most successful and most widely used methods of studying written material was the SQ3R method, first developed at The Ohio State University. Researchers had noted that students who were more successful were more active readers. More recently, this method has been updated to the PQ4R Method, which adds an additional step. This method teaches you the same skills that have made many thousands of students successful. If you use this method when you read and study, you will be more successful, too. I have outlined the steps below and the text describes this method in Chapter 13.

The P stands for PREVIEW. After you have read the overview or chapter outline, and the list of learning objectives, you should survey the chapter in the text. This is also called skimming. Look at the headings and subheadings, and get the gist of the major points in this chapter. Check off each point in the outline of this Study Guide as you pass it in the pages of the text.

The Q stands for QUESTION. Reading is greatly enhanced if you are searching for the answers to questions. For this text, the Student Study Guide provides learning objectives that can serve as questions. For other texts, make up questions for yourself, based on the chapter overview or on your own survey of the chapter. Be sure that you have at least one question for each major unit in the chapter; you will be less efficient at studying those units for which you do not have questions.

The first of the four Rs is for READ. As you read, look for the answers to the questions you posed, or to the study or learning objectives furnished for you. When you find material that answers these questions, put a mark (X) or a "post-it" note in the margin next to that material. This will help now, since you are actively involved, and later, when you review. It is a good idea to wait to underline or highlight lines of text until after you have read the entire chapter at least once, so you will know what is and what is not most important. (In fact, while some "authorities" suggest you underline or highlight no more than 10% of what you are reading, I find that when most of us begin to underline or highlight, we wind up doing it to most of the chapter--I suggest not doing it at all because it becomes too passive, which counteracts your attempts to read "actively.")

The second R stands for REFLECT. As you are reading, stop every so often and reflect on the material to increase its meaningfulness. This includes analyzing the material, thinking about how to apply it to your own life, interpreting the information, and connecting it with information you already have in your long-term memory.

The third R is for RECITE. One of the oldest classroom techniques in the world (Aristotle used it) is recitation. In the classroom version, the teacher asks the questions and the students answer them. Unless you can get your teacher to study with you regularly, you'll have to play both roles. Periodically stop in your reading and say aloud (if possible) what the author is telling you. Try to put it in your own words, but be sure to use technical terms as you learn them. If you are not in a situation where you can recite out loud, do it in writing. Just thinking it is not enough. When should you pause to recite? A good rule of thumb is that each time you come to the end of a major subheading, you should recite. One professor encourages his students to recite at least one sentence at the end of each paragraph, and two or three or more sentences at the end of each subunit (when you come to a new heading).

People who do not use recitation usually forget half of what they read in one hour, and another half of the half they remembered by the end of the day. People who use recitation often remember from 75 to 90 percent of what they studied. This technique pays off. By the way, if anyone questions why you are talking to yourself, tell them that a psychologist recommended it.

The fourth R is for REVIEW. You should review a chapter soon after you have studied it (using the PQ and first 3Rs). You should review it again the day or evening before a test. It is not usually helpful to cram the night before a test, and particularly not the day of the test! That type of studying does not produce good memory, and is likely to make you more anxious during the test itself.

Taking Tests

One of the things students fear most is failure. Failure signifies that things are not going well, and alerts us to the possibility that we may not achieve our goals. Unfortunately, many students see tests and exams as opportunities to fail. They prepare by becoming anxious and fearful, and trying to cram as much as possible right before the exam. These students rarely do well on the exam. They often fail, thus accomplishing just what they feared.

Taking tests requires strategy and planning. First, it is helpful to know what type of tests you will have. Your instructor probably told you during the first class meeting, or it may be in the class syllabus or course outline. If you do not know, ask.

If you are going to be taking essay exams, the best way to prepare is by writing essays. Before you do this, it is a good idea to find out what types of questions the instructor asks, and what is expected in a response. Again, it is helpful to ask the instructor for this material. Perhaps you can even see some examples of essay questions from previous years--some instructors at some colleges have copies of their exams on file in the department office or in the library. By finding out what is expected, you can formulate a model against which you can evaluate your answers.

Now, using the learning objectives, or some essay questions you wrote, actually sit down and write out the answers. I have prepared at least two essay questions for each chapter in this text. HINT: If you usually feel more anxious during a test, it may help you to practice writing your essays in the room in which the test will be given. Simply find a time when the room is vacant, and make yourself at home.

If your instructor gives multiple-choice tests, then you should practice taking multiple-choice tests. For each chapter, either use questions provided in the Student Study Guide, or make up your own. You may find it helpful to work out an arrangement to pool questions with other students, thereby reducing the amount of work you have to do, and developing a network of friends. Or, you may ask your professor if he or she would entertain the idea of having students write some of the exam questions--some of my professors did that in my undergraduate classes, and it is something I sometimes have my students do.

Whichever way you do it, the important thing is to prepare for tests and exams. Preparation is about 95 percent of the secret to getting a good grade. (Yes, there is some actual luck or chance involved in test scores, as even your instructor will admit!) Preparation is not only a good study and review technique, but also helps to reduce anxiety.

Dealing With Test Anxiety

Anxiety can be a helpful response when it occurs at low levels. In 1908, Yerkes and Dodson showed that the amount of anxiety that could benefit performance was a function of the difficulty and complexity of the task. As the difficulty of the task rose, anxiety became less helpful and more likely to interfere with performance.

If you have ever been so anxious in a test situation that you were unable to do well, even though you knew the information, you have test anxiety. If you get your exams back, and are surprised that you marked wrong answers when you knew the correct answers, or if you can only remember the correct answers after you leave the examination room, you too may have test anxiety.

Strategy Number One: Effective Study

Use study habits that promote learning and make the best use of time. Strategies, such as scheduling your time and using the PQ4R system, reduce anxiety by increasing confidence. As you come to realize that you know the material, your confidence rises and anxiety retreats.

Strategy Number Two: Relaxation

Each of us develops a unique pattern of relaxation. Some people relax by going to a specific place, either in person or mentally. Others relax by playing music, by being with friends, by using autogenic relaxation phrases, or by meditating. Whatever you do, be aware of it, and try to practice relaxation techniques. If you are good at relaxing, try thinking about those situations that make you anxious, and relax while you think of them. To do this, allow yourself to think only briefly (fifteen to thirty seconds at a time) of the situation that makes you anxious, and then relax again. After a number of such pairings, you will find that thinking about that situation no longer makes you anxious. At this point, you may be surprised to find that the situation itself also no longer produces anxiety. You may find that it is helpful to think about these anxiety-provoking situations in a sequence from those that produce very little anxiety to those that are more anxiety-evoking. Such a list, from low to high anxiety, might look something like this:

1. Your instructor announces that there will be a test in four weeks.
2. Your instructor reminds you of the test next week.
3. As you study, you see on the course outline the word *test*, and remember next week's test.
4. One of your friends asks you if you want to study together for the test, which is the day after tomorrow.
5. You choose not to go out with your friends because of the test tomorrow.
6. As you get up in the morning, you remember that today is the day of the test.
7. You are walking down the hall toward the classroom, thinking about what questions might be on the test.
8. The instructor enters the classroom, carrying a sheaf of papers in hand.
9. The instructor distributes the papers, and you see the word *test* or *exam* at the top.
10. After reading the first five questions, you have not been able to think of the answer to any of them.

If you work at it gradually and consistently, pairing these types of thoughts (briefly) with relaxation and remembering to let go and relax after each one, this will dispel test anxiety and make test taking a more productive and successful experience.

Strategy Number Three: Thinking Clearly

Most students who have test anxiety think in unclear and unproductive ways. They say to themselves things like: "I can't get these answers correct . . . I don't know this stuff . . . I don't know anything at all . . . I'm going to fail this test . . . I'm probably going to flunk out of school . . . I'm just a dumb nerd." These thoughts share two unfortunate characteristics: they are negative and they are absolute. They should be replaced.

When we tell ourselves negative and absolute thoughts, we find it impossible to focus on the test material. The result is that we miss questions even when we know the answers. Our thinking prevents us from doing well.

A good strategy for replacing these negative and absolute thoughts is to practice thinking positive and honest thoughts, such as: "I may not know all the answers, but I know some of them . . . I don't know the answer to that right now, so I will go on to the next one and come back to that . . . I don't have to get them all right . . . I studied hard and carefully, and I can get some of them correct . . . I am a serious student, and have some abilities . . . I am prepared for this test, and know many of the answers . . . This test is important, but it is not going to determine the course of my entire life and if I don't do well, it doesn't mean I'm a horrible person or a dummy."

By thinking clearly, honestly, and positively, we quiet the flood of anxiety and focus on the task at hand. Students who use this technique invariably do better on the tests. It takes practice to think clearly, but it is worth the effort. After a while, you will find that it becomes natural and does not take any noticeable effort. And as anxiety is reduced, more energy is available for studying and for doing well on examinations. The eventual outcome is more enjoyment with learning, better learning, more success in college, and the achievement of your goals.

Strategy Number Four: Guided Imagery

Something I often do with my students before a test is to have them relax (see strategy Two), close their eyes, and visualize themselves walking into a tall building. They go into the elevator in the building and take it to the top floor, which is fifty-six stories up. They walk out of the elevator, and go to the stairwell, then climb to the top of the building. There is no railing on the top of the building. I direct them to walk over to the very edge of the building and put their toes at the very edge, then look down. I ask them to think about how they are feeling as they are looking down onto the street from the top of this building. I then tell them to back up, have the realization that they can fly--just spread out their arms and they can fly. Then they are directed back to the edge of the building, knowing that they can fly. They put their toes on the edge, look down, then spread their arms and fly, eventually flying down to land safely on the ground below. Next I have them visualize themselves in the classroom; on the desk before them is their test. They look at the test and see themselves reading the questions, saying "I know that answer. Yes, I remember learning that." They visualize themselves being successful, answering all the questions correctly, feeling good about themselves. Then I have them visualize getting their tests back, with a big "A" on the test.

Some students are much better able to visualize than others. You can try combining strategy two with this strategy to help you improve your visualization, since it can be an effective success strategy.

Strategy Number Five: Do the Easy Ones First
One technique I learned while studying for the GRE (Graduate Record Exam) was to read each question and answer the ones I knew, then go back to the harder ones. Two things to watch out for on this: first, be sure you get the answers in the right place--sometimes when we skip a question or two, we wind up marking the wrong space, so check that your answer to question 10 is in space 10; second, you may find you're stumped by the first several questions--don't let that throw you, just keep going because there is bound to be one you jump on and say, "Yes! I know that one." Answer the easy ones first, then go back to the others after you've built up your confidence seeing you DO know "stuff." Then, always go back over the whole test to be sure you answered every question (the exception here is if you have a professor who takes more than one point off for wrong answers--in that case, it's better not to answer than to answer wrong, but I don't know anyone who does that).

Strategy Number Six: State Dependent Learning
Research has found that we remember information best when we are in the same "state" we were in when we first learned the information. So, for example, you might remember a certain song when prompted by a specific stimulus (seeing someone who reminds you of your "first true love"); or, we will remember

things we learned when we were particularly happy if we are again in that mood. This goes for physical contexts as well--so that we have an advantage if we take an exam in the same room where we learned the information in the first place. But it also goes to physical context in terms of our bodies--if you drink coffee or caffeine-laden sodas when you study, try to do the same before your exam. On the other hand, if you don't consume caffeine when you study, by all means, DO NOT suddenly have a cup of coffee before your exam. Because of the power of this phenomenon, you may want to create a particular mental context for yourself when you study so that you can put yourself into the same mental context when you take your exams.

Strategy Number Seven: Take a Break

If you find yourself getting stressed out during the test, take a break. Put your pencil down, breath deeply, you may even want to put your head down on the desk (please, do not fall asleep!). Use the relaxation techniques or the guided imagery strategy; visualize yourself looking at the test and suddenly realizing that you DO know the answers to at least most of the questions. Then go back to taking the test.

Remember, that with all of these test taking strategies, if you don't do the first one, none of the others will help! Passing the course requires that you actively study the material.

Memory Techniques

No matter how much you read, it won't help you if you don't remember *what* you read. The most critical factor in remembering is being able to apply what you have learned. Of course, some things such as people's names, or certain dates, or statistical information are not easily applied to your life, so you'll have to use other techniques. But first, let's talk about the "easy way."

Apply It To Your Life

If you can take the material you are learning and use it in your everyday life, you will remember it without any problem. Connect it with what you already know, either from life experience or other courses you have taken. Sometimes what you are learning fits nicely with what you already knew; sometimes it will contradict what you learned before. This is an opportunity to look at how the new information fits in with the old--were there new research findings? Or, is it merely a difference of opinion? Make these associations--don't keep the information for any class neatly compartmentalized--if you do, you'll have a hard time trying to find it when you need it.

Teach It to Someone Else!

When we start teaching something to someone else, we find we HAVE TO learn it, and by trying to explain the material to another person, we examine it and think about it differently. So, take the material you are learning in this class (or any class) and teach it to someone else. When they ask you questions, you can look them up and find the answers, or think them out together, or ask someone else. As you explain these concepts to someone else (your children, your friends, or even your dog), you will suddenly see them in a totally different light.

Mnemonic Techniques

Some things are just really difficult to apply to your own life. Dates, names, places, statistics, and such may not have a great deal of meaning for you. In that event, use the tricks that memory specialists use-- mnemonics. There are many different types. For example, one famous mnemonic is an acronym for remembering the Great Lakes: HOMES=Huron, Ontario, Michigan, Erie, and Superior; or the colors of the rainbow is a man's name: ROY G. BIV=Red, Orange, Yellow, Green, Blue, Indigo, and Violet (if not for this "man," I'd never remember indigo!) You can make up your own acronyms by taking the first initial of any term, person, etc. It's easiest, though, if it's something that makes sense to you.

Another mnemonic technique is called the "method of loci," and I've been told it's one that medical students use to remember body parts. You list the things you need to remember, then visualize yourself walking around a familiar place (like your living room), putting one item on a particular piece of furniture. Then, when you need to remember that item, you go through your "living room" to see where it is.

One other mnemonic technique is the story method. Take the information you need to remember and put it into a story.

Be an "Information Dropper"

This is similar to the suggestion to teach, but less formal. Ask your friends to "indulge" you by listening to what you learned in your Life Span Development class (or any other class). Then *tell* them what you are learning. You may, in fact, find that you have managed to help one of your friends by sharing this information!

Rote Memory

If you can remember back to grade school, when you learned to multiply, somehow the only way that seems to happen is by repeating the multiplication tables over and over and over again. Personally, I think this is about the worst way to learn most anything, but for some things (like multiplication tables) it works. The Flashcards that are included in each chapter of this Study Guide are a way to help you learn through repeating the material you don't know until you are able to answer the questions posed without looking at the reverse side of the cards. Hopefully you will then go further, and apply the information to other areas of your life.

Most Important

Remember this: professors don't actually "teach" their students, rather, they facilitate learning so students end up teaching themselves. While we try really hard to motivate our students, keep them interested, and present information in a way that helps students to understand, the ultimate responsibility for learning rests with the student. Some students have learned *despite* their professors, others don't learn even with the very best of professors. So, keep your goals in mind, study hard, ask questions, and aim for success!

Further Resources

Making the Grade Student CD-ROM

Packaged for **FREE**, this user-friendly CD-ROM gives students an opportunity to test their comprehension of the course material in a manner which is most comfortable and beneficial to them. Included are practice tests for each chapter that cover topics in the adolescent development course and an internet primer.

On-Line Learning Center http://www.mhhe.com/santrocka8

An expansive resource for students, this site includes:

- Self-assessment quizzes for each chapter
- Study tools, including crossword puzzles
- Links to relevant web sites
- PowerPoint Presentations
- Adolescent Development Image Gallery

McGraw-Hill Developmental Psychology Supersite http://www.mhhe.com/developmental

This website provides valuable resources to help you , such as Interactive exercises and simulations and links to some of the best developmental psychology sites on the web.

For those of you with "Print Disabilities" including blindness, visual impairment, learning disabilities or other physical disabilities, please check out the **Recording for the Blind and Dyslexic website** at **www.rfbd.org/** or call customer service at **(800) 221-4792**. This educational library has 77,000 taped titles including textbooks, and reference and professional materials for people who cannot read standard print because of a disability.

We Want to Hear from You!

Help us to improve the quality of future supplements. Take a moment to visit our website and share your thoughts by completing our supplements evaluation form. Your feedback will greatly help us in the future. The form is located at:

http://www.com/developmental

APA Style

For information on APA writing style and guidelines, please refer your students to the American Psychological Association's web site at http://www.apa.org, or link to this site by visiting Santrock's *Adolescence* On-Line Learning Center at http://www.mhhe.com/santrocka8

Using the Internet in Teaching Adolescence

There are numerous possibilities or ways to use the Internet when Adolescence courses. In fact, the shear vastness of available information is often overwhelming for both instructors and students alike. Most of you have some idea about how to search for information available on the Internet, but you need to have the critical thinking skills necessary to discern whether the information you are locating is valid and useful. The following five criteria may be helpful in assisting you with analyzing the appropriateness of information available on the Internet.

1. **Accuracy**

2. **Authority**

3. **Objectivity**

4. **Currency**

5. **Coverage**You can often struggle with search strategies or become easily frustrated if you cannot locate the type of information you want. There are several excellent tutorials available online which can assist in this process and most libraries have resources designed to help students create more sophisticated searching methodologies. The following sites may provide some assistance. **Tutorial for beginning users:** http://www.lib.berkeley.edu/TeachingLib/Guides/Internet/FindInfo.html

Created by the library staff at Berkeley this is an excellent place for both instructors and students to learn more about using the Internet. The tutorial is divided into two sections with the first providing information about how to access the Internet and use Netscape. The second part of the tutorial discusses how to search for information and includes a comparative chart of the best five search engines, explanations of meta-search tools, and convenient handouts which can be used for class exercises. Also available in the handouts section are Power Point slides and instructor's notes.

Guide to Meta-search engines:

http://www.indiana.edu/~librcsd/search/meta.html

This is a useful description of 13 meta-search engines with links to each and can aid both instructors and students in searching for Internet resources.

◆ Chapter 1   Introduction

Learning Objectives with Key Terms and Key People in Boldface

1.0   What is the Historical Perspective on Adolescence?
  A.   Early History
    1.1   How would you compare Plato and Aristotle's views of adolescence?
    1.2   What is the difference between society's views of childhood and adolescence during the Middle Ages and those expressed during the eighteenth century by **Jean-Jacques Rousseau**?
  B.   The Twentieth Century
    1.3   How did the concept of adolescence emerge between 1890 and 1920?
    1.4   What were the origins of **G. Stanley Hall**'s concept of adolescence?
    1.5   What was Hall's **storm-and-stress view** concept of adolescence?
    1.6   How important was Hall to the study of adolescence?
    1.7   What are the main points of **Margaret Mead**'s sociocultural view of adolescence and the most common criticisms of those views?
    1.8   What is the **inventionist view** of adolescence?
    1.9   Why do historians call the period of 1890 to 1920 the "age of adolescence?"
    1.10   How are schools, work, and economics important dimensions of the inventionist view?
    1.11   What were the consequences of the youth-related work and education laws enacted between 1890 and the 1920?
    1.12   How would you delineate the changes in the adolescent experience for each decade from the 1920s through the 1970s?
    1.13   What females and ethnic minority individuals have contributed to the study of adolescents?
  C.   Stereotyping Adolescents
    1.14   What is a **stereotype**, and what are the contemporary stereotypes of adolescence?
    1.15   What did Joseph Adelson mean by the **adolescent generalization gap**?
    1.16   What did research by **Daniel Offer** and his colleagues reveal about stereotypes of adolescence?
    1.17   How do personal experience and media portrayals contribute to stereotypical public attitudes toward adolescents?
2.0   What Are Adolescents Like Today?
  A.   Current Status
    2.1   Why is today both the best of times and the worst of times for adolescents?
    2.2   How would you compare the current status of adolescents and public attitudes toward them with that of adolescents of several decades ago?
    2.3   What differences in development among adolescents render them a heterogeneous group?
    2.4   What do we mean by **contexts** of development?
    2.5   What are the **sociocultural contexts** of development?

Key Terms

Write a sentence using each of these key terms by either defining the term or giving an example of it. For instance, you might write, "The storm-and-stress view of adolescence holds that..." or, "(give examples) are examples of behaviors that typify the storm-and-stress view of adolescence." Compare your definitions with those given at the end of study guide chapter; check your examples by referring to the text. Review the text for those terms you don't know or define incorrectly.

1. storm-and-stress view

   _____

   _____

2. inventionist view

   _____

   _____

3. stereotype

   _____

   _____

4. adolescent generalization gap

   _____

   _____

5. contexts

   _____

   _____

6. social policy

   _____

   _____

7. generational inequity

   _____

   _____

8. development

   _____

   _____

9. biological processes

   _____

   _____

10. cognitive processes

   _____

   _____

11.　socioemotional processes

_____

_____

12.　prenatal period

_____

_____

13.　infancy

_____

_____

14.　early childhood

_____

_____

15.　middle and late adulthood

_____

_____

16.　adolescence

_____

_____

17.　early adolescence

_____

_____

18.　late adolescence

_____

_____

19.　youth

_____

_____

20.　early adulthood

_____

_____

21.　middle adulthood

_____

_____

22.　late adulthood

_____

_____

23. maturation

_____

_____

24. nature-nurture controversy

_____

_____

25. continuity of development

_____

_____

26. discontinuity of development

_____

_____

27. early-later experience issue

_____

_____

Key People in the Study of Adolescence
Match the name with the concept, issue, or topic related to adolescence with which they are associated.

___	1. G. Stanley Hall	A.	Studied teenagers in Samoa
___	2. Margaret Mead	B.	Coined the term "youth"
___	3. Leta Hollingsworth	C.	The father of the scientific study of adolescence
___	4. Daniel Offer	D.	His work challenged the negative stereotypes of adolescents
___	5. Marian Wright Edelman	E.	First used the term "gifted" and challenged the theory of male superiority.
___	6. Bernice Neugarten	F.	Describe the importance of improving opportunities for at risk adolescents
___	7. Ruby Takanishi	G.	A child's rights advocate, who champions improvements in social policies affecting young people and their families
___	8. Kenneth Kenniston	H.	Believes that many segments of society, not just adolescents, are affected by inequities in our social and economic policies

Historical Perspective
Guided Review
Plato believed that (1) _____ made its first appearance in adolescence. Aristotle argued that the most important aspect of adolescence is (2) _____. In the Middle Ages, children and adolescents were viewed as (3) _____ and were treated with (4) _____ discipline. French philosopher Jean-Jacques Rousseau believed that development has (5) _____. The scientific exploration of adolescence began in the (6) _____ century. (7) _____ is considered the father of the scientific study of adolescence. His ideas were first published in (8) _____, and indicated the biological influence of (9) _____. Hall expressed the (10) _____ view, meaning that adolescence is a (11) _____ time charged with (12) _____ and _____. Margaret Mead believed that the basic nature of adolescents is (13) _____ and that adolescence is more stressful in cultures like the United States because (14) _____. The (15) _____ view says that adolescence is a (16)

5

_____ creation of the (17) _____ century. The important dimensions of the inventionist view are (18) _____, (19) _____, and (20) _____. Historians agree that the period of (21) _____was the "age of adolescence," mainly due to legislation concerning (22) _____ and _____. (23) _____ and (24) _____ characterized adolescence in the 1920s; the (25) _____ arrived in the 1930s, followed by (26) _____ in the 1940s. The 1950s saw a focus on (27) _____, while attention to (28) _____ characterized the 1960s. The 1970s were rocked by (29) _____ and the beginnings of the (30) _____ movement.

A stereotype is (31) _____ . Common stereotypes of adolescence are that they are all (32) _____, (33) _____, (34)_____, (35)_____, and (36) _____. Joseph Adelson called these widespread generalizations about adolescents the (37) _____, which comes from information about a (38) _____, but highly (39)_____ group of adolescents. Public attitudes about adolescence come from a combination of (40) _____ experience and (41) _____, neither of which are accurate.

Historical Perspective
Section Review

1. Compare and contrast Hall's storm-and-stress perspective of adolescence with Margaret Mead's sociocultural view.

_____

_____

2. Describe the social, economic, and political events between 1890 and 1920 that account for that period being known as the "age of adolescence."

_____

_____

3. a. Compare and contrast widespread stereotypes about adolescents with what Offer and his colleagues found out about how adolescents described themselves.

_____

_____

   b. What accounts for this adolescent generalization gap?

_____

_____

Today's Adolescents
Guided Review

Today we study adolescents in the (1) _____ of their development, meaning the (2)_____ in which development occurs. These are influenced by (3)_____, (4) _____, (5) _____, and (6) _____ factors, and consist of (7) _____, (8) _____, (9)_____, (10) _____, (11) _____, and (12) _____.

A government's course of action designed to influence the welfare of its citizens is known as its (13) _____. Some say that Americans engage in (14) _____, evidenced by the fact that older adults get more government resources than younger citizens.

Adolescents are not a (15) _____ group; they are (16) _____. (17) _____, (18) _____, (19) _____, (20) _____, (21) _____, and (22) _____ differences influence the development of every adolescent.

Today's Adolescents
Section Review
1.   List three facts of contemporary life that makes today "the best of times" for adolescents.

_____

_____

2.   List three facts of contemporary life that makes today "the worst of times" for adolescents.

_____

_____

3.   What are four examples that suggest that today's adolescents are growing up in a less stable environment than that of adolescents several decades ago.

_____

_____

4.   Why should the well being of adolescents be one of the major concerns for maker of social policy?

_____

_____

The Nature of Development
Guided Review
       The pattern of movement or change that occurs throughout the life span is known as (1) _____. (2) _____ processes involve changes in the individual's physical makeup. Cognitive processes involve changes in (3) _____ and (4) _____. Socioemotional processes involve changes in (5) _____, (6) _____, (7) _____, and (8) _____ contexts.
       Development is commonly divided into these periods: (9)_____; (10) _____, (11) _____; (12) _____, (13) _____, and (14) _____, (15) _____ and (16) _____ adulthood. Adolescence is the period of transition between (17) _____ and (18) _____ that involves (19) _____, (20) _____, and (21) _____ changes. In most cultures, adolescence begins at about ages (22) _____ to _____ and ends about ages (23) _____ to _____. Kenniston called the period between adolescence and adulthood (24) _____, and believed that it was a time of (25) _____ and (26) _____ temporariness that could last (27) _____ to _____ years or longer.
       The debate over whether development is primarily due to (28) _____ or (29)_____ is another version of the (30) _____ controversy. The issue involves whether development is (31) _____ or (32) _____ and whether (33) _____ experiences are more important to development than (34)_____ experiences. Most developmentalists refrain from taking an (35) _____ position on these issues.

7

The Nature of Development
Section Review
1.   Complete the table by giving the name and a brief description of the eight periods of development corresponding to the given ages.

Age	Name	Description
Prenatal		
Birth to 18–25 months		
2 to 5 years		
6 to 10–11 years		
10–13 to 18–22 years		
Late teens to early 20s and 30s		
35–45 to 55–65 years		
60–70 years to death		

2.   Explain the nature/nurture controversy in your own words, using any facet of adolescent physical, cognitive, or emotional development as an example.

_____

_____

Understanding Adolescence and Careers in Adolescence
Guided Review
        Those who study adolescent development are concerned with the roles of (1) _____, (2) _____, (3) _____, and (4) _____ as factors in adolescent biological processes. We need to know more about the cognitive processes of (5) _____ skills and (6) _____, as well as the nature of (7) _____. The key contexts or settings in which adolescent development occurs are (8) _____, (9) _____, (10) _____, and (11) _____. The components of adolescent social and personality development include (12) _____ and _____, (13) _____, (14) _____, (15) _____ development, and (16) _____. There is special interest in the (17) _____ of and (18) _____ in such adolescent problems and disorders as (19) _____, (20) _____, (21) _____, (22) _____ , and (23) _____ disorders. We need (24) _____ studies to help correct our (25) _____ and (26) _____ of adolescents. (27) _____ thinking is a key aspect too understanding adolescent development. Careers in adolescent development that require graduate and post-graduate education and training include (28) _____ and _____ teaching; (29)_____ or _____ psychology, (30) _____ counseling, or going to medical school and becoming a (31) _____.

Understanding Adolescence and Careers in Adolescent Development
Section Review
List ten characteristics and cognitive processes of critical thinkers.

_____

_____

Explorations in Adolescence

1.   Discuss how and why early alcohol use, drug experimentation, and poor success in school can lead a teenage boy to drop out of school and get in trouble with the law. How do these behaviors impact each other?

2.   Consider how growing up with an abusive father and having poor self-esteem could lead a teenage girl to sexual promiscuity and pregnancy. How do these behaviors impact each other?

3.   Considering your answers to numbers 1 and 2, do you think it is as important to provide opportunities to at-risk teenagers as it is to have programs to help them when they get into trouble?

Adventures for the Mind

1.   Choose any ethnic group other than your own. Imagine how your experiences would have been different in the following domains. Write the ethic group or culture that you have chosen here:
     _____

     a.   relationship with your parents

     _____

     b.   relationship with your peers

     _____

     c.   high school experience

     _____

     d.   your physical health and development

     _____

     e.   your moral and spiritual development

     _____

     f.   your intellectual development

     _____

     g.   your dating behavior and romantic relationships

     _____

     h.   the neighborhood in which you lived

     _____

     i.   your family's socioeconomic status

     _____

     j.   how you would be different today as a result of these variations in experience

     _____

2. Referring to the list of areas in number 1, pick the five areas that you think were the most influential in making you who you are today. Discuss the impact of your experiences in these areas on your adult development.

Adolescence in Research
Concerning Margaret Mead's 1928 study of Samoan adolescents, state the hypothesis, the research methods (if known), the research conclusions, and the implications and applications for adolescent development.

Comprehensive Review
1. That these times are the best of times for today's adolescents is indicated by the observation that
    a. crack cocaine is more addictive and deadly than marijuana.
    b. individuals have longer life expectancies that ever before.
    c. most families include a father who is the breadwinner, a mother, and children.
    d. television transmits powerful messages about sex and violence.

2. According to Plato, the distinguishing feature of the adolescent period was the development of
    a. reason.
    b. self-determination.
    c. virtues and morals.
    d. conformity to societal standards.

3. Stanley Hall described adolescence as a period of
    a. emotional stability.
    b. passivity and conformity.
    c. considerable turmoil.
    d. gradual socioemotional development.

4. Margaret Mead proposed that adolescents develop easily into adulthood if their environments are appropriately designed, after observing adolescents in
    a. Samoa.
    b. the Philippines.
    c.   the Trobriand Islands.
    d.   Mangia.

5. One of the most unconventional recommendations Margaret Mead made to Americans involved reducing adolescent turmoil by
    a. releasing adolescents from school at age 13.
    b. requiring all adolescents to work full time.
    c. encouraging sex play.
    d. requiring adolescents to live apart from their parents.

6. The current view of Margaret Mead's research on Samoan adolescents is that
    a. it was unbiased and error-free.
    b. it supports the inventionist view rather than G. Stanley Hall's view of adolescence.
    c. it exemplifies the adolescent generalization gap.
    d. their lives are more stressful than Mead observed.

7. Which of the following factors did *not* contribute to the invention of the concept of adolescence?
   a. child-saving legislation
   b. increased adolescent employment during the Great Depression
   c. the separation of work and the home
   d. the creation of a system of compulsory education

8. As compulsory laws regarding youth were enacted in the early twentieth century, employment of adolescents _____ and school attendance _____ .
   a. decreased; increased
   b. decreased; decreased
   c. increased; decreased
   d. increased; increased

9. You are reading a book about how children and adolescents have historically been treated by their parents. The book describes how a mother tries to imitate her daughter's dance steps. The historical passage probably referred to the
   a. 1890s.
   b. 1920s.
   c. 1940s.
   d. 1960s.

10. Which of the following is most likely to be true concerning perceptions of adolescents of the mid 1970s to the 1980s?
   a. They are less interested in physical fitness.
   b. They are more achievement-oriented.
   c. They engage in more radical protests than in the 1970s.
   d. They are less sexually permissive.

11. If you categorized all adolescents as rebellious, lazy, smart alecks, you would be using a(n)
   a. Sturm and Drang view.
   b. inventionist view.
   c. stereotype.
   d. generation gap view.

12. When you were an adolescent, your parents accused your generation of being lazy and having no respect for authority. Based on the research concerning parents' and adolescents' attitudes, you might have told your parents:
   a. "I guess we just have an insurmountable generation gap."
   b. "What you call a generation gap, I would call a generalization gap."
   c. "Although the majority of adolescents have a generation gap, I don't."
   d. "Only the parents of deviant adolescents have a generalization gap."

13. The research by Daniel Offer and his colleagues in 1988, which examined the self-images of adolescents around the world, had what effect on the belief that adolescents are highly stressed?
   a. It supported that belief.
   b. It challenged its accuracy.
   c. It proved that such a belief is inaccurate.
   d. It was inconclusive and therefore had no impact.

14. Sociocultural context refers to
    a. the setting in which development occurs.
    b. studies that allow comparisons between different cultures.
    c. the most important influences on development according to G. Stanley Hall.
    d. a term associated with inferiority and deficits in the cultural group in questions.

15. Ethnicity refers to
    a. one's cultural heritage, nationality, race, religion, and language.
    b. the fact that some ethnic groups in a society benefit disproportionately more than other ethnic groups in terms of national allocations of resources.
    c. a sociocultural dimension of femaleness and maleness.
    d. a sense of shared membership with an ethnic group.

16. A national government's actions that influence the welfare of its citizens defines the concept of
    a. family values.
    b. generational inequity.
    c. the inventionist viewpoint.
    d. social policy.

17. According to Marian Wright Edelman, president of the Children's Defense Fund, the most important function of our society should be
    a. eliminating violence.
    b. restructuring our educational system.
    c. parenting and nurturing the next generation.
    d. developing a healthy knowledge of the body and sexuality.

18. The concern that older members of the society benefit disproportionately more than younger members of the society in terms of national allocations of resources is the concept of
    a. generational inequity.
    b. social policy.
    c. the adolescent generalization gap.
    d. the storm and stress view.

19. Which of the following is *not* a major process contributing to the scientific study of development?
    a. cognitive
    b. biological
    c. socioemotional
    d. personal

20. According to G. Stanley Hall, the dominant process of adolescent development would be
    a. biological.
    b. cognitive.
    c. sexual.
    d. socioemotional.

21. Developmentalists subdivide the period of development before adolescence into _____ periods.
    a. two
    b. six
    c. four
    d. eight

22. If Kenneth Kenniston is correct, a youth would be expected to
    a. live in several different places.
    b. be confused about sexual orientation.
    c. avoid dating.
    d. be unable to secure full-time employment.

23. On the issue of maturation and experience, most developmentalists
    a. agree with the position of G. Stanley Hall.
    b. agree with the position of Margaret Mead.
    c. agree with the inventionist viewpoint.
    d. recognize the importance of their interaction.

24. Many developmentalists believe that humans progress through a number of defined stages in the course of their lives. John Santrock, the author of *Adolescence*, would say that these developmentalists see human development
    a. as discontinuous.
    b. as unstable.
    c. as dominated by environment.
    d. much as G. Stanley Hall did.

25. Most developmentalists avoid taking extreme positions on major developmental issues because
    a. differences between male and female adolescents are growing larger.
    b. heredity is nearly always a stronger force than environment
    c. adolescents are beginning their sexual encounters at earlier ages.
    d. simplistic explanations deny the complexity of human development.

Adolescence on the Screen

- *Cider House Rules* is about an orphaned boy whose identity search leads him back to what his foster father wanted for him.

- *The Talented Mr. Ripley* depicts a highly educated and charming sociopath.

- *Girl, Interrupted* concerns an adolescent's 1960s hospitalization in a private psychiatric facility.

- *October Sky* tells the story of budding rocket scientists in the 1950s in rural West Virginia.

- *Good Will Hunting* portrays the life and friends of a boy who grew up in foster homes and has learned to be self-sufficient, working as a janitor and living in a lower socioeconomic class neighborhood.

- *Tumbleweeds* follows a displaced single mother and her teenage daughter as they move from place to place and live on a shoestring while the mother looks for a man who will give them a better life.

- *Liberty House* depicts the changing sociopolitical climate of the 1950s, including integration, interracial dating, and changing family structure and influence.

Adolescence in Books

- *You and Your Adolescent* (*Second Edition*), by Laurence Steinberg (Harper Perennial, 1997), provides a broad, developmental overview of adolescence, with parental advice mixed in.

- *The Rise and Fall of the American Teenager*, by Thomas Hine (Avon, 1999), traces the evolution of American adolescence as a social invention shaped by the needs of the 20th century.

Answer Key

Key Terms
1. **storm-and-stress view** G. Stanley Hall's concept that adolescence is a turbulent time charge with conflict and mood swings
2. **inventionist view** The view that adolescence is a sociohistorical creation. Especially important in this view are the sociohistorical circumstances at the beginning of the Twentieth century, a time when legislation was enacted that ensured the dependency of youth and made their move into the economic sphere more manageable.
3. **stereotype** A broad category that reflects our impressions and beliefs about people. All stereotypes refer to an image of what the typical member of a particular group is like.
4. **adolescent generalization gap** Adelson's concept of widespread generalizations about adolescents based on information about a limited, highly visible group of adolescents.
5. **contexts** Settings in which development occurs. These settings are influenced by historical, economic, social, and cultural factors.
6. **social policy** A national government's course of action designed to influence the welfare of its citizens.
7. **generational inequity** The unfair treatment of younger members of an aging society in which older adults pile up advantage by receiving inequitably large allocations of resources, such as Social Security and Medicare.
8. **development** The pattern of change that begins at conception and continues through the life cycle. Most development involves growth, although it also includes decay (as in death and dying).
9. **biological processes** Changes in an individual's physical nature.
10. **cognitive processes** Changes in an individual's thinking and intelligence.
11. **socioemotional processes** Changes in an individual's relationships with other people, emotions, personality, and social contexts.
12. **prenatal period** The time from conception to birth.
13. **infancy** The developmental period that extends from birth to 18 or 24 months.
14. **early childhood** The developmental period extending from the end of infancy to about 5 or 6 years of age; sometimes called the preschool years.
15. **middle and late childhood** The developmental period extending from about 6 to about 11 years of age; sometimes called the elementary school years.
16. **adolescence** The developmental period of transition from childhood to early adulthood; it involves biological, cognitive, and socioemotional changes.
17. **early adolescence** The developmental period that corresponds roughly to the middle school or junior high school years and includes most pubertal change.
18. **late adolescence** Approximately the latter half of the second decade of life. Career interests, dating, and identity exploration are often more pronounced in late adolescence than in early adolescence.
19. **youth** Kenniston's term for the transitional period between adolescence and adulthood that is a time of economic and personal temporariness.
20. **early adulthood** The developmental period beginning in the late teens or early twenties and lasting into the thirties.
21. **middle adulthood** The developmental period that is entered at about 35 to 45 years and exited at about 55 to 65 yeas of age.
22. **late adulthood** The developmental period that lasts from about 60 to 70 years of age until death.
23. **maturation** The orderly sequence of changes dictated by a genetic blueprint.

24. **nature-nurture controversy** *Nature* refers to an organism's biological inheritance, *nurture* to environmental experiences. "Nature" proponents claim that biological inheritance is the most important influence on development; "nurture" proponents claim that environmental experiences are the most important.
25. **continuity of development** Gradual, cumulative change from conception to death.
26. **discontinuity of development** Development progressing through distinct stages in the life span.
27. **early-later experience issue** This issue focuses on the degree to which early experiences (especially early in childhood) or later experiences are the key determinants of development.

Key People in the Study of Adolescence

1. C	3. E	5. G	7. F
2. A	4. D	6. H	8. B

Historical Perspective
Guided Review

1. reason
2. self-determination
3. miniature adults
4. harsh
5. distinct phases
6. Twentieth
7. G. Stanley Hall
8. 1904
9. Charles Darwin
10. storm-and-stress
11. turbulent
12. conflict/mood swings
13. sociocultural
14. children are considered different

15. inventionist
16. sociohistorical
17. Twentieth
18. schools
19. work
20. economics
21. 1890–1920
22. school/employment
23. Autonomy
24. conformity to peers
25. Great Depression
26. World War II
27. laws
28. education
29. protests

30. feminist
31. broad category
32. rebellious
33. faddish
34. delinquent
35. self-centered
36. conflicted
37. adolescent generalization gap
38. limited
39. visible
40. personal
41. media portrayals

Historical Perspective
Section Review

1. Hall believed that adolescence is a turbulent time charged with conflict and mood swings. Mead believed that when a culture proves a smooth, gradual transition from childhood to adulthood, little storm and stress occurs.

2. Compulsory education and labor laws with strict enforcement provisions.

3.
   a.   The stereotype that adolescence is highly stressful and disturbed is not born out by studies of adolescents around the world, who indicate positive feelings toward themselves and their families and confidence in their ability to cope with life's stresses.
   b.   Personal experience and media portrayals, neither of with produces an objective view.

Today's Adolescents
Guided Review

1. contexts
2. settings
3. historical
4. economic
5. social
6. cultural
7. families
8. peers
9. schools
10. churches
11. neighborhoods
12. communities
13. social policy
14. generational inequity
15. homogenous
16. heterogeneous
17. socioeconomic
18. ethnic
19. cultural
20. gender
21. age
22. lifestyle

Today's Adolescence
Section Review

1. computers; longer life expectancies; television, satellites, and air travel
2. crack cocaine; television images of violence and sex; contradictory messages about sex
3. high divorce rates; high adolescent pregnancy rates; increased geographic mobility of families; adolescent drug use.
4. The future of youth is the future of society. If adolescents don't reach their full potential they will be able to contribute less to society.

The Nature of Development
Guided Review

1. development
2. Biological
3. thinking
4. intelligence
5. relationships with people
6. emotion
7. personality
8. social
9. prenatal
10. infancy
11. early childhood
12. middle childhood
13. adolescence
14. early
15. middle
16. late
17. childhood
18. adulthood
19. biological
20. cognitive
21. socioemotional
22. 10 - 13
23. 18 - 22
24. youth
25. personal
26. economic–8
27. 2–8
28. maturation
29. experience
30. nature/nurture
31. continuous
32. discontinuous
33. early
34. later
35. extreme

The Nature of Development
Section Review

Age	Name	Description
Conception to birth	Prenatal	Growth from a single cell to a complete organism
Birth to 18–25 months	Infancy	Dependency on adults; early psychological development
2 to 5 years	Early childhood	Children lean to care for self, develop school readiness, and play with peers
6 to 10–11 years	Middle and late childhood	Master reading, writing, and arithmetic, exposure to culture; self-control increases; achievement becomes a theme.
10–13 to 18–22 years	Adolescence	Biological, cognitive, and emotional changes; career interests, dating, and identity options explored in late adolescence.
Late teens to early 20s and 30s	Early adulthood	Establishing personal and economic independence; career development; starting a family
35–45 to 55–65 years	Middle adulthood	Transmitting values to the next generation; enhanced concerns about one's body; reflection on meaning of life
60–70 years to death	Late adulthood	Adjusting to decreasing strength and health, retirement and reduced income; adapting to changing social roles; increased freedom; parenthood

2. For instance, nature influences physical differences between boys and girls; but nurture accounts for changing gender roles.

Understanding Adolescence and Careers in Adolescence
Guided Review

1. heredity
2. environment
3. evolution
4. health
5. thinking
6. decision making
7. intelligence
8. families
9. peers
10. schools
11. culture
12. self/identity
13. gender
14. sexuality
15. moral
16. achievement
17. prevention
18. intervention
19. drug abuse
20. juvenile delinquency
21. depression
22. suicide
23. eating
24. scientific
25. individual observations
26. personal interpretations
27. Critical
28. high school/college
29. clinical/counseling
30. school
31. psychiatrist

Understanding Adolescence and Careers in Adolescent Development
Section Review
Critical thinkers think reflectively and productively and evaluate evidence. They are open-minded, intellectually curious, and look for multiple determinants of behavior. They analyze, infer, connect, synthesize, criticize, evaluate, think, and rethink.

Explorations in Adolescence
No answers given—personal reflection

Adventures for the Mind
No answers given—personal reflection

Adolescence in Research
Mead used observational methods to test her hypothesis that the basic nature of adolescence is not biological, but sociocultural. She concluded that the lives of Samoan adolescents had little storm and stress, because adolescents were not sheltered from observing sex, birth, and death, whereas in cultures like the United States where children are treated very differently than adults, adolescents experience more stress.

Comprehensive Review

1. b	6. d	11. c	16. d	21. c
2. a	7. b	12. b	17. c	22. a
3. c	8. a	13. b	18. a	23. d
4. a	9. b	14. a	19. d	24. a
5. c	10. b	15. a	20. a	25. d

◆ Chapter 2   The Science of Adolescent Development

Learning Objectives with Key Terms and Key People in Boldface

1.0   What Are the Nature and Characteristics of the Scientific Research Approach?
   A.   Why Research On Adolescent Development Is Important?
      1.1   Why is research on adolescent development important?
2.0   What is the Scientific Research Approach?
   A.   The Scientific Research Approach
      2.1   What are the steps in the **scientific method**?
      2.2   What is the difference between a **theory** and **hypotheses**?
3.0   What Are the Theories of Adolescent Development?
   A.   Psychoanalytic Theories
      3.1   What are the characteristics of Sigmund Freud's **psychoanalytic theory**?
      3.2   What are the **id**, **ego**, and **superego**?
      3.3   What are **defense mechanisms**?
      3.4   What is **repression**?
      3.5   What are the characteristics of Freud's **oral**, **anal**, **phallic**, **genital**, and **latency** stages?
      3.6   What did Freud mean by **erogenous zones**?
      3.7   What is the **Oedipus complex**?
      3.8   How does Erik Erikson's theory differ from that of Freud?
      3.9   What are the characteristics of Erikson's eight life span stages—**trust versus mistrust, autonomy versus shame and doubt, initiative versus guilt, industry versus inferiority, identity versus identity confusion, intimacy versus isolation, generativity versus stagnation, and integrity versus despair**?
   B.   Cognitive Theories
      3.10   What are the three major theories of **cognitive development**?
      3.11   What are the characteristics of Piaget's stages cognitive development—the **sensorimotor**, **preoperational**, **concrete operational**, and **formal** stages?
      3.12   How does the cognitive theory of **Lev Vygotsky** differ from that of **Piaget**?
      3.13   What are the main concerns of the **information processing** theory?
   C.   Behavioral and Social Cognitive Theories
      3.14   What do **behavioral** and **social cognitive** theories emphasize?
      3.15   What is the main emphasis of **behaviorism**?
      3.16   What is the essence of Bandura's **social cognitive theory**?
   D.   Ecological, Contextual Theories
      3.17   How does Urie Brofenbrenner's **ecological theory** explain adolescent development?
      3.18   What are the characteristics of the five systems that make up Brofenbrenner's ecological theory—the **microsystem**, **mesosystem**, **exosystem**, **macrosystem**, and **chronosystem**?
      3.19   What is the emphasis of Glenn Elder's **life course theory**?
   E.   Eclectic Theoretical Orientation
      3.20   What is meant by an **eclectic theoretical orientation**?

4.0   **What Research Methods Are Used to Study Adolescent Development?**

    A.   **Research Methods**

        4.1   What is the difference between observation in a **laboratory** and **naturalistic observation**?

        4.2   How are **interviews** and **questionnaires** used to study adolescent development?

        4.3   What do **standardized tests** contribute to our understanding of adolescent development?

        4.4   What are **case studies**?

        4.5   What is the goal of **correlational research**?

        4.6   What does **experimental research** allow us to conclude about behavior?

        4.7   What is the difference between the **independent variable** and the **dependent variable**?

        4.8   What are the functions of the **experimental group** and the **control group**?

        4.9   What is **random assignment**?

        4.10   What is the advantage of using **multiple measures**, **sources**, and **contexts** to study adolescent development?

        4.11   What is the difference between **cross-sectional research** and **longitudinal research**?

    B.   **The Field of Adolescent Development Research**

        4.12   What are the main outlets for research about adolescent development?

        4.13   What organizational format is used in research journals?

5.0   **What Are the Main Challenges Faced by Researchers of Adolescent Development?**

    A.   **Research Challenges**

        5.1   What are the main challenges faced by researchers in adolescent development?

    B.   **Ethics**

        5.2   What **ethical considerations** guide researchers?

    C.   **Gender**

        5.3   What **gender considerations** do researchers need to take into account?

    D.   **Culture and Ethnicity**

        5.4   What do **ethnicity** and **culture** have to do with research into adolescent development?

        5.5   What is **ethnic gloss**?

        5.6   What is **nomothetic research**?

        5.7   What is meant by **idiographic needs**?

    E.   **Being a Wise Consumer of Information About Adolescent Development**

        5.8   What six rules should you follow in order to be a wise consumer of information about adolescent development?

6.0   **Explorations in Adolescent Development**

        6.1   In what way did Leo Vygotsky influence Bronfenbrenner's beliefs about human development?

        6.2   What was Glen Elder's contribution to Bronfenbrenner's theories?

7.0   **Adventures for the Mind**

        7.1   How do your personal views about adolescence compare to those of psychologists?

Key Terms
Write a sentence using each of these key terms by either defining the term or giving an example of it. For instance, you might write, "The storm-and-stress view of adolescence holds that..." or, "(give examples) are examples of behaviors that typify the storm-and-stress view of adolescence." Compare your definitions with those given at the end of study guide chapter, and check your examples by referring to the text. Review the text for those terms you don't know or define incorrectly.

1. scientific research

_____

_____

2. scientific method

_____

_____

3. theory

_____

_____

4. hypotheses

_____

_____

5. id

_____

_____

6. ego

_____

_____

7. superego

_____

_____

8. defense mechanisms

_____

_____

9. repression

_____

_____

10. erogenous zones

_____

_____

11.   oral stage

_____

_____

12.   anal stage

_____

_____

13.   phallic stage

_____

_____

14.   latency stage

_____

_____

15.   genital stage

_____

_____

16.   trust versus mistrust

_____

_____

17.   autonomy versus shame and doubt

_____

_____

18.   initiative versus guilt

_____

_____

19.   industry versus inferiority

_____

_____

20.   identity versus identity confusion

_____

_____

21.   intimacy versus isolation

_____

_____

22. generativity versus stagnation

_____

_____

23. integrity versus despair

_____

_____

24. sensorimotor stage

_____

_____

25. preoperational stage

_____

_____

26. concrete operational stage

_____

_____

27. formal operational stage

_____

_____

28. information processing

_____

_____

29. behavioral and social cognitive theories

_____

_____

30. behaviorism

_____

_____

31. social cognitive theory

_____

_____

32. ecological theory

_____

_____

33. microsystem

_____

_____

34. mesosystem

_____

_____

35. exosystem

_____

_____

36. macrosystem

_____

_____

37. chronosystem

_____

_____

38. life course theory

_____

_____

39. eclectic theoretical orientation

_____

_____

Key People in the Study of Adolescence

Match the name with the concept, issue, or topic related to adolescence with which they are associated.

____	1.	Sigmund Freud	A. Associated with social cognitive theory
____	2.	Peter Blos	B. Eight psychosocial stages
____	3.	Anna Freud	C. Four cognitive stages
____	4.	Karen Horney	D. Five systems in which adolescents develop
____	5.	Nancy Chodorow	E. Associated with behaviorism
____	6.	Erik Erikson	F. Contextual life course theory
____	7.	Jean Piaget	G. Five psychosexual stages
____	8.	B. F. Skinner	H. Believed that regression is a normal aspect of puberty
____	9.	Albert Bandura	I. Believed that women define themselves in terms of relationships
____	10.	Walter Mischel	J. Believed that defense mechanisms are the key to understanding adolescent adjustment
____	11.	Urie Bronfenbrenner	K. Coined the term cognitive social learning theory; associated with Albert Bandura
____	12.	Glenn Elder, Jr.	L. Believed that planful competence in late adolescence was linked with adult success
____	13.	John Clausen	M. Associated with the first feminist-based criticism of Freud's theory

Why Research on Adolescent Development is Important/Scientific Research Approach
Guided Review

We get information from personal (1) _____ and (2) _____ or _____. Because these sources often do not agree, we need (3) _____ research. (4)_____ research is (5) _____, (6) _____, and (7) _____. It reduces the probability that information will be based on (8) _____, (9) _____, or (10) _____. Scientific research is based on the scientific method, which includes these steps: (11) _____, (12) _____, (13) _____, and (14) _____. A theory is a (15) _____ set of (16) _____ that helps to (17) _____ and make (18) _____. (19) _____ are derived from theories.

Why Research on Adolescent Development is Important/Scientific Research Approach
Section Review

Label each stage and describe what would be done in each stage of a scientific study of mentoring.

Number	Name	Description
One		
Two		
Three		
Four		

Theories of Adolescent Development
Guided Review

The four major theories of adolescent development are (1) _____, (2) _____, (3) _____, and (4) _____-learning. For (5) _____ theorists, development is primarily (6) _____. The main psychoanalytic theorist is (7) _____. He believed that personality is made up of three structures: (8) _____, (9) _____, and (10) _____. The conflicting demands of these structures produce (11) _____. People use (12) _____ to help resolve this anxiety. Two psychoanalytical theorists who thought that defense mechanisms were important to understanding adolescent development are (13) _____ and (14) _____. Freud believed that problems develop because of (15) _____ experiences. He thought that individuals go through five stages, called (16) _____ stages. The stages are (17) _____, (18) _____, (19) _____, (20)_____, and (21) _____. During the (22) _____ stage the (23) _____ conflict is the major source of conflict. There have been many revisions of Freud's theory, include those of feminist theorists (24) _____ and (25) _____. The most important revision of Freud's theory was undertaken by (26) _____, who believed that individuals develop in eight stages. These stages are: (27) _____, (28) _____, (29) _____, (30) _____, (31) _____, (32) _____, (33)_____, and (34) _____.

25

Whereas psychoanalytic theories stress the importance of adolescent's (35) _____ thoughts, cognitive theories emphasis their (36) _____ thoughts. Important cognitive theories are those of (37) _____ and (38)_____. (39) _____ believed that people go through four stages in understanding the world. Those stages are: (40) _____, (41) _____, (42)_____, and (43) _____. Russian (44) _____ believed that cognitive skills have their origins in (45) _____ relations and thus must be analyzed in the context of the individual's (46) _____ context. He thus emphasized that knowledge is (47) _____ and (48) _____. The (49) _____ approach is concerned with how individuals (50) _____ information, such as how information (51) _____ the mind, how it is (52) _____ and (53) _____, and how it is (54) _____ in order that people can (55) _____ and (56) _____.

Behavioral and social cognitive theories emphasize the importance of studying (57) _____ experiences and (58) _____. According to B.F. Skinner, the (59) _____ is not needed to explain behavior and development, for development is (60) _____, which has been determined by (61) _____ and (62) _____. Social cognitive theory states that (63) _____, (64) _____, and (65) _____ factors are important in understanding development. (66) _____ and (67) _____ are the main social cognitive theorists. (68) _____ emphasizes (69) _____ interactions between the (70) _____, (71) _____, and the (72) _____. Bandura believes that the person factor of (73) _____ is especially important in children's development. Two environmental theories that emphasize the importance of contextual factors are those of (74) _____ and (75) _____. Bronfenbrenner's ecological view of development stresses that five environmental systems impact on development. They are the: (76) _____, (77) _____, (78) _____, (79) _____, and (80) _____. Glenn Elder's (81) _____ theory emphasizes the study of lives in historical (82) _____ and (83) _____.

Because no single theory can explain the complex nature of adolescent development, it is useful to follow an (84) _____ theoretical orientation.

Theories of Adolescent Development
Section Review
1.   For each of the Freudian stages, state the age and focus of development and pleasure.

Stage	Age	Focus of Development/Pleasure
Oral		
Anal		
Phallic		
Latency		
Genital		

2. For each of the Erikson stages, provide the age range and focus of psychosocial development.

Stage	Age	Focus of Development
Trust vs. mistrust		
Autonomy vs. shame and doubt		
Initiative vs. guilt		
Industry vs. inferiority		
Identity vs. identity confusion		
Intimacy vs. isolation		
Generativity vs. stagnation		
Integrity vs. despair		

3. For each of Piaget's cognitive stages, state age and manner in which the child/adolescent thinks and understands the world.

Stage	Age	Way of Thinking and Understanding
Sensorimotor		
Preoperational		
Concrete operational		
Formal operational		

4. Using any behavior of your choice, explain how, according to B.F. Skinner's view of behaviorism, you learned that behavior though receiving or not receiving a reward.

5.   Explain any achievement of your choice (getting a job, getting the grade you wanted, getting the date you wanted) using Bandura's concept of reciprocal influences, stating how the environment and your own personal, cognitive factors influenced your behavior.

_____

_____

6.   Give an example of an environmental influence for each of Bronfenbrenner's five systems:
     a. microsystem

_____

     b. mesosystem

_____

     c. exosystem

_____

     d. macrosystem

_____

     e. chronosystem

_____

7.   Explain how the four aspects of Glenn Elder's life course theory have influenced or may influence any one experience in your life.
     a. social timing
     b. historical time and place
     c. linked lives
     d. human agency and social constraints

_____

_____

Research: Methods, Adolescent Development Research, and Research Challenges
Guided Review
        Researchers use many different methods to study adolescent development. Scientific observation requires (1) _____ what to look for, observing in an (2) _____ manner, (3) _____ recording and (4) _____ what you saw, and effectively (5) _____ your observations. Observations can be made in (6) _____ or (7) _____ settings. (8) _____ technique involves participants observing their own behavior.
        Researchers use (9) _____ and (10)_____ to ask adolescents about their feelings, experiences, and beliefs. Most interviews are (11) _____ but questionnaires can be done (12) _____, by (13) _____, or on the (14) _____. One of the problems with interviews and surveys is that people give (15) _____ answers or even (16) _____. (17) _____ assess adolescents' performance in different domains. The most widely used standardized test of adolescent personality is the (18) _____. A (19) _____ is an in-depth look at one person. Because each person in unique, this method alone cannot be used to make (20) _____ about other people. The goal of correlational research is to describe the (21) _____ between two or more events or characteristics. Correlation does not mean the same thing as (22) _____. Only (23)_____ research allows us to determine the causes of behavior. With this method, the event being manipulated is the (24) _____ variable; the factor that is being measured is the (25) _____ variable. Research subjects are assigned to either the (26) _____ group or the (27) _____ group by a method known as (28) _____ assignment. Because all methods have their strengths and weaknesses, researchers are increasingly adopting a multiple (29) _____, (30) _____, and (31) _____ approach to their subjects.

Researchers may sometimes need to decide the time span of the research. Studying individuals of different ages all at *one* time is known as (32) _____ research, while studying the same individuals *over a period* of time is known as (33) _____- research. The main outlets for adolescent development research are (34) _____ and (35) _____ presented at meetings. Research journal articles follow this format: (36) _____, (37) _____, (38) _____, (39)_____, and (40)_____.

Researchers face several challenges. Three ethical requirements of research are that researchers keep the (41) _____ of participants foremost, the requirement that participants give (42) _____ to the research, and that they have the right to (43)_____ from the research. Some believe that psychological research has entailed

(44) _____ and (45) _____ bias. Researchers need to include more (46) _____ minorities in their research and avoid ethnic (47) _____, which means using an ethnic label in a (48) _____ way that may make an ethnic group look more (49)_____ than it really is. (50) _____ research does not focus on individuals but on the characteristics of the (51) _____ subjects. (52) _____ needs are the (53) _____ concerns that research may not address.

Research: Methods, Adolescent Development Research, and Research Challenges
Section Review
Using your own words, list six guidelines to follow when evaluating information about adolescents that you read about in newspapers, magazines, or research journals or hear about on television.

1.

_____

2.

_____

3.

_____

4.

_____

5.

_____

6.

_____

Explorations in Adolescent Development
1.   How did Glenn Elder and Urie Bronfenbrenner influence each other's developmental theories?

_____

_____

2.   What are the similarities between their theories?

_____

_____

3.   What are the differences in their theories?

_____

_____

Adventures for the Mind

Find an article in a research journal (such as Developmental Psychology, Child Development, Journal of Research on Adolescence, Journal of Early Adolescence, or Journal of Youth and Adolescence) about any topic in the text. Then look for an article on the same subject in either a newspaper or are a magazine. Compare how the research article on the topic differs from the newspaper or magazine article. What are the differences between the nature, type, and quality of information presented?

Research in Adolescence

Concerning John Clausen's (1993) research about individual's planning their life course, state the hypothesis, the research methods (if known), the research conclusions, and the implications and applications for adolescent development.

_____

_____

Comprehensive Review

1.   The science of adolescent development is
       a.   a systematic body of testable theories that can be verified or refuted.
       b.   a set of specific, testable worldviews that describe adolescent development.
       c.   a descriptive catalogue of methods used to collect information about adolescent development.
       d.   a chronological identification of the stages of socioemotional, cognitive, and physical changes in adolescent.

2.   Predicting that dependent adolescents will become alcoholics is an example of a(n)
       a.   theory of personality.
       b.   hypothesis.
       c.   scientific fact.
       d.   unscientific question.

3.   Developing a study schedule is a function of the
       a.   id.
       b.   ego.
       c.   superego.
       d.   ego-ideal.

4.   History reveals that Sigmund Freud's psychosexual theory may have been influenced by his adolescent experiences. Apparently, Freud as a teenager was
       a.   unusually shy and sexually repressed.
       b.   normally expressive.
       c.   oversexed and overactive.
       d.   completely disinterested in sex.

5. According Peter Blos and Anna Freud,
    a. it is permissible to make generalizations about the role of defense mechanisms in adolescent development on the basis of small or clinical samples of subjects.
    b. research on adolescent defense mechanisms should be nonsexist.
    c. defense mechanisms are a normal aspect of adolescent development.
    d. Sigmund Freud's original analysis of the role of defense mechanisms in adolescent development has been confirmed many times.

6. Louella believes all boys have "cooties." She devotes herself to athletics and caring for various pets. A psychoanalyst would say Louella is
    a. behaving normally for someone in the latency stage.
    b. being overly controlled by her superego.
    c. experiencing unconscious conflicts between her ego and id.
    d. fixated at the phallic stage of development.

7. According to Freudians, identification occurs when the individual
    a. regresses to a form of behavior that characterized her adolescent years.
    b. experiences conflict between sexual and aggressive instincts and reality contact.
    c. develops intellectual and physical skills while identifying with a competent adult.
    d. resolves sexual desires for the opposite-sex parent by patterning herself after the same-sex parent.

8. Erik Erikson's theory emphasized
    a. repeated resolutions of unconscious conflicts about sexual energy.
    b. success in confronting specific conflicts at particular ages in life.
    c. changes in adolescent thinking as they matured.
    d. the influence of sensitive periods in the various stages of biological maturation.

9. Susan changed her major three times in college, and now that she has graduated, she still cannot decide what type of job she wants. Erik Erickson would describe Susan as going through a period of
    a. shame and doubt.
    b. identity confusion.
    c. despair.
    d. generativity and stagnation.

10. In the futuristic film *2001:A Space Odyssey*, a computer named HAL performs many humanlike activities in outer space. Psychologists might justifiably argue that while HAL could memorize and pay attention, he could never have arguments with his family nor be a "social" machine. These criticisms could also be leveled against the _____ view of adolescents.
    a. information-processing
    b. Piagetian
    c. social learning
    d. psychoanalytic

11. Dotty can't stand to be seen in public with her parents. It is most likely that Dotty is in Piaget's
    a. sensorimotor stage.
    b. preoperational stage.
    c. concrete operational stage.
    d. formal operational stage.

12. The information processing approach emphasizes
    a. the quality of thinking among adolescent of different ages.
    b. overcoming age related problems or "crises."
    c. age appropriate expressions of sexual energy.
    d. perception, memory, reasoning ability, and problem solving.

13. A social learning theorist would agree with which one of the following statements?
    a. Adolescents are not passive responders; they judge, expect, plan, and imagine behaviors.
    b. Adolescent behaviors change solely as a result of reward and punishment.
    c. Adolescent development researchers underestimate the role of biologically based changes in behavior.
    d. An eclectic approach is always preferred in explaining a particular behavior.

14. One of the strong points of behavior theory is its
    a. belief that cognitive processes are irrelevant for understanding development.
    b. emphasis on the relationship between environmental stimuli and adolescent behavior.
    c. emphasis on reducing adolescent behavior to fine-grained elements.
    d. emphasis on the role of information processing as a mediator between behavior and environment.

15. To increase the number of times your spouse does the dishes, B. F. Skinner would tell you to
    a. yell at your spouse for not doing the dishes.
    b. kiss your spouse for doing the dishes.
    c. leave the sink full of dishes until your spouse does them.
    d. ask your spouse nicely to do the dishes.

16. From B. F. Skinner's point of view, the best way to explain adolescent behavior is to
    a. pay attention to the external consequences of that behavior.
    b. pay attention to the self-produced consequences of that behavior.
    c. focus on adolescent cognitive interpretation of her environmental experiences.
    d. identify the biological processes that determine adolescent maturation.

17. The frequent finding that adults who abuse their children and adolescents typically come from families in which they themselves were abused supports which theory of development?
    a. Freudian psychoanalytic theory
    b. information processing theory
    c. ecological theory
    d. social learning theory

18. Which of the following is an achievement of the ecological perspective?
    a. It emphasizes the interconnectedness of social settings.
    b. It accounts for the adolescent's biological heritage.
    c. It is concerned with cognition's role.
    d. All of these answers are correct.

19. A major strength of ecological theory is its framework for explaining
    a. environmental influences on development.
    b. biological influences on development.
    c. cognitive development.
    d. affective processes in development.

20. The development of adolescents in Somalia was negatively affected by the recent famine. Such events are examples of the
    a. macrosystem.
    b. exosystem.
    c. mesosystem.
    d. chronosystem.

21. Many developmentalists have chosen to subscribe to an eclectic viewpoint because
    a. they cannot afford to subscribe to all the other viewpoints; the annual dues are too high.
    b. none of the current theories is at all correct.
    c. they believe that not enough data have been collected so far to even begin proposing a definitive theory.
    d. each of the major theories has both valid points and flaws.

22. Which of the following is true about theories that endeavor to explain adolescent development?
    a. If theorists keep working at it they will eventually come up with one theory that explains development.
    b. Cognitive, psychoanalytic, and humanistic theories have nothing in common and can never be reconciled.
    c. The theories proposed should be thought of as complementary rather than competitive.
    d. One theory from biology, one theory from cognitive psychology, and one theory from social psychology are all that is needed to explain development.

23. One difficulty of doing research on adolescents in a laboratory setting is that
    a. an unnatural behavior may occur.
    b. random assignment is impossible.
    c. extraneous factors are difficult to control.
    d. the experimenter's judgments are of unknown reliability.

24. An investigator interested in gender differences in helping behavior spends three hours a day in the mall watching who opens doors for shoppers burdened with packages. Which of the following methods of data collection is being used?
    a. naturalistic observation
    b. experimental
    c. correlational
    d. case studies

25. How is a questionnaire study different from one that uses interviews?
    a. Questionnaires usually involve in-depth probing into the details of a person's life.
    b. Interviews may be carried out over the phone, while questionnaires are always completed with the researcher present.
    c. Questionnaires ask respondents to indicate their answers on paper instead of answering orally.
    d. Interviews are best for cross-cultural research.

Adolescence on the Screen

- *Good Will Hunting* concerns an adolescent named Will (played by Matt Damon) in treatment for attachment problems brought on by his being abandoned by his biological parents and abused by his foster parents. Will's therapist Sean (played by Robin Williams) uses a psychodynamic treatment model.

- *Ordinary People* portrays a surviving son's guilt and suicidal depression over what he feels was his role in his brother's death. He pulls through with the help of hospitalization and a psychodynamic therapist whom he trusts.

Adolescence in Books

Two recent biographies about Erikson and Freud demonstrate how individual life events—as well as historical events, time, and place—influenced their theories:

- *Freud: A Life for Our Time*, by Peter Gay (W.W. Norton, 1998), is a balanced and comprehensive biography of Sigmund Freud that places his theories in the context of the times

- *Identity's Architect: A Biography of Erik H. Erikson*, by Lawrence J. Friedman (Simon & Schuster, 1999), traces the origins of Erikson's concern with identity and identity crises to his early life experiences.

Answer Key

Key Terms

1. **scientific research** Research that is objective, systematic, and testable.
2. **scientific method** An approach that can be used to discover accurate information. It includes the following steps: conceptualize the problem, collect data, draw conclusions, and revise research conclusions and theory.
3. **theory** An interrelated, coherent set of ideas that helps to explain and make predictions.
4. **hypotheses** Specific assumptions and predictions that can be tested to determine their accuracy.
5. **id** The part of the Freudian structure of personality that consists of instincts, which are an individual's reserve of psychic energy.
6. **ego** The part of the Freudian structure of personality that deals with the demands of reality.
7. **superego** The part of the Freudian structure of personality that is the moral branch of personality.
8. **defense mechanisms** The psychoanalytic term for unconscious methods used by the ego to distort reality in order to protect itself from anxiety.
9. **repression** The most powerful and pervasive defense mechanism; it pushes unacceptable id impulses out of awareness and back into the unconscious mind.
10. **erogenous zones** Freud's concept of the parts of the body that have especially strong pleasure-giving qualities at each stage of development.
11. **oral stage** The first Freudian stage of development, occurring during the first 18 months of life, when the infant's pleasure centers on the mouth.
12. **anal stage** The second Freudian stage of development, occurring between 1 1/2 and 3 years of age. The child's greatest pleasure involves the anus or the eliminative functions associated with it.
13. **phallic stage** The third Freudian stage of development, occurring between the ages of 3 and 6, named after the Latin word phallus, meaning penis.
14. **latency stage** The fourth Freudian stage, occurring between approximately 6 years of age and puberty, when the child represses all interest in sexuality and develops social and intellectual skills.
15. **genital stage** The fourth and final Freudian stage of development, that occurs from puberty on; a sexual reawakening in which the source of sexual pleasure now becomes someone outside of the family.
16. **trust versus mistrust** Erikson's first psychosocial stage, experienced in the first year of life; a sense of trust requires a feeling of physical comfort and a minimal amount of fear and apprehension about the future.
17. **autonomy versus shame and doubt** Erikson's second stage of development, which occurs in late infancy and todddlerhood (1 to 3 years). After gaining trust in their caregivers, infants begin to discover that their behavior is their own.

18. **initiative versus guilt** Erikson's third stage of development, which occurs during the preschool years. As preschool children encounter a widening social world, they are challenged more than they were as infants.

19. **industry versus inferiority** Erikson's fourth stage of development, which occurs approximately in the elementary school years. Children's initiative brings them into contact with a wealth of new experiences, and they direct their energy toward mastering knowledge and intellectual skills.

20. **identity versus identity confusion** Erikson's fifth stage of development, which occurs during the adolescent years. Adolescents are faced with finding out who they are, what they are all about, and where they are going in life.

21. **intimacy versus isolation** Erikson's sixth stage of development, which occurs during the early adulthood years. Young adults face the developmental task of forming initiate relationships with others.

22. **generativity versus stagnation** Erikson's seventh stage of development, which occurs during middle adulthood. A chief concern is to assist the younger generation in developing and leading useful lives.

23. **integrity versus despair** Erikson's eighth and final stage of development, which occurs during late adulthood. In the later years of life, we look back and evaluate what we have done with our lives.

24. **sensorimotor stage** The first of Piaget's stages that lasts from birth to about 2 years of age, when infants construct an understanding of the world by coordinating sensory experiences (such as seeing and hearing) with motoric actions.

25. **preoperational stage** The second Piagetian developmental stage that lasts from about 2 to 7 years of age, when children begin to represent the world with words, images, and drawings.

26. **concrete operational stage** Piaget's third stage, which lasts from approximately 7 to 11 years of age, when children can perform operations, and logical reasoning replaces intuitive thought as long as the reasoning can be applied to specific concrete examples.

27. **formal operational stage** Piaget's fourth and final stage, which occurs between the ages of 11 and 15, when individuals move beyond concrete experiences and think in more abstract and more logical ways.

28. **information processing** How individuals process information about their world, how information enters the mind, how it is stored and transformed, and how it is retrieved to perform such complex activities as problem solving and reasoning.

29. **behavioral and social cognitive theories** Emphasis is placed on the importance of studying environmental experiences and observable behavior. Social cognitive theorists emphasize person/cognitive factors in development.

30. **behaviorism** The scientific study of observable behavioral responses and their environmental determinants.

31. **social cognitive theory** States that behavior, environment, and person/cognitive factors are important in understanding development.

32. **ecological theory** Bronfenbrenner's view of development, involving five environmental systems—microsystem, exosystem, ecosystem, macrosystem, and chronosystem. These emphasize the role of social contexts in development.

33. **microsystem** The setting or context in which an individual lives, including the person's family, peers, school, and neighborhood.

34. **mesosystem** Relationships between microsystems or connections between contexts, such as the connection between family experience and the school experience.

35. **exosystem** The level at which experiences in another social setting in which the individual does not have an active role influence what the individual experiences in an immediate context.

36. **macrosystem** The culture in which individuals live.

37. **chronosystem** The patterning of environmental events and transitions over the life course and their sociohistorical contexts.

38. **life course theory** Glenn Elder's theory that human development can be best understood by considering lives in their historical time and place, the timing of social roles and life events, the interdependence or connections among lives, and the role of human agency and social constraints in decision making.

39.   **eclectic theoretical orientation** Not following any one theoretical approach, but rather selecting from each theory whatever is considered the best in it.

Key People in the Study of Adolescence

1. G	4. M	7. C	10. K
2. H	5. I	8. E	11. D
3. J	6. B	9. A	12. F
			13. L

Why Research on Adolescent Development is Important/Scientific Research Approach
Guided Review

1. personal experiences
2. authorities/experts
3. scientific
4. Scientific
5. objective
6. systematic
7. testable

8. personal beliefs
9. opinion
10. feelings
11. conceptualize the problem
12. collect data
13. draw conclusions
14. revise theory

15. coherent
16. ideas
17. explain
18. predictions
19. hypotheses

Why Research on Adolescent Development is Important/Scientific Research Approach
Section Review

Number	Name	Description
One	Conceptualize the problem	Identify the problem; develop hypothesis that mentoring will improve achievement of adolescents from impoverished backgrounds.
Two	Collect information (data)	Conduct the mentoring program for six months and collect data before and after program begins.
Three	Draw conclusions	Analyze the data that shows improvement over period of program; conclude that mentoring helped increase achievement.
Four	Revise research conclusions and theory	Research will increase likelihood that mentoring will be considered an important component to help improve achievement of low-income adolescents.

Theories of Adolescent Development
Guided Review

1. psychoanalytic
2. cognitive
3. behavioral
4. social
5. psychoanalytic
6. unconscious
7. Sigmund Freud
8. id
9. ego
10. superego
11. anxiety
12. defense mechanisms
13. Peter Blos
14. Anna Freud
15. early
16. psychosexual
17. oral
18. anal
19. phallic
20. latent
21. genital
22. phallic
23. Oedipus
24. Karen Horney
25. Nancy Chodorow
26. Erik Erikson
27. trust vs. mistrust
28. autonomy vs. shame and doubt
29. initiative vs. guilt
30. industry vs. inferiority
31. identity vs. confusion
32. intimacy vs. isolation
33. generativity vs. stagnation
34. integrity vs. despair
35. unconscious
36. conscious
37. Jean Piaget
38. Lev Vygotsky
39. Piaget
40. sensorimotor
41. preoperational
42. concrete operational
43. formal operational
44. Lev Vygotsky
45. social
46. sociocultural
47. situated
48. collaborative
49. information processing
50. process
51. enters
52. stored
53. transformed
54. retrieved
55. reason
56. solve problems
57. environmental
58. observable behavior
59. mind
60. behavior
61. rewards
62. punishments
63. behavior
64. environment
65. person/cognitive
66. Albert Bandura
67. Walter Mischel
68. Bandura
69. reciprocal
70. person
71. behavior
72. environment
73. self-efficacy
74. Urie Bronfenbrenner
75. Glenn Elder
76. microsystem
77. mesosystem
78. exosystem
79. macrosystem
80. chronosystem
81. life course
82. place
83. time
84. eclectic

Theories of Adolescent Development
Section Review

1.

Stage	Age	Focus of Development/pleasure
Oral	0–1 1/2 years	Pleasure focused on the mouth; sucking reduces tension.
Anal	1 1/2–3 years	Pleasure involves the anus; eliminative functions reduce tension.
Phallic	3–6 years	Pleasure focuses on the genitals; child discovers self-manipulation is enjoyable.
Latency	6 years–puberty	Child represses interest in sexuality and develops social and intellectual skills
Genital	Adolescence–adulthood	Sexual pleasure is focused on those outside of the family.

2.

Stage	Age	Focus of Development
Trust vs. mistrust	Infancy	Feeling of physical comfort and minimal amount of fear and apprehension.
Autonomy vs. shame and doubt	1–3 years	Begin to assert independence or autonomy in behavior.
Initiative vs. guilt	3–5 years	Engage in active, purposeful behavior to cope with challenges of the world.
Industry vs. inferiority	6 years–puberty	Direct energy toward mastering knowledge and intellectual skills.
Identity vs. identity confusion	10–20 years	Finding out who they are, what they are about, and where they are going in life.
Intimacy vs. isolation	20s and 30s	Forming intimate relationships.
Generativity vs. stagnation	40s and 50s	Assist younger generation in developing and leading useful lives.
Integrity vs. despair	60s to death	Look back and evaluate life's accomplishments.

3.

Stage	Age	Way of Thinking and Understanding.
Sensorimotor	Birth–2	Coordinates sensory experiences with physical actions.
Preoperational	2–7	Uses words and images to represent the world.
Concrete operational	7–11	Reason logically about concrete events and classify objects.
Formal operational	11–adulthood	Reasons in abstract, idealistic, and logical ways.

4.   Example: You transfer to a new school and try to be friendly by introducing yourself (behavior). People don't respond in a friendly manner (lack of reward) so you withdraw and don't try to fit in (behavior).

5.   Example: Using same example as in # 4, the students (environment) influenced your behavior because when you tried to be friendly and they did not respond, you assume that they don't want your friendship (personal, cognitive) and so you withdraw (behavior).

6.   Examples:
   a. Microsystem—family, peers, school, neighborhood
   b. Mesosystem—school and parents; parents and friends
   c. Exosystem—lack of facilities for a handicapped person
   d. Macrosystem—ethnic or racial group
   e. Chronosystem—wider range of gender roles for men and women

7.   Examples: Today, women may put off having children for a long time (social timing), because it is accepted that they may want to have a career first (historical place and time). The woman's parents and spouse may be more active in grandparenting than they would have been years ago, giving her more support in combining career and family (linked lives). Her employer may be more supportive of her need to take time off when her children are sick (human agency/social constraint).

Research: Methods, Adolescent Development Research, and Research Challenges
Guided Review

1. knowing	15. socially desirable	29. measure	43. withdraw
2. unbiased	16. lie	30. source	44. gender
3. accurately	17. standardized tests	31. context	45. ethnic
4. categorizing	18. MMPI-A	32. cross-sectional	46. ethnic
5. communicating	19. case study	33. longitudinal	47. gloss
6. laboratory	20. generalizations	34. journals	48. superficial
7. naturalistic	21. relationships	35. papers	49. homogenous
8. video-recall	22. causation	36. abstract	50. nomothetic
9. interview	23. experimental	37. introduction	51. group
10. surveys	24. independent	38. methods	52. idiographic
11. in person	25. dependent	39. results	53. individual
12. in person	26. expert	40. discussion	
13. mail	27. control	41. best interests	
14. Internet	28. random	42. informed consent	

Research: Methods, Adolescent Development Research, and Research Challenges
Section Review
1. Be cautious.
2. Avoid assuming that individual needs can be determined from group research.
3. Don't over generalize about small or clinical samples.
4. Be aware that a single study is usually not conclusive about a topic or issue.
5. Remember that correlational studies don't prove causal relationships.
6. Evaluate the source of the information.

Explorations in Adolescent Development
1. Elder influenced Bronfenbrenner's interest in the role that time plays in development. They discussed their views with each other and reviewed each other's manuscripts. Bronfenbrenner influenced Elder to more directly address issues in developmental psychology.

2. Both of their theories emphasize the interrelatedness of development to biological, cognitive, emotional, social, and cultural domains.

3. The main difference is that Elder's life-course theory focuses primarily on the kinds of environments people live in over the long term, ("macro" environments), while Bronfenbrenner's theory focuses on person-environment interaction in "micro" environments during child and adolescent years.

Adventures for the Mind
Individual reflection—no answers provided.

Research in Adolescence
The hypothesis was that planful competence in early life was associated with later life success. The methods were longitudinal life-history interviews. Analyzing nearly 50 years of 60 male and female subjects, Clausen found that adolescents who manifest self-confidence, dependability, and intellectual investment, the components of planful competence, had occupational and family success in the adult years. A few adolescents low in planful

competence became effective adults, and a few adolescents high in planful competence had dismal lives, but they were the exception. Clausen concluded that personality development can involve stability and change.

Comprehensive Review

1. a	6. a	11. d	16. a	21. d
2. b	7. d	12. d	17. d	22. c
3. b	8. b	13. a	18. a	23. a
4. a	9. b	14. b	19. a	24. a
5. c	10. a	15. b	20. b	25. c

◆ Chapter 3   Biological Foundations, Puberty and Health

Learning Objectives with Key Terms and Key People in Boldface

1.0   **What is the Relationship Between the Theory of Evolution and Adolescent Development?**
    A.   **Natural Selection**
        1.1   That is the theory of **natural selection**?
    B.   **Evolutionary Psychology**
        1.2   What is evolutionary **psychology**?
    C.   **Stress and Resilience**
        1.3   What can the evolutionary perspective tell us about stress and resilience?
    D.   **The Social Cognitive View of Evolution**
        1.4   What is the social cognitive view of evolution?

2.0   **What is the Relationship Between Heredity and Environment?**
    A.   **The Nature of Genes**
        2.1   What is the nature of genes?
        2.2   What are the biochemical agents of the genetic code?
        2.3   What is the difference between **genotype** and **phenotype**?
        2.4   What is the difference between **reaction range** and **canalization**?
    B.   **Methods**
        2.5   What are the research methods of **behavioral genetics**?
        2.6   What is a **twin study**?
        2.7   How do twin studies examine the difference between **identical twins** and **fraternal twins**?
        2.8   What is an **adoption study**?
    C.   **Temperament**
        2.9   What is **temperament**?
        2.10   What are the characteristics of the **easy**, **difficult**, and **slow-to-warm up** child?
        2.11   What are the relative influences of **heredity** and **environment**?
        2.12   What is the **goodness-of fit** model?
    D.   **Exploring Heredity and Environment**
        2.13   What distinguishes Sandra Scarr's concepts of **passive genotype-environmental interactions, evocative genotype-environmental interactions**, and **active (niche-picking) genotype-environmental interactions**?
        2.14   What is the difference between **shared environmental influences** and **nonshared environmental influences**?
        2.15   What are the most reasonable conclusions we can make about the interaction of heredity and environment?

3.0   **What is Puberty and What Developmental Changes Does It Involve?**
    A.   **Physical Changes**
        3.1   What changes occur in **puberty**?
        3.2   When does puberty take place for boys and girls?
        3.3   How do **menarche** and the menstrual cycle affect girls in puberty?
        3.4   What are the determinants of heredity?

Key Terms

Write a sentence using each of these key terms by either defining the term or giving an example of it. For instance, you might write, "Evolutionary psychology is…" Or, you might give an example of how an evolutionary psychologist might view an aspect of adolescence. Compare your definitions with those given at the end of study guide chapter and check your examples by referring to the text. Review the text for those terms you don't know or define incorrectly.

1.   natural selection

2.   evolutionary psychology

_____

_____

3.   genotype

_____

_____

4.   phenotype

_____

_____

5.   reaction range

_____

_____

6.   canalization

_____

_____

7.   behavior genetics

_____

_____

8.   twin study

_____

_____

9.   identical twins

_____

_____

10.   fraternal twins

_____

_____

11.   adoption study

_____

_____

12.   temperament

_____

_____

13.   easy child

_____

_____

14. difficult child

_____

_____

15. slow-to-warm-up child

_____

_____

16. goodness-of-fit model

_____

_____

17. passive genotype-environment correlations

_____

_____

18. evocative genotype-environment correlations

_____

_____

19. active (niche-picking) genotype-environment correlations

_____

_____

20. shared environmental influences

_____

_____

21. nonshared environmental influences

_____

_____

22. puberty

_____

_____

23. menarche

_____

_____

24. hormones

_____

_____

25. hypothalamus

_____

_____

26. pituitary gland

_____

_____

27. gonads

_____

_____

28. androgens

_____

_____

29. estrogens

_____

_____

30. testosterone

_____

_____

31. estradiol

_____

_____

Key People in Adolescent Development

Match the person with the event or concept in adolescent development with which they are associated.

___	1. Charles Darwin	A.	Three temperament types
___	2. David Buss	B.	Evolutionary psychology
___	3. Mihalyi Csikszentmihalyi	C.	Conducts research in behavioral genetics
___	4. Albert Bandura	D.	Studies puberty's role in adolescent development
___	5. Alexander Chess and Stella Thomas	E.	Studied stress and resilience from evolutionary perspective
___	6. Sandra Scarr	F.	Critic of "one-sided" evolutionism
___	7. Roberta Simmons and Dale Blyth	G.	Associated with theory of natural selection
___	8. Jeanne Brooks Gunn	H.	Conducted longitudinal study of early and late maturation

Evolution and Adolescent Development
Guided Review

(1) _____ is the evolutionary process that favors individuals of a species that are best adapted to (2) _____ and (3) _____. (4) _____ is credited with promulgating this theory, which he wrote about in his book, (5) _____. Evolutionary psychology emphasizes the importance of (6) _____, (7) _____, and the (8) _____ of the _____ in explaining behavior. Evolutionary psychology's emphasis on adaptation reflects the earlier views of the perspective known as (9) _____. (10) _____, from the University of Texas at Austin, has ushered in a new wave of interest in evolution. Mihalyi Csikszentmihalyi and Jennifer Schmidt have examined (11) _____ and (12) _____ from a evolutionary perspective. They argue that the body has been (13) _____ to act in (14) _____ ways from puberty. Albert Bandura acknowledges the role of evolution in human adaptation but argues for a (15) _____ view that enables organisms to (16) _____ and (17) _____ their environment.

Heredity and Environment
Guided Review

Each adolescent inherits a (1) _____ code from his or her parents that is carried by biochemical agents called (2) _____ and (3) _____. A (4) _____ is a person's genetic heritage, the actual genetic heritage. A (5) _____ is the way an individual's genotype is (6) _____ in observed and measurable characteristics. Phenotypes include (7) _____ traits as well as (8) _____ characteristics. Genetic codes (9) _____ adolescents to develop in a particular way, and (10) _____ are either responsive or unresponsive to the code. The importance of the environment's restricting or enriching effect on the phenotype is known as the (11) _____ range, the range of possible phenotypes for each genotype. The process by which some genotypic characteristics appear to be immune from environmental effects is known as (12) _____. (13) _____ is the study of the degree and nature of heredity's influence on behavior. The research method that explores the varying influences of heredity and environment is (14) _____ studies. Identical twins, called (15) _____ twins, develop from a single egg and are identical to each other. Fraternal twins, also known as (16) _____ twins, develop from separate and eggs and sperm, making them no more genetically similar than any other sibling. By comparing identical and fraternal twins, behavior geneticists can study the relative influences of (17) _____ and (18) _____. (19) _____ studies compare the psychological and behavior characteristics of (20) _____ children to their (21) _____ and (22) _____ parents. These studies seek to ascertain if children are more like their (23) _____ or (24) _____ parents.

(25) _____ is an individual's behavioral style and characteristic way of responding to the environment. Alexander Chess and Stella Thomas believe that there are three basic temperamental types: (26) _____, (27) _____, and (28) _____. The (29) _____ model suggests that an adolescent's development is best when there is a (30) _____ between the temperament of the adolescent and the expectations of (31) _____, (32) _____, and (33) _____.

Behavior geneticists study the ways in which (34) _____ and (35) _____ work together in development. They believe that environment and heredity are correlated in three ways: (36) _____, (37) _____, and (38) _____. Adolescent siblings living in the same home are not necessarily exposed to the same environment because their (39) _____ are different. Behavioral geneticists Robert Plomin and others study the influence of (40) _____ and (41) _____ environmental influences. The most reasonable conclusion about heredity and environment is that both (42) _____ to make us who we are.

Heredity and Environment
Section Review

Match the temperament cluster with the description of the behavior, using Chess and Thomas's model of temperamental types. Put "E" for easy child, "D" for difficult child, and SW for "slow-to-warm-up child."

_____   1. low expression of mood when happy or sad
_____   2. generally expresses positive affect
_____   3. generally expresses negative affect
_____   4. easily approaches new people and situations
_____   5. high degree of physical energy
_____   6. irregular eating, sleeping, and toileting habits
_____   7. high expression of pleasure when happy
_____   8. easily tolerates changes in routine
_____   9. low level of physical energy
_____   10. regular sleeping, eating, and toileting habits

Puberty
Guided Review

The period of rapid maturation involving hormonal and bodily changes that occur primarily during early adolescence is known as (1) _____. (2) _____ is a girl's first menstruation, and it occurs at just over (3) _____ years of age. The determinants of puberty include (4) _____, (5) _____, (6) _____, and (7) _____. The powerful chemical substances that are secreted by the endocrine glands and carried through the body by the bloodstream are (8) _____. The endocrine system interacts with the part of the brain known as the (9) _____, the (10) _____ gland, and the (11) _____ glands, known as (12) _____. The male sex glands are (13) _____; the female sex glands are (14) _____. The main class of female hormones is (15)_____, of which (16)_____ plays the most important role in puberty. The main class of male hormones is (17) _____ and (18) _____ is the most important in pubertal development.

The most noticeable physical changes occurring during puberty are increases in (19) _____, (20) _____, and (21) _____ maturation. The growth spurt occurs approximately (22) _____ years earlier for girls than for boys, with the mean year of the spurt being (23) _____ years of age for girls and (24) _____ for boys. (25) _____maturation is a key feature in pubertal development. There is (26) _____ variation in individual pubertal development. For boys, puberty usually occurs between the ages of (27) _____ and _____; for girls menarche may appear between the ages of (28) _____ and _____.

The psychological dimensions of puberty focus mainly on (29) _____ image. Adolescent (30) _____ have more negative body images than do adolescent (31) _____. Early maturation favors (32) _____, and early maturing (33) _____ are at risk for a number of problems. However, some scholars believe that puberty's effects on development are (34) _____, as most early- and late-maturing adolescents get through its challenges (35) _____.

Puberty
Section Review
1. Give a brief explanation of how each of the components of the endocrine system affects pubertal development.

    a.   Pituitary gland

    _____

    _____

    b.   Adrenal gland

    _____

    _____

    c.   Hypothalamus

    _____

    _____

    d.   Thyroid gland

    _____

    _____

    e.   Gonads

    _____

    _____

2. Describe each of the five pubertal stages of male and female sexual development.

    a.   Male

    _____

    _____

    b.   Female

    _____

    _____

Adolescent Health
Guided Review

Health goals for adolescence include reducing health compromising behaviors, such as (1) _____, (2) _____, and (3) _____, and (4) and increasing health-enhancing behaviors, such as (5) _____, (6) _____, (7) _____, (8) _____, and (8) _____.

(9) _____ and (10) _____ are blamed for the poor physical condition of adolescents. (11) _____ may provide a buffer to adolescent stress, in addition to providing adolescents with a more (12) _____. The three leading causes of death in adolescents are (13) _____, (14) _____, and (15) _____. More than half of all deaths in adolescents ages 10 to 19 involve (16) _____. In about 50 percent of the motor vehicle fatalities involving an adolescent, the driver has a blood alcohol level of (17) _____ percent. Suicide accounts for (18) _____ percent of deaths in the 15–19 age group. Since the 1950s, the adolescent suicide rate has (19) _____. Homicide is especially high among

(20) _____ adolescents. They are (21) _____ times more likely to be killed by guns than natural cause.

      Among the cognitive factors in adolescents' health behavior are concepts of health (22) _____, (23) _____ about health, and heath (24) _____. Adolescents and adults (25) _____ their vulnerability to harm, particularly risk from (26) _____ and (27) _____. One of the main social contexts that influence the health of ethnic minority group adolescents is (28) _____ status. (29) _____ is related to poor health in adolescents, and affect the adolescent's access to (30) _____ care. Positive health behaviors are best achieved when adolescents develop a sense of (31) _____ within a (32) _____ family context. Schools can contribute to adolescent health through (33) _____ and (34) _____ programs, and by adopting a (35) _____ curriculum. Gender differences also affect adolescent health. (36) _____ tend to underreport physical symptoms and are less willing to change their health attitudes and behavior than (37) _____ adolescents. Adolescents (38) _____ health-care systems. Among the chief barriers to better health services for adolescents are (39) _____, poor (40) _____, (41) _____ of services, and (42) _____ of care.

Explorations in Adolescence
Describe the model of the full-service school and state how it can improve adolescent health.

_____
_____
_____

Adventures for the Mind
List ten characteristics relating to your physical, emotional, and cognitive development. Think about their origins. Did them come from your mother? Your father? Your experiences? What does this tell you have the role of nature and nurture in your own development?

_____
_____
_____
_____
_____
_____
_____
_____
_____
_____

Adolescence in Research

Concerning Simmons and Blyth's 1987 research about early and late maturation, state the hypothesis, the research methods (if known), the research conclusions, and the implications and applications for adolescent development.

_____

_____

_____

Comprehensive Review

1. The unique arrangement of chromosomes and genes inherited by each adolescent is referred to as the
   _____ , whereas the adolescent's observed characteristics are called the _____ .
   a. phenotype; genotype
   b. phenotype; reaction range
   c. genotype; reaction range
   d. genotype; phenotype

2. The concept of reaction range is really very simple: _____ cause(s) most of the reaction, and
   _____ determine(s) most of the range.
   a. genes; environment
   b. environment; genes
   c. genes; hormones
   d. environment; hormones

3. _____ is the area concerned with the degree and nature of the hereditary basis of behavior.
   a. Genetic psychology
   b. Behavioral psychology
   c. Behavior genetics
   d. Developmental genetics

4. A behavioral geneticist comparing the IQs of monozygotic twins with those of dizygotic twins is applying
   the
   a. twin-study method.
   b. family-of-twins method.
   c. kinship method.
   d. habitability method.

5. An individual's behavioral style or characteristic way of behaving is referred to as the individual's
   a. life style.
   b. personality.
   c. mannerisms.
   d. temperament.

6. The whole issue of temperament can be
   a. dismissed as having no genetic determinants.
   b. measured early in life.
   c. distinguished from behavioral style, which may be genetically influenced.
   d. discovered and mapped by behavior-genetics techniques.

7. Barry's parents are pretty "laid back" while Barry himself is quite tense, always in a hurry, and critical. According to the _____ model, there are likely to be some problems in the parent-adolescent relationship.
   a. connecting
   b. communication-fit
   c. goodness-of-fit
   d. temperament

8. Sandra Scarr proposed all the following heredity-environment interactions except:
   a. passive genotype-environmental interactions.
   b. heritable genotype-environmental interactions.
   c. evocative genotype-environmental interactions.
   d. active genotype-environmental interactions.

9. Glenda and Betty are sisters. Although they are both high achievers in school, their personalities are quite different: Glenda is extroverted and Betty is introverted. Behavioral geneticists would be most likely to explain this situation by emphasizing that
   a. Glenda and Betty both received family encouragement to do well in school.
   b. intellectual performance is controlled by different gene pathways than personality style.
   c. while personality is polygenetically determined, intelligence is not.
   d. both genes and an environment are necessary for adolescents to exist.

10. The principal conclusion is that genes and environment affect development by a process of
    a. multiplication.
    b. subtraction.
    c. interaction.
    d. reaction.

11. On average, females enter puberty at an earlier age than males, and that's why
    a. women are typically shorter than men.
    b. fifth- and sixth-grade girls are usually taller than boys.
    c. girls and boys do not get along well during puberty.
    d. boys are more muscular, and girls have more fat.

12. Sue started her menstrual period about two years earlier than Mary, even though both girls are very healthy. A likely explanation for this event is that
    a. Sue is an athlete.
    b. Sue has greater body mass than Mary.
    c. Mary has greater body mass than Sue.
    d. Sue has better genes than Mary.

13. Which of the following represents the correct sequence of endocrine-system control?
    a. Pituitary gland, hypothalamus-gonadotropin secretion, estradiol/testosterone production
    b. Hypothalamus, estradiol/testosterone production, pituitary, gonadotropin secretion
    c. Hypothalamus-pituitary-gonadotropin secretion, estradiol/testosterone production
    d. Estradiol/testosterone production, gonadotropin secretion, pituitary, hypothalamus

14. Androgens are to females as _____ are to males.
    a. testosterone
    b. gonadotropins
    c. hormones
    d. estrogens

15. _____ is important in the pubertal development of females.
    a. Thyroxin
    b. Estradiol
    c. Androgen
    d. Estrogen

16. Your son and daughter are fraternal twins, both in the sixth grade. Your son gets angry because people tease him about his sister being taller than he. You can legitimately tell your son that
    a. although his sister is taller, his sexual maturation is more advanced.
    b. his sister is probably taller because she doesn't eat as much junk food.
    c. he needn't worry, because he'll probably catch up with or surpass his sister's height by the end of the eighth grade.
    d. since his sister was taller than he during childhood, she'll be taller than he during adolescence.

17. The fact that some adolescent males begin puberty as early as 10 years of age and others as late as 17 years (or even later) is an example of
    a. environmental influences.
    b. individual differences.
    c. biologically caused psychological disturbance.
    d. behavior genetics in action.

18. In the California Longitudinal Study, males who matured early
    a. perceived themselves as more successful in peer relations.
    b. perceived themselves more negatively because of additional parental pressure.
    c. were perceived by peers as unattractive due to the accompanying occurrence of acne.
    d. perceived themselves more negatively because they were "ahead of the others."

19. In a college course in human sexuality, Jill was asked to describe her initial reactions to menarche. She described the experience very negatively, emphasizing the discomfort and messiness. Jill probably was
    a. well prepared for the event.
    b. unlikely to tell her mother about the event.
    c. an early maturer.
    d. on time in her pubertal development.

20. Stephanie is a late-maturing female. She has an increased probability of
    a. being tall and thin.
    b. being shorter and stockier.
    c. having no skin problems.
    d. having to visit the dermatologist.

21. Early-maturing adolescents often date at an earlier age than their later-maturing friends. For females, at least, this early social involvement may be welcomed uneasily by the adolescent, because many adolescent females are
    a. unprepared for puberty.
    b. emotionally secure.
    c. unattractive.
    d. not interested in heterosexual interactions.

22. Which of the following is not a model explaining pubertal change and behavior?
    a. connections with social events
    b. goodness-of-fit
    c. direct hormonal effects
    d. indirect effects via secondary sex characteristics

23. Which of the following statements about the Graber, Brooks-Gunn, and Warren (1995) article illustrating research on adolescent development is most accurate?
    a. This article presents an example of research that is applied rather than basic.
    b. The primary research measure of menarcheal age.
    c. This articles presents research that uses a correlational rather than experimental strategy.
    d. The results reveal gender similarities rather than differences.

Adolescence on the Screen
■ *My Left Foot* addresses how a boy deals with physical deformity.

■ *Trainspotting* depicts the decadent lifestyle of Scottish teenagers bent on self-destruction through heroin addiction.

■ *Ordinary People* tell of an adolescent boy's struggle with suicidal tendencies arising out of the guilt he feels for an accident that took his young brother's life.

Adolescence in Books
■ *The What's Happening to My Body? Book for Boys,* by Lynda Madaras & D. Ssveddra (Newmarket, 1991), is written for parents and focuses on how to help boys cope with pubertal transitions.

■ *You're in Charge*, by Niels Lauersen & Eileen Stukane (Fawcett, 1993), is written for teenage girls and describes the changing female body.

Answer Key

Key Terms
1. **natural selection** The evolutionary process that favors individuals of a species that are best adapted to survive and reproduce.
2. **evolutionary psychology** Psychology's newest approach that emphasizes the importance of adoption, reproduction, and "survival of the fittest" in explaining behavior
3. **genotype** A person's genetic heritage; the actual genetic material.
4. **phenotype** The way an individual's genotype is expressed in observed and measurable characteristics.
5. **reaction range** The range of phenotypes for each genotype, suggesting the importance of the environment's restrictiveness or enrichment.

6. **canalization** The process by which characteristics takes a narrow path or developmental course. Apparently, preservative forces help protect a person from environmental extremes.

7. **behavior genetics** The study of the degree and nature of behavior's hereditary basis.

8. **twin study** A study in which the behavioral similarity of identical twins is compared with the behavioral similarity of fraternal twins.

9. **identical twins** Twins who develop from a single fertilized egg, which splits into two genetically identical replicas, each of which becomes a person. Also called monozygotic twins.

10. **fraternal twins** Twins who develop from separate eggs and separate sperm, making them genetically no more similar than nontwin siblings. Also called dizygotic twins.

11. **adoption study** A study in which investigators seek to discover whether, in behavior and psychological characteristics, adopted children and adolescents are more like their adoptive parents, who provided a home environment, or their biological parents, who contributed their heredity. Another form of adoption study is to compare adoptive and biological siblings.

12. **temperament** An individual's behavioral style and characteristic way of responding.

13. **easy child** A temperament category that involves being in a positive mood, quickly establishing routines, and adapting easily to new experiences.

14. **difficult child** A temperament category that involves reacting negatively, fussing a lot, engaging in irregular daily routines, and being slow to accept new experiences.

15. **slow-to-warm-up child** A temperament category that involves having a low activity level, being somewhat negative, showing low adaptability, and displaying a low intensity of mood.

16. **goodness-of-fit model** According to this model, an adolescent adapts best when there is a congruence, or match, between the adolescent's temperament and the demands of the social environment (such as the expectations and attitudes of parents, peers, and teachers).

17. **passive genotype-environment correlations** Occur when parents who are genetically related to the child provide a rearing environment for the child.

18. **evocative genotype-environment correlations** Occur when the adolescent's genotype elicits certain types of physical and social environments.

19. **active (niche-picking) genotype-environment correlations** Occur when adolescents seek out environments they find compatible and stimulating.

20. **shared environmental influences** Adolescents common environmental experiences that are shared with their sibling, such as their parents' personalities and intellectual orientation, the family's social class, and the neighborhood in which they live.

21. **nonshared environmental influences** The adolescent's own unique experiences, both within a family and outside the family that are not shared by another sibling.

22. **puberty** A period of rapid physical maturation involving hormonal and bodily changes that occur primarily in early adolescence.

23. **menarche** A girl's first menstruation.

24. **hormones** Powerful chemical substances secreted by the endocrine glands and carried through the body by the bloodstream.

25. **hypothalamus** A structure in the higher portion of the brain that monitors eating, drinking, and sex.

26. **pituitary gland** An important endocrine gland that controls growth and regulates other glands.

27. **gonads** The sex glands—the ovaries in females, the testes in males.

28. **androgens** The main class of male sex hormones.

29. **estrogens** The main class of female sex hormones.

30. **testosterone** A hormone associated in boys with genital development, an increase in height, and a change in voice.

31. **estradiol** A hormone associated in girls with breast, uterine, and skeletal development.

Key People in Adolescent Development

1. G
2. B
3. E
4. F
5. A
6. C
7. G
8. E

Evolution and Adolescent Development
Guided Review

1. Natural selection
2. survive
3. reproduce
4. Charles Darwin
5. *On the Origin of Species*
6. adaptation
7. reproduction
8. survival of the fittest
9. functionalism
10. David Buss
11. stress
12. resilience
13. programmed
14. predictable
15. bi-directional
16. alter
17. construct

Heredity and Environment
Guided Review

1. code
2. genes
3. chromosomes
4. genotype
5. phenotype
6. observed
7. physical
8. psychological
9. predispose
10. environments
11. reaction
12. canalization
13. Behavior genetics
14. twin
15. monozygotic
16. dizygotic
17. heredity
18. environment
19. Adoption
20. adopted
21. biological
22. adoptive
23. biological
24. adoptive
25. temperament
26. easy
27. difficult
28. slow-to-warm-up
29. goodness-of-fit
30. congruence (match)
31. parents
32. peers
33. teachers
34. heredity
35. environment
36. passively
37. evocatively
38. actively
39. personality
40. shared
41. nonshared
42. interact

Heredity and Environment
Section Review

1. SW
2. E
3. D
4. E
5. D
6. D
7. D
8. E
9. SW
10. E

Puberty
Guided Review

1. puberty	**8.** hormones	**15.** estrogens	**22.** 2	**29.** boys
2. menarche	**9.** hypothalamus	**16.** estradiol	**23.** 9	**30.** girls
3. 13	**10.** pituitary	**17.** androgens	**24.** 11	**31.** boys
4. nutrition	**11.** sex	**18.** testosterone	**25.** sexual	**32.** boys
5. health	**12.** gonads	**19.** height	**26.** wide	**33.** girls
6. heredity	**13.** testes	**20.** weight	**27.** 13/17	**34.** exaggerated
7. body mass	**14.** ovaries	**21.** sexual	**28.** 9/15	**35.** competently

Puberty
Section Review

1.
   a.   Pituitary gland—sends gonadotropins to the testes and ovaries.
   b.   Adrenal gland—involved in male adolescent behavior.
   c.   Hypothalamus—brain structure that interacts with pituitary gland to monitor regulation of hormones.
   d.   Thyroid gland—interacts with pituitary gland to influence grow.
   e.   Gonads—testes in males, ovaries in females. Strongly involved in the appearance of secondary sex characteristics, such as facial hair in males and breast development in females.

2.
   a.   Male
      1.   No public hair; penis, testes, and scrotum the same size and shape as those of a child.
      2.   A little soft, long, lightly colored hair at the base of the penis; testes and scrotum enlarged; penis grown a little; scrotum, sack holding testes, has lowered.
      3.   Pubic hair is darker and coarser and more curled; penis has grown in length; testes and scrotum have grown and dropped lower.
      4.   Pubic hair is dark, curly, and coarse and has spread to the thighs. Penis is larger and wider. Glans of penis is bigger. Scrotum is larger and bigger.
      5.   Hair has spread to thighs, and penis, scrotum, and testes are the size and shape of those of an adult male.
   b.   Female
      1.   Nipple raised.
      2.   Nipple raised more; breast is a small mound.
      3.   Areola and breast larger.
      4.   Areola and nipple make a mound that stick up.
      5.   Breasts fully developed.

Adolescent Health
Guided Review
1. drug abuse
2. violence
3. unprotected sex
4. driving dangerously
5. eating nutritiously
6. exercising
7. wearing seat belts
8. getting adequate sleep
9. television
10. schools
11. physical exercise
12. positive identity
13. accidents
14. suicide
15. homicide
16. motor vehicles
17. 10
18. 12
19. tripled
20. African American male
21. three
22. behavior
23. beliefs
24. knowledge
25. underestimate
26. substance abuse
27. unprotected sex
28. socioeconomic
29. poverty
30. health
31. autonomy
32. supportive
33. school lunch
34. physical education
35. life sciences
36. boys
37. girl
38. underutilize
39. cost
40. organization
41. availability
42. confidentiality

Explorations in Adolescence
The full-service school provides primary health clinics, youth service programs, and other services to improve access to health and social services. It is a partnership with community agencies and includes parents. Recent research suggests that this model improves mental and physical health, and helps decrease substance abuse, dropout rates, pregnancy, and truancy.

Adventures for the Mind
No answers provided—individual reflection and response.

Adolescence in Research
This was a longitudinal study, following more than 450 individuals in Milwaukee, Wisconsin, or 5 years, from sixth to tenth grade. The students were individually interviewed, and their achievement test scores and grade point averages were obtained. The researchers found that early-maturing girls had more problems in school, were more independent, and were more popular with boys than late-maturing girls were.

Comprehensive Review
1. d
2. b
3. c
4. a
5. d
6. b
7. c
8. b
9. a
10. c
11. b
12. b
13. c
14. d
15. b
16. c
17. b
18. a
19. c
20. a
21. a
22. b
23. c

◆ Chapter 4   Cognitive Development

Learning Objectives with Key Terms and Key People in Boldface

1.0   What is the Cognitive Developmental View of Adolescence?
- **A.   Piaget's Theory**
  - 1.1   What is the nature of Piaget's theory of cognitive processes?
  - 1.2   What is a **schema**?
  - 1.3   What roles do **assimilation** and **accommodation** play in cognitive development?
  - 1.4   What did Piaget mean by **equilibration**?
  - 1.5   What are names and defining characteristics of Piaget's four stages of cognitive development?
  - 1.6   How does an infant learn about the world in the **sensorimotor stage**?
  - 1.7   What happens in the **preoperational stage**?
  - 1.8   What are the characteristics of the **concrete operational stage**?
  - 1.9   What did Piaget mean by **operations**?
  - 1.10   What are the characteristics of **conservation** and **classification**?
  - 1.11   What are the indicators of the **formal operational stage**?
  - 1.12   What is **hypothetical-deductive reasoning**?
  - 1.13   What has been the significance of Piaget's theory for adolescent education?
  - 1.14   What were Piaget's main contributions to understanding cognitive development?
  - 1.15   What are the major criticisms of Piaget's theory?
  - 1.16   What are the distinctions between **early formal operational thought** and **late** formal operational thought?
- **B.   Vygotsky's Theory**
  - 1.17   Who are the **neo-Piagetians** who expanded and modified Piaget's theory?
  - 1.18   What were Vygotsky's main contributions to cognitive developmental theory?
  - 1.19   What did Lev Vygotsky mean by the **zone of proximal development (ZPD)**?
  - 1.20   How do the concepts of **scaffolding**, **cognitive apprenticeship**, **tutoring**, **cooperative learning**, and **reciprocal teaching** contribute to cognitive development and learning?
  - 1.21   Why do we say that Piaget and Vygotsky both were proponents of **constructivism**?
  - 1.22   What is the difference between a cognitive constructivist approach and a social constructivist approach?

2.0   What is the Information Processing View of Cognitive Development?
- **A.   Characteristics**
  - 2.1   What, according to Robert Siegler, are the three main characteristics of the information processing approach to cognitive development?
  - 2.2   What are the components of thinking, change mechanisms, and self-modification?
  - 2.3   According to Robbie Case, why are adolescents better at processing information than children?
  - 2.4   What is **automaticity**?
- **B.   Attention and Memory**
  - 2.5   What are **attention** and **memory** and why are they such important adolescent cognitive processes?
  - 2.6   What are the functions of **short-term memory** and **long-term memory**?

Key Terms

Write a sentence using each of these key terms by either defining the term or giving an example of it. For instance, you might write, "A schema is..." or, "(give examples) is an example of a schema." Compare your definitions with those given at the end of study guide chapter and check your examples by referring to the text. Review the text for those terms you don't know or define incorrectly.

1.   schema

_____

_____

2.   assimilation

_____

_____

3.   accommodation

_____

_____

4.   equilibration

_____

_____

5.   sensorimotor stage

_____

_____

6.   preoperational stage

_____

_____

7.   concrete operational thought

_____

_____

8.   operations

_____

_____

9.   conservation

_____

_____

10.   classification

_____

_____

11.   formal operational thought

_____

_____

12.   hypothetical-deductive reasoning

_____

_____

13.   early formal operational thought

_____

_____

14.   late formal operational thought

_____

_____

15.   neo-Piagetians

_____

_____

16.   zone of proximal development (ZPD)

_____

_____

17.   scaffolding

_____

_____

18.   cognitive apprenticeship

_____

_____

19.   cooperative learning

_____

_____

20. reciprocal teaching

_____

_____

21. constructivism

_____

_____

22. automaticity

_____

_____

23. attention

_____

_____

24. memory

_____

_____

25. short-term memory

_____

_____

26. long-term memory

_____

_____

27. strategies

_____

_____

28. critical thinking

_____

_____

29. Jasper Project

_____

_____

30. creativity

_____

_____

31.   convergent thinking

_____

_____

32.   divergent thinking

_____

_____

33.   brainstorming

_____

_____

34.   metacognition

_____

_____

35.   metacognitive knowledge

_____

_____

36.   metacognitive activity

_____

_____

37.   self-regulatory learning

_____

_____

38.   psychometric/intelligence point of view

_____

_____

39.   intelligence

_____

_____

40.   mental age (MA)

_____

_____

41.   intelligent quotient (IQ)

_____

_____

42.   normal distribution

_____

_____

43. triarchic theory of intelligence

_____

_____

44. emotional intelligence

_____

_____

45. culture-fair tests

_____

_____

46. social cognition

_____

_____

47. adolescent egocentrism

_____

_____

48. imaginary audience

_____

_____

49. personal fable

_____

_____

50. perspective taking

_____

_____

51. implicit personality theory

_____

_____

Key People in the Study of Adolescence

Match the name with the concept, issue, or topic related to adolescence with which they are associated.

___	1. Jean Piaget	A. Multiple intelligences
___	2. Lev Vygotsky	B. Mental age (MA)
___	3. Barbara Rogoff	C. Four stages of cognitive development
___	4. Annamarie Palincsar & Ann Brown	D. General intelligence
___	5. Robert Siegler	E. Triarchic theory of intelligence
___	6. Robbie Case	F. Zone of proximal development
___	7. Daniel Keating	G. Cognitive apprenticeships
___	8. J.P. Guilford	H. Information processing view
___	9. Mihalyi Csikszentmihalyi	I. Reciprocal teaching
___	10. Michael Pressley	J. Automaticity
___	11. Deanna Kuhn	K. Creativity
___	12. Alfred Binet	L. Metacognition & critical thinking
___	13. William Stern	M. Strategies
___	14. David Wechsler	N. Primary abilities related to intelligence
___	15. Charles Spearman	O. Developed IQ tests with several subscales
___	16. L. L. Thurstone	P. Emotional intelligence
___	17. Robert Sternberg	Q. Imaginary audience & personal fable
___	18. Howard Gardner	R. Perspective taking
___	19. Daniel Goleman	S. Adolescent decision-making
___	20. David Elkind	T. Convergent & divergent thinking
___	21. Robert Selman	U. Intelligence quotient (IQ)

The Cognitive Developmental View
Guided Review

The most well known theory of adolescent cognitive development is that of (1) _____. He believed that adolescents use (2) _____ to construct their world, by the (3) _____ of new information, and the (4) _____ to new information. New information and experiences may cause (5) _____, which causes a shift from one stage of thought to the next. He believed that individuals develop through four cognitive stages: (6) _____, (7) _____, (8) _____, and (9) _____. The (10) _____ stage last from birth to about 2 years, and children construct their understanding of the world through their (11) _____ and (12) _____ actions. The (13) _____ stage lasts from about 2 to 7 years of age. In this stage children begin to represent the world with (14) _____, (15) _____, and (16) _____. The third stage, the (17) _____ stage, lasts from about 7 to 11 years of age. In this stage children can perform operations, which are another word for (18) _____ actions. The most characteristic skills learned in this stage are (19)_____ and (20) _____. However, in this stage children cannot reason (21) _____ about objects. The last stage, that of (22) _____ thought, occurs between the ages of 11 - 15 years, and is characterized by (23) _____, (24) _____, and (25) _____-_____ thinking. Some experts thing that this stage has two phases: (26) _____ and (27) _____. Critics of this theory say that Piaget did not sufficiently take into account (28) _____ and (29) _____. A group of theorists known as (30) _____ have proposed substantial changes in Piaget's theory.

The most well known neo-Piagetian is (31) _____. He believed that knowledge is (32) _____ and (33)_____. One of his most important concepts is that of the (34) _____ of (35) _____, which involves children being guided by (36) _____ and skilled (37) _____. Vygotsky stressed that learning (38) _____ skills is a key aspect of development. Some contemporary concepts linked to Vygotsky's theory include (39) _____, (40) _____ apprenticeship, (41) _____, (42) _____ learning and (43) _____ teaching.

Both Piaget and Vygotsky's views are considered (44) _____. Piaget's is (45) _____ and Vygotsky's is (46) _____. In both of their views, teachers should be (47) _____, not directors of learning.

The Cognitive Developmental View
Section Review

1. Using any event or experience of your choice, describe how an existing schema was changed as a result of disequilibrium, assimilation, and accommodation.

_____

_____

2. Explain how each of these contemporary cognitive concepts would be utilized in a secondary high school classroom.

a. Scaffolding

_____

b. cognitive apprenticeship

_____

c. tutoring

_____

d. cooperative learning

_____

e. reciprocal teaching

_____

_____

3. Fill in the boxes with the descriptions comparing the views of Piaget and Vygotsky.

Topic	Vygotsky	Piaget
Constructivism		
Stages		
View on Education		
Teaching Implications		

The Information Processing Approach
Guided Review

Robert Siegler described the three main characteristics of the information processing approach as (1) _____, (2) _____ which include (3) _____, (4) _____, (5) _____ construction, and (6) _____, and (7) _____. Adolescents have better (8) _____ and (9) _____ skills than children. Adolescence is time of increased (10) _____ making, and adolescents are better at it than children. However, breadth of (11) _____ is important in making decisions in every-day life. Critical thinking involves thinking (12) _____, (13) _____, and (14) _____ the evidence. The cognitive changes taking place in adolescence that are important to critical thinking are increased (15) _____, (16) _____, and capacity of (17) _____, breadth of (18) _____ knowledge, increased ability to construct new (19) _____ of knowledge, and a greater range of spontaneous use of (20) _____. The videodisc based educational program that focuses on solving real-world math problems is the (21) _____ Project. Debates about critical thinking center on whether it should be taught in a (22) _____ way or tied to (23) _____ subject matter, and whether it resides in an adolescent's (24) _____ or is (25) _____. Creative thinking involves thinking about something in (26) _____ and (27) _____ ways and coming up with (28) _____ solutions to problems. J.P. Guilford distinguished between (29) _____ thinking, which produces one correct answer, and (30) _____ thinking, which is more characteristic of creativity. (31) _____ is a useful strategy to stimulate creative thinking. Knowing about knowing is called (32) _____. According to Michael Pressley, education should help students learn a rich repertoire of (33) _____ that lead to solutions to problems. Deanna Kuhn argues that metacognition is the key to developing (34) _____ skills. Self-generation and self-monitoring of thoughts, feelings, and behaviors is known as (35) _____ learning, a hallmark of high-achieving students.

Information Processing Approach
Section Review

1.   List seven strategies for encouraging adolescent creative thinking.

_____

_____

_____

2.   What did Sternberg's research disclose about the relationship between short-term memory and problem solving?

_____

_____

3.   What are the characteristics of self-regulatory learners?

_____

_____

The Psychometric/Intelligence View
Guided Review

The psychometric/intelligence view of cognitive development emphasizes the importance of (1) _____ differences in (2) _____. Many advocates of this view argue that intelligence should be assess by (3) _____. One generally accepted definition of intelligence is that it consists of (4) _____ ability, (5) _____ skills, and the ability to (6) _____ to (7) _____. The first intelligence test was developed by (8) _____- and (9) _____ in order to find out which students would not benefit from (10) _____. Binet developed the concept of (11) _____, an individual's level of mental development relative to others. In 1912, (12) _____ created the concept of (13) _____-, which refers to a person's (14) _____ age divided by (15) _____ age, multiplied by (16) _____. The equation is expressed as: (17) _____. If a mental age is the same as his or her chronological age, the person's IQ is (18) _____. If mental age is above chronological age, the IQ is (19) _____100, and (20)_____ 100 if mental age is below chronological age. The revised Binet test

is known as the (21)_____. When the majority of test scores fall in the middle of the possible range of score, with few scores at the extreme ends, the scores are said to be a (22)_____.
American (23) _____ developed a widely used intelligence test known as the (24) _____. The scales provide a (25) _____ IQ, as well as (26) _____ and (27)_____ IQ. Charles Spearman proposed that people have a (28) _____ intelligence, which he called (29) _____, and specific intelligences, which he called (30) _____. L.L. Thurstone believed that people have (31) _____ specific abilities, which he called (32) _____ mental abilities. Robert Sternberg's (33) _____ theory of intelligence states that the three forms of intelligence are: (34) _____, (35) _____, and (36) _____. Howard Gardner developed the theory of (37) _____ intelligences, or (38) _____ of mind. They are: (39) _____, (40) _____, (41) _____, (42) _____, (43) _____, (44) _____, (45) _____, and (46) _____. Daniel Goleman has argued for a form of social intelligence called (47) _____ intelligence, that involves the ability to monitor one's own and others' (48) _____ and (49) _____ in order to guide one's own thinking and action. Goleman believes that the four main processes of this form of intelligence are emotional (50) _____, (51) _____ emotions, (52) _____ emotions, and (53) _____ relationships. Controversies and issues in the intelligence view of cognitive development involve those related to (54) _____ and _____; (55) _____ and _____; and the (56) _____ and _____ of intelligence tests. As for the latter controversy, it is always important to remember that intelligence tests are an indicator of (57) _____ performance, not (58) _____ potential.

The Psychometric/Intelligence View
Section Review

1.   Describe how each of components of Sternberg's triarchic theory of intelligence would be utilized in writing a book report.

_____

_____

2.   Match the skills indicative of each of Gardner's eight frames of mind with the profession or vocation they are most likely to be associated with.

_____ 1. scientists, engineers, accountants	A. verbal skills
_____ 2. farmers, botanists, landscapers	B. intrapersonal
_____ 3. teachers and mental health professionals	C. mathematical
_____ 4. surgeons, dancers, athletes	D. naturalist
_____ 5. composers and musicians	E. spatial
_____ 6. theologians and psychologists	F. interpersonal
_____ 7. authors, journalists, speakers	G. bodily-kinesthetic
_____ 8. architects, artists, sailors	H. musical

3. Summarize the current status of the following debates about intelligence:
   a. Nature and nurture

   _____

   _____

   b. Ethnicity and culture

   _____

   _____

   c. Use and misuse of intelligence tests

   _____

   _____

Social Cognition
Guided Review

The way people conceptualize and reason about their social world is known as (1) _____. The heightened self-consciousness of adolescents is known as (2) _____, which David Elkind says consists of (3) _____, the adolescent belief that everyone is as interested in them as they are in themselves , and the (4) _____ _____, thinking that they are unique. Elkind says that egocentrism is the result of what Piaget called (5) _____. Robert Selman proposed a developmental theory of (6) _____, which is the ability to assume another person's perspective and understand his or her thoughts and feelings. Selman believes that this characteristic develops in (7) _____ stages. The layperson's conception of personality is known as (8) _____ personality theory. Adolescent personality theory is more like that of (9) _____ than the theories of children. Adolescents seem to take into account (10) _____ and _____ information when evaluating people, and to look at (11) _____ and (12) _____ variants in personality. Social cognition will be an important part of several chapters of the text, including those relating to (13) _____, (14) _____. (15) _____ and _____, and (16) _____ development.

Social Cognition
Section Review

1. Fill in the blanks with the name, age, and description of each of Selman's Stages of Perspective Taking.

Stage #	Stage name	Ages	Description
0			
1			
2			
3			
4			

2. Do you have a personal fable? What does it consist of? Do you think that it is important to have a personal fable? Why or why not?

_____

_____

Explorations in Adolescence
How does the Fostering a Community of Learners school program encourage reflection and discussion?

_____

_____

Adventures for the Mind
Think of a situation in which it might be against your best interests to be egocentric. Now think of one in which it might be very adaptive to act as if all eyes are on you. It is reasonable to conclude that adolescent egocentrism should, under some circumstances, continue throughout life?

_____

_____

Adolescence in Research
Concerning Lewis's 1981 research about adolescent decision making, state the hypothesis, the research methods (if known), the research conclusions, and the implications and applications for adolescent development.

_____

_____

Comprehensive Review
1. According to Jean Piaget, the fundamental ways in which adolescents adapt their thinking entails
    a. conservation and classification.
    b. social information processing and perspective taking.
    c. the imaginary audience and the personal fable.
    d. assimilation and accommodation.

2. When children begin representing their worlds in images and words, they are in which stage of cognitive development?
    a. sensorimotor
    b. preoperational
    c. concrete operational
    d. informal operational

3. A child begins to pull toys from her toy box; in so doing, she sorts them into piles of cars, trucks, and animals. She also understands that some toys can be switched from one pile to another or can form new piles based on types having similar colors. This behavior reflects the cognitive ability called
    a. perspective taking.
    b. classification.
    c. organization.
    d. conservation.

4. Unlike the concrete operational child, the formal operational adolescent can demonstrate
    a. assimilation.
    b. reversible mental operations.
    c. conservation ability.
    d. hypothetical-deductive reasoning.

5. Compared to the early formal operational problem solver, the late formal operational solver
    a. derives her hypothesis from the problem data.
    b. looks for a general hypothesis to explain what has happened.
    c. is satisfied with general statements about cause and effect.
    d. searches for necessary and sufficient conditions to explain the results.

6. Which of the following statements does not describe one of Jean Piaget's contributions to the field of cognitive development?
    a. Jean Piaget contributed a number of important concepts such as conservation and object permanence.
    b. Jean Piaget demonstrated that culture and education influence cognitive development.
    c. Jean Piaget demonstrated that we adapt to our environment.
    d. Jean Piaget made many insightful and systematic observations of children.

7. Which group of developmentalists believes that cognitive development is more specific in many respects than did Piaget?
    a. Piagetians
    b. Neo-Piagetians
    c. competency-based developmentalists
    d. information processing developmentalists

8. Perhaps the greatest general criticism is that Piaget's theory tends to underestimate the importance of ____ in cognitive development.
    a. culture and education
    b. arts and entertainment
    c. authority and mystery
    d. sexuality and role playing

9. Tasks too difficult for an individual that can be mastered with the help of more skilled individuals defines what
    a. Jean Piaget called hypothetical-deductive reasoning.
    b. Lev Vygotsky called the zone of proximal development.
    c. Kurt Fisher called abstract relations.
    d. Neo-Piagetians called social information.

10. The study of social cognition has been related to all of the following except
    a. the nature of physical development.
    b. moral reasoning.
    c. social intelligence.
    d. the nature of friendship.

11. Adolescent egocentrism is represented by two types of thinking referred to as
    a. the imaginary audience and the personal fable.
    b. the abiding self and the transient self.
    c. narcissism and the imaginary audience.
    d. the indestructible self and the transient self.

12. Your 20-year-old friend confesses to you that she has always thought that somehow she was very different from everyone she knew, in her feelings and her understanding of the world. You might suspect that her sense of herself reflects
   a. David Elkind's notion of the personal fable.
   b. an organic pathology, perhaps a temporal lobe tumor.
   c. a failure to achieve formal operational thought.
   d. developmental delay of adolescence.

13. Perspective taking refers to the adolescent's
   a. ability to infer and adopt the perspective of another.
   b. formation of concepts about himself and others.
   c. egocentric assumption that others are preoccupied with his behavior.
   d. ability to form impressions of others.

14. Your adolescent sister says that people with red hair cannot be trusted. Your recognize that she is developing
   a. an inability to take another person's perspective.
   b. a dangerous form of prejudice.
   c. an implicit personality theory.
   d. a personal fable.

15. While taking an IQ test, a series of numbers is read aloud to a student, with the student being asked to repeat them as quickly as possible. Which kind of memory is being assessed?
   a. long-term
   b. short-term
   c. digital
   d. conceptual

16. Which term includes the ability to learn from and adapt to our everyday lives?
   a. self
   b. intelligence
   c. knowable self
   d. learned personality

17. Alfred Binet developed intelligence tests to
   a. show that intelligence is largely the result of heredity.
   b. identify students who would not profit from typical schooling.
   c. identify students who were gifted, and needed extra challenges in their schooling.
   d. distinguish convergent thinkers from divergent thinkers.

18. One of the main advantages of the Wechsler scales over the Binet test is that the Wechsler scales include measures that are
   a. progressive.
   b. culturally specific.
   c. not verbal.
   d. screen for brain damage.

19. The _____ intelligence test is often employed in assessing older adolescents because it is particularly good in identifying specific strengths and weaknesses in mental performance.
    a. Stanford-Binet
    b. WAIS-R
    c. WC-R
    d. Terman Intelligence Scale

20. Which of the following individuals did not propose a theory of intelligence?
    a. L.L. Thurstone
    b. Lewis Terman
    c. Charles Spearman
    d. Howard Gardner

21. The type or aspect of intelligence measured by the Binet and Wechsler tests is most closely matched to the aspect Sternberg calls
    a. componential intelligence.
    b. experiential intelligence.
    c. contextual intelligence.
    d. tacit knowledge.

22. According to Howard Gardner
    a. it is better to administer intelligence tests to individuals than to groups.
    b. intelligence is best defined in terms of seven frames of mind.
    c. individuals have a general intelligence rather than various specific intelligences.
    d. intelligence is best defined in terms of three main components.

23. In addition to the question of whether intelligence is primarily inherited, another important question about intelligence concerns
    a. the arbitrary distinction between aptitude and achievement tests.
    b. cultural and ethnic differences in test scores.
    c. using the computer as a model for information processing.
    d. the emotional and social adjustment of gifted individuals.

24. Intelligence tests explicit designed to minimize the differences between ethnic groups are called
    a. bias liberated.
    b. culture fair.
    c. socially equitable.
    d. psychometrically equivalent.

25. A psychology professor asks his students to think of as many uses as possible for a paper clip. The professor is encouraging
    a. brainstorming.
    b. divergent thinking.
    c. convergent thinking.
    d. ideational originality.

Adolescence on the Screen

■ *Phenomenon* explores the problems that come with high levels of intelligence.

■ *Searching for Bobby Fischer* depicts parents facing the dilemma of raising a gifted chess prodigy.

Adolescence in Books

■ *Teaching and Learning Through Multiple Intelligences (Second Edition)*, by Linda Campbell, Bruce Campbell, and Dee Dickonson (Allyn & Bacon, 1999), provides applications of Gardner's eight intelligences to classrooms.

■ *How People Learn*, by Committee on Developments in the Science of Learning (National Academy Press, 1999), describes the current state of knowledge about how children and youth think and learn.

Answer Key

Key Terms

1. **schema** Piaget's theory of a concept or framework that exists in the individual's mind to organize and interpret information.
2. **assimilation** Occurs when individuals incorporate new information into existing knowledge.
3. **accommodation** Occurs when individuals adjust to new information.
4. **equilibration** A mechanism in Piaget's theory that explains how children or adolescents shift from one stage of thought to the next. The shift occurs as they experience cognitive conflict or a disequilibrium in trying to understand the world. Eventually, the child or adolescent resolves the conflict and reaches a balance or equilibrium.
5. **sensorimotor stage** Piaget's first stage of development, lasting from birth to about 2 years of age. In this stage, infants construct an understanding of the world by coordinating sensory experiences with physical, motoric actions.
6. **preoperational stage** Piaget's second stage, which lasts from about 2 to 7 years of age. In this stage children begin to represent their world with words, images, and drawings.
7. **concrete operational thought** Piaget's third stage, which lasts from about 7 to 11 years of age. In this stage, children can perform operations. Logical reasoning replaces intuitive thought as long as the reasoning can be applied to specific or concrete examples.
8. **operations** Mental actions that let the individual do mentally what was only done before physically; also involves engaging in mental actions that are reversible.
9. **conservation** Piaget's term for an individual's ability to recognize that length, number, mass, quantity, area, weight, and volume of objects and substances do not change through transformations that alter their appearance
10. **classification** Also called class inclusion reasoning, this concept in concrete operational thought requires individuals to systematically organize objects into hierarchies of classes and subclasses
11. **formal operational thought** Piaget's fourth and final stage of cognitive development, which he believes emerges between 11 to 15 years of age. It is characterized by abstract, idealistic, and logical thought.
12. **hypothetical-deductive reasoning** Piaget's term for adolescents' ability, in the formal operational stage, to develop hypotheses, or best guesses, about ways to solve problems; they then systematically deduce, or conclude the best path to follow in solving the problem.
13. **early formal operational thought** Involves adolescents' increased ability to think in hypothetical ways, which produces unconstrained thoughts with unlimited possibilities. Formal operational thought submerges reality as the world is perceived too idealistically and subjectively.

14. **late formal operational thought** Involves a restoration of cognitive balance; adolescents now test out the products of their reasoning against experience and a consolidation of formal operational thought takes place.

15. **neo-Piagetians** They argue that Piaget got some things right, but that his theory needs considerable revisions. In their revision, they give more emphasis to information processing that involves attention, memory, and strategies; they also seek to provide more precise explanations of cognitive changes.

16. **zone of proximal development (ZPD)** Vygotsky's concept that refers to the range of tasks that are too difficult for individuals to master alone, but that can be mastered with the guidance or assistance of adults or more skilled peers.

17. **scaffolding** Refers to changing levels of support over the course of a teaching session; a more skilled person (teacher or a more advanced peer) adjusts the amount of guidance to fit the adolescent's current level of performance.

18. **cognitive apprenticeship** Involves a novice and an expert, who stretches the novice's understanding of and use of the culture's skills.

19. **cooperative learning** Involves students working in small groups to help each other learn.

20. **reciprocal teaching** Involves students taking turns leading a small group discussion. Reciprocal teaching can also involve an adult and an adolescent.

21. **constructivism** Emphasizes that individuals actively construct knowledge and understanding.

22. **automaticity** The ability to process information with little or no effort.

23. **attention** The concentration and focusing of mental effort.

24. **memory** The retention of information over time.

25. **short-term memory** A limited-capacity memory system in which information is retained for as long as 30 seconds, unless the information is rehearsed, in which case it can be retained longer.

26. **long-term memory** A relatively permanent memory system that holds huge amounts of information for a long period of time.

27. **strategies** Activities that are under the learner's conscious control; they sometimes are called control processes. For example, organization is one important strategy.

28. **critical thinking** Thinking reflectively, productively, and evaluating the evidence.

29. **Jasper Project** Twelve videodisc-based adventures that focus on solving real-world math problems.

30. **creativity** The ability to think about something in novel and unusual ways and come up with unique solutions to problems.

31. **convergent thinking** According to Guilford, a pattern of thinking in which individuals produce one correct answer; characteristic of the terms on conventional intelligence tests.

32. **divergent thinking** According to Guilford, a pattern of thinking in which individuals produce many answers to the same question; more characteristic of creativity than convergent thinking.

33. **brainstorming** A technique in which individuals are encouraged to come up with creative ideas in a group, play off each other's ideas, and say practically whatever comes to mind relevant to a particular issue.

34. **metacognition** Cognition about cognition, or "knowing about knowing."

35. **metacognitive knowledge** Involves monitoring and reflecting on one's recent thoughts.

36. **metacognitive activity** Occurs when individuals use self-awareness to adapt to and manage strategies during actual problem solving and thinking.

37. **self-regulatory learning** Consists of the self-generation and self-monitoring of thoughts, feelings, and behaviors to reach a goal.

38. **psychometric/intelligence view** Emphasizes the importance of individual differences in intelligence. Many advocates of this view also argue that intelligence should be assessed with intelligence tests.

39. **intelligence** Mental ability related to verbal and problem-solving skills, and the ability to adapt to and learn from life's everyday experiences. Not everyone agrees on what constitutes intelligence.

40. **mental age (MA)** Developed by Binet, an individual's level of mental development relative to others.

41. **intelligent quotient (IQ)** A person's tested mental age divided by chronological age, multiplied by 100.

42. **normal distribution** A symmetrical distribution of values or scores with a majority of scores falling in the middle of the possible range of scores and few scores appearing toward the extremes of the range; a distribution that yields what is called a "bell-shaped curve."

43. **triarchic theory of intelligence** Sternberg's view that intelligence comes in three main forms: analytical, experiential, and contextual.

44. **emotional intelligence** A form of social intelligence that involves the ability to monitor one's own and others' feelings and emotions, to discriminate among them, and to sue this information to guide one's thinking and action.

45. **culture-fair tests** Tests of intelligence that attempt to be free of cultural bias.

46. **social cognition** How individuals conceptualize and reason about their social world—the people they watch and interact with, relationships with those people, the groups in which they participate, and how they reason about themselves and others.

47. **adolescent egocentrism** The heightened self-consciousness of adolescents, which is reflected in their belief that others are as interested in them as they are in themselves.

48. **imaginary audience** According to Elkind, the imaginary audience involves attention-getting behavior—the desire to be noticed, visible, and "on stage."

49. **personal fable** An adolescent's sense of personal uniqueness.

50. **perspective taking** The ability to assume another person's perspective and understand his or her thoughts and feelings.

51. **implicit personality theory** The layperson's conception of personality.

Key People

1. C	7. S	13. U	19. P
2. F	8. T	14. O	20. Q
3. G	9. K	15. D	21. R
4. I	10. M	16. N	
5. H	11. L	17. E	
6. J	12. B	18. A	

The Cognitive Developmental View
Guided Review

1. Jean Piaget	13. preoperational	25. hypothetical/ deductive	36. adults
2. schemas	14. words	26. early	37. peers
3. assimilation	15. images	27. late	38. cultural
4. accommodation	16. drawings	28. culture	39. scaffolding
5. disequilibrium	17. concrete operational	29. education	40. cognitive
6. sensorimotor	18. mental	30. neo-Piagetian	41. tutoring
7. preoperational	19. conservation	31. Lev Vygotsky	42. cooperative
8. concrete operational	20. classification	32. situated	43. reciprocal
9. formal operational	21. abstractly	33. collaborative	44. constructivist
10. sensorimotor	22. formal operational	34. zone	45. cognitive
11. senses	23. abstract	35. proximal	46. social
12. motoric	24. idealistic		47. facilitators

Cognitive Developmental View
Section Review

1. No answer provided—personal reflection. However, the answer should describe the preexisting schema, the disequilibrium that resulted as the result of the new information or experience, indicate the new information that was assimilated, and state how the old schema accommodated the new information.

2.
a. Scaffolding involves direct teaching, with less guidance provided by teacher or more advanced peer as student learns more.
b. Cognitive apprenticeship involves an adult or expert modeling thinking strategies and allowing students to anticipate or complete the expert's next step or idea.
c. Tutoring involves a cognitive apprenticeship between and adult or more skilled adolescent. Fellow students are more effective tutors, and peer tutoring also benefits the tutor.
d. Cooperative learning involves working and learning in small groups.
e. Reciprocal teaching involves students taking turns leading a small group discussion. The teacher gradually assumes a less active role, letting the student assume more initiative.

3.

Topic	Vygotsky	Piaget
Constructivism	Social constructivist	Cognitive constructivist
Stages	No general stages of development proposed.	Strong emphasis on stages—sensorimotor, preoperational, concrete operational, and formal operational.
View on Education	Education plays a central role in helping children learn the tools of the culture.	Education merely refines the child's cognitive skills that already have emerged.
Teaching Implications	Teacher is facilitator and guide, not director; establishes learning opportunities for children to learn with teacher and more skilled peers	Teacher is facilitator and guide, but not director; teacher provides support for children to explore their world and discover knowledge.

The Information Processing Approach
Guided Review

1. thinking
2. change mechanisms
3. encoding
4. automaticity
5. strategy
6. generalization
7. self-modification
8. attention
9. memory
10. decision
11. experience
12. reflectively
13. productivity
14. evaluating
15. speed
16. automaticity
17. information processing
18. content
19. combinations
20. strategies
21. Jasper
22. general
23. specific
24. heads
25. situated
26. novel
27. unusual
28. unique
29. convergent
30. divergent
31. brainstorming
32. metacognition
33. strategies
34. critical thinking
35. self-regulatory

Information Processing Approach
Section Review
1. a. Encourage adolescents to use brainstorming.
    b. Provide an environment that stimulates creativity.
    c. Don't over control the situation.
    d. Encourage internal self-motivation.
    e. Foster flexible and playful thinking.
    f. Introduce adolescents to creative people.
    g. Talk with adolescents about creative people or have them read about them.

2. Adolescents had better problem-solving skills than children because their short-term memory had greater capacity. Children seemed to run out of short-term memory before they were able to think through the problem.

3. Self regulatory learners (1) set goals for extending their knowledge and sustaining their motivation; (2) are aware of their emotional make-up and have strategies for managing their emotions; (3) periodically monitor their progress toward a goal; (4) fine tune or revise their strategies based on the progress they are making; and (5) evaluate obstacles that may arise and make the necessary adaptations.

Psychometric/Intelligence View
Guided Review
1. individual
2. intelligence
3. intelligence tests
4. verbal
5. problem-solving
6. adapt
7. experience
8. Alfred Binet
9. Theophile Simon
10. classroom education
11. mental age (MA)
12. William Stern
13. IQ
14. mental age
15. chronological
16. 100
17. IQ=MA/CA × 100
18. 100
19. above
20. below
21. Stanford-Binet
22. normal distribution
23. David Wechsler
24. Wechsler scales
25. full-scale
26. performance
27. verbal
28. general
29. "g"
30. "s"
31. seven
32. primary
33. triarchic
34. analytical
35. creative
36. practical
37. multiple
38. eight
39. verbal
40. math
41. spatial
42. movement
43. self-insight
44. insight about others
45. musical
46. naturalist
47. emotional
48. feelings
49. emotions
50. self-awareness
51. emotions
52. reading
53. handling
54. nature/nurture
55. ethnicity/culture
56. use/misuse
57. current
58. fixed

Psychometric/Intelligence View
Section Review
1. a. Analytical —Analyze the book's main themes.
    b. Creative—Generate new ideas about how the book might have been written better.
    c. Practical—Think about how the book's themes can be applied to real life.

2. **1.** C; **2.** D; **3.** F; **4.** G; **5.** H; **6.** B; **7.** A; **8.** E.

3.   a.   Nature and nurture—Heredity is an important part of intelligence.

       b.   Ethnicity and culture—There are ethnic differences in the average scores on standardized intelligence tests between African American and White American adolescents, but the differences are believed to be the result of environmental factors such as social, economic, and educational opportunities.

       c.   Use and misuse of intelligence tests—Intelligence tests can lead to stereotypes and expectations about adolescents and should not be used as the main or sole characteristic of competence. Further, intelligence tests do not take into account the many domains of intelligence, such as those described by Sternberg and Gardner.

Social Cognition
Guided Review

1. social cognition
2. egocentrism
3. imaginary audience
4. personal fable
5. formal operational thought
6. perspective taking
7. five
8. implicit
9. psychologists
10. past/present
11. situational
12. contextual
13. family
14. peers
15. self/identity
16. moral

Social Cognition
Section Review

1.

Stage #	Stage name	Ages	Description
0	Egocentric	3—6	No distinction between social perspective of self and others.
1	Social-informational perspective taking	6—8	Ability to focus on one social perspective rather than coordinating viewpoints.
2	Self-reflective perspective taking	8—10	Can form coordinated chain of perspectives but cannot understand simultaneous mutuality.
3	Mutual perspective taking	10–12	Understands simultaneous mutuality between two people and can also view the interaction from an additional third person perspective.
4	Social and conventional system perspective taking	12–15	Adolescent realizes mutual perspective taking is a necessary social convention.

2. No answer provided—personal reflection.

Explorations in Adolescence

The three strategies that foster reflection and discussion in the FCL classroom are (1) using visiting experts and teachers to model thinking and self-reflection about a topic; (2) letting students teach each other, especially cross-age teaching; and (3) providing access to experts on-line, by way of e-mail.

Adventures for the Mind
An example of maladaptive egocentrism would be when you have to give a report in class, for which you are well-prepared, and you are so concerned that if you make a mistake people will notice and think how terrible you are that you cannot relax and do your best. An example when it is appropriate to think all eyes are on you is when you are caring for or teaching children who look up to you as a role model.

Adolescence in Research
The hypothesis, that older adolescents are better at decision making than younger adolescents, was supported by the research. Eight-, tenth-, and twelfth-grade students were presented with dilemmas involving the choice of a medical procedure. The oldest students were most likely to spontaneously mention a variety of risks, to recommend outside consultation, and to anticipate future consequences. Eighth-graders had a more short-terms view, such as the effects of getting turned down for a date, or being teased by peers.

Comprehensive Review

1. d	**6.** b	**11.** a	**16.** b	**21.** a
2. b	**7.** b	**12.** a	**17.** b	**22.** b
3. b	**8.** a	**13.** a	**18.** c	**23.** b
4. d	**9.** b	**14.** c	**19.** b	**24.** b
5. d	**10.** a	**15.** b	**20.** b	**25.** b

◆ Chapter 5   Families

Learning Objectives with Key Terms and Key People in Boldface

1.0   What Family Processes Affect Adolescent Development?

A.   Reciprocal Socialization, Synchrony, and the Family As A System

1.1   What is reciprocal socialization and how does it affect adolescent development?

1.2   What is meant by parent-adolescent **synchrony**?

1.3   What defines a family's social system?

B.   Developmental Construction of Relationships

1.4   What is the developmental construction of relationships?

1.5   What are the main variations of the **developmental construction views**?

1.6   What is the difference between the **continuity view** and the **discontinuity view**?

1.7   What research evidence exists in support of each view?

C.   Maturation of the Adolescent and Maturation of Parents

1.8   What parental and adolescent maturation processes affect parent-adolescent interaction?

1.9   What are the major changes in adolescence that influence parent-adolescent relationships?

1.10   What parental changes contribute to parent-adolescent relationships?

1.11   How does the timing of parenthood affect parent-adolescent interaction?

D.   Sociocultural and Historical Changes

1.12   What sociocultural and historical changes affect family processes?

1.13   What sociocultural changes have made families different than they were 50 years ago?

E.   The Roles of Cognition and Emotion in Family Relationships

1.14   What roles do cognition and emotions play in family socialization?

1.15   What parental cognitive factors affect their children's social development?

1.16   What processes help us understand family relationships?

2.0   What Factors Influence Parent-Adolescent Relationships?

A.   Parents as Managers

2.1   What do we mean when we say that parents should manage their adolescent's lives?

B.   Parenting Techniques

2.2   What are the four main parenting categories and which one is most closely associated with socially competent behavior?

2.3   What is the nature of **authoritarian, authoritative, neglectful**, and **indulgent** parenting styles?

C.   Parent-Adolescent Conflict

2.4   What is the nature and extent of parent-adolescent conflict?

2.5   At what point in adolescence does conflict peak?

2.6   What is the subject of most parental-adolescent conflict?

2.7   What beneficial effects may conflict have on adolescents?

2.8   What is the generation gap?

2.9   What percentage of families is parent-adolescent conflict high?

2.10   What problems are associated with intense, prolonged conflict?

D.   Autonomy and Attachment

2.11   How important are autonomy and attachment in an adolescent's successful adaptation to adulthood?

2.12   What is the difference between autonomy and **emotional autonomy**?

2.13   What is the appropriate time for adolescents to achieve autonomy from their parents?

2.14   What problems do parents have with their adolescent's achieving autonomy?

2.15   What developmental transition signals autonomy?

2.16   Why do some adolescents run away from home, and what problems might they be susceptible to as a result?

2.17   What is the best advice to give a parent about their adolescent's need for autonomy?

2.18   Why is it important that adolescents be both autonomous and attached to their parents?

2.19   What is the difference between **secure attachment** and **insecure attachment**?

2.20   Why is secure attachment related social competence and successful adaptation to the world?

2.21   What is the Adult Attachment Interview (AAI)?

2.22   What is the difference between **dismissing/avoidant attachment, preoccupied/ambivalent attachment**, and **unresolved/disorganized attachment**?

3.0   What are the Components of Sibling Relationships?

A.   Sibling Roles

3.1   What is the nature and extent of conflict in many sibling relationships?

B.   Developmental Changes

3.2   How do sibling relationships change over time?

C.   Birth Order

3.3   How does birth order affect sibling and parent relationships?

3.4   Is an only child likely to be a "spoiled brat"?

3.5   What is the most reasonable conclusion to be gained from research about the effects of birth order on adolescent behavior and achievement?

4.0   How is Today's Family Changing, and What Society and Social Policy Developments Help Account for the Changes?

A.   Divorce

4.1   How do adolescents adjust to divorce in their families?

4.2   Should parents stay together for the sake of their children and adolescents?

4.3   How much to post-divorce family processes affect adolescent adjustment to divorce?

4.4   What factors contribute to adolescent risk and vulnerability to divorce?

4.5   What role does socioeconomic status play in the lives of adolescents in divorced families?

B.   Stepfamilies

4.6   What adjustment problems are associated with adolescents who live in stepfamilies?

4.7   What is the most difficult time for adolescents to experience their parents' remarriage?

4.8   What is **boundary ambiguity**?

4.9   How do you compare adolescent's relationships with their biological and stepparents?

4.10   What is the difference between complex and simple stepfamilies and in which do adolescents have more problems?

C.   Working Parents

4.11   What is the effect of parental work on the development of children and adolescents?

4.12   What effect do working mothers have on adolescent development?

4.13   What are the special adjustment problems of latchkey adolescents?

4.14   What are the effect of relocation on adolescent development?

4.15   How does parental unemployment affect adolescents?

D.   **Culture and Ethnicity**

4.16   What roles do culture and ethnicity play in families?

4.17   What is the effect of culture on parental roles and discipline styles and family support systems?

4.18   In what ways do ethnic minority families differ from White American families?

4.19   What are the main differences between White American families and African American and Latino families?

E.   **Gender and Parenting**

4.20   How do gender and gender roles affect families?

4.21   What is the mother's role in the family today?

4.22   What is the father's role in today's family?

4.23   How can mothers and fathers become cooperative and effective parenting partners?

5.0   **How Does Social Policy Affect Families With Adolescents?**

A.   **Social Policies and Families**

5.1   What changes in social policy would benefit families with adolescents?

6.0   **Explorations in Adolescent Development**

6.1   What are the similarities and differences in the extended-family systems of African American and Mexican American families and how is it changing?

7.0   **Adventures for the Mind**

7.1   What are some strategies for reducing parent-adolescent conflict?

7.2   What is the best way for parents to communicate with children about their plans for divorce?

Key Terms

Write a sentence using each of these key terms by either defining the term or giving an example of it. For instance, you might write, "Secure attachment is...", or you might give an example of secure attachment. Compare your definitions with those given at the end of study guide chapter; check your examples by referring to the text. Review the text for those terms you don't know or define incorrectly.

1.   reciprocal socialization

_____

_____

2.   synchrony

_____

_____

3.   developmental construction views

_____

_____

4.   continuity view

_____

_____

5.   discontinuity view

_____

_____

6.   authoritarian parenting

_____

_____

7.   authoritative parenting

_____

_____

8.   neglectful parenting

_____

_____

9.   indulgent parenting

_____

_____

10.   emotional autonomy

_____

_____

11.   insecure attachment

_____

_____

12.   secure attachment

_____

_____

13.   dismissing/avoidant attachment

_____

_____

14.   preoccupied/ambivalent attachment

_____

_____

15.   unresolved/disorganized attachment

_____

_____

16.   boundary ambiguity

_____

_____

Key People in Adolescent Development

Match the person with the event or concept in adolescent development with which they are associated.

___	1. Andrew Collins	A. Parenting styles
___	2. Diana Baumrind	B. Infant attachment research
___	3. Laurence Steinberg	C. Adolescent cognitive changes
___	4. John Bowlby and Mary Ainsworth	D. Adolescent adjustment to parental divorce
___	5. Joseph Allen	E. Adolescent-parental attachment
___	6. E. Mavis Hetherington	F. Studied autonomy and conflict in adolescent-parental relationships
___	7. Lois Hoffman	G. Studied effects of maternal employment

The Nature of Family Processes
Guided Review

The process by which parents and adolescents socialize with each other is known as (1) _____. An important aspect of parent-adolescent relationships is they way they interact with are attuned to each other, otherwise known as (2) _____. Reciprocal socialization takes place with the social system of a family, which consists of subsystems defined by its members (3) _____, (4) _____, and (5) _____. Each family member participates in several subsystems, some (6) _____, involving only two people, and some (7) _____, involving more than two people. The mother-father-adolescent are a (8) _____ subsystem. Two (9) _____ views describe how individuals acquire modes of relating to others as they grow up. In the (10) _____ view, emphasis is on the role of early parent-child relationships in constructing a basic way of relating to people throughout the life span. In the (11) _____ view, emphasis is on change and growth in relationships over time.

Adolescents and parents change and mature together and these changes influence their relationships. Among the change in the adolescent that can influence parent-adolescent relationships are (12) _____, (13) expanded _____ reasoning, increased (14) _____ thought, (14) _____ expectations, changes in (15) _____, (16) _____, (17) _____ and (18) _____, and movement toward (19) _____. The conflict between parents and adolescents is the most stressful during the (20) _____ of pubertal growth, especially between (21) _____ and (22) _____. Parental changes that affect the relationship with their adolescent involve (23) _____ satisfaction, (24) _____ burdens, (25) _____ reevaluation, and (26) _____ and _____ concerns.

Historical influences, such as (27) _____, (28) _____, and (29) _____, and cultural influences like (30) _____, (31) _____, and (32) general _____ and _____ influence family processes. Parental cognitive processes such as (33) _____, (34) _____, and (35) _____ about their parental role, as well as how parents (36) _____, (37) _____, and (38) _____ their adolescent's behaviors and beliefs. Family emotional processes affect the development of emotional (39) _____, (40) _____ and (41) _____.

Parent-Adolescent Relationships
Guided Review

Increasingly, parents are seen as (1) _____ of adolescents' lives, especially as they (2) _____, (3) _____, and (4) _____ opportunities and relationships. Parenting techniques fall into four main categories: (5) _____, a restrictive, punitive style; (6) _____, in which adolescents are encouraged to be independent but limits and controls are placed on their behavior, (7) _____, a style in which parents are uninvolved in the adolescent's lives, and (8) _____, a style in which parents are highly involved but place few demands or controls. The (9) _____ style is most associated with social competence, the (10) _____ with social incompetence. The misperception that there is a huge gulf that separates parents and adolescents is called the (11) _____ gap; this is mostly an inaccurate (12) _____. Most adolescents share their parents values of (13) _____, (14) _____, and (15) _____ aspirations, and also share their (16) _____ and _____ beliefs. Parent-adolescent conflict generally peak during (17) _____ adolescence, and then decreases. Most conflict involves everyday events of (18) _____ life. Adolescents have the most conflict with their (19) _____. About (20) _____ percent of adolescents have prolonged and intense conflict with their parents. In many of these cases, the problems began in (21) _____.

Many parents have a hard time handling their adolescent's autonomy, a term associated with (22) _____ and (23) _____. (24) _____ autonomy is especially important, and it involves the capacity to relinquish (25) _____ _____ on the parents. Expectations about the appropriate timing of autonomy achievement vary across (26) _____, (27) _____, and (28) _____, but it is most often triggered when individuals leave for (29) _____. Autonomy does not mean lack of parental (30) _____, an important factor in an adolescent's social (31) _____ and (32) _____ exploration of the world. Adolescent attachment is generally classified in one (33) _____ category _____ and three categories of (34) _____ attachment: (35) _____, (36) _____, and (37) _____.

Parent-Adolescent Relationships
Section Review
Match the terms with the correct definitions or descriptions.

_____	1. autonomy	A. Parents are uninvolved
_____	2. emotional autonomy	B. Highly restrictive, punitive parenting style
_____	3. authoritarian parenting style	C. Adolescents de-emphasize the importance of attachment
_____	4. authoritative parenting style	D. Adolescents are hypertuned to attachment issues
_____	5. indulgent parenting style	E. Parenting style associated with social competence
_____	6. neglectful parenting style	F. Parenting style associated with social incompetence
_____	7. dismissing/avoidant attachment	G. Relinquishing childlike dependence on parents
_____	8. preoccupied/ambivalent attachment	H. Adolescent has an unusually high fear
_____	9. unresolved/disorganized attachment	I. An important foundation for child, adolescent, and adult development
_____	10. secure/autonomous attachment	J. Related with independence and self-direction

Sibling Relationships
Guided Review
More than (1) _____ percent of American adolescents have (2) _____, another term for brothers and sisters. Adolescent siblings do more than fight. They (3) _____, (4) _____ each other, (5) _____, (6) _____ together. They act as (7) _____ supports, (8) _____, and (9) _____ partners. Sibling conflict is lower in (10) _____ than in (11) _____, due in part to a (12) _____ in the amount of (13) _____ they spend together, as well as a change in the sibling (14) _____ structure. (15) _____ order plays a role in sibling relationships Firstborns tend to be more (16) _____-oriented and less (17) _____. They also tend to be high (18) _____. Later-borns are not so easy to characterize since they occupy so many different sibling (19) _____, but they usually enjoy (20) _____ relationships with their (21) _____ than do firstborns. Middle-borns tend to be more (22) _____, often playing the role of family (23) _____. It is a misconception that an only child is a (24) _____. They generally have a (25) _____ personality and are (26) _____ oriented. An increasing number of researchers think that birth order has been (27) _____ and _____. Far more important family factors influencing development are (28) _____, (29) _____ treatment by parents.

The Changing Family in a Changing Society and Social Policy
Guided Review

Children from (1) _____ families show poorer (2) _____ than do children from (3) _____ families. They are more likely to have (4) _____ problems, externalized problems such as (5) _____ and (6) _____, internalized problems such as (7) _____ and (8) _____, be less (9) _____ responsible, have less (10) _____ intimate relationships, (11) _____ school, become (12) _____ active at an earlier age and (12) _____ drugs, associate with (13) _____ peers, and have (14) _____. Although there is disagreement about the size and extent of these effects, many argue that approximately (15) _____ of adolescents in divorced families have these types of problems, in contrast to only (16) _____ in non-divorced families. Sometimes divorce may be advantageous to the adolescent, especially if there is high (17) _____ between parents and between (18) _____ and their parents. Post-divorce adjustment is improved if parents maintain a (19) _____ relationship with each other and both use a (20) _____ parenting styles. Non-custodial (21) _____ often have better relationships with their children because they are less likely to (22) _____, (23) _____, and (24) _____ the adolescent's behavior. Noncustodial mother's (25) _____, (26) _____, and (27) _____ can improve adolescent post-divorce adjustment. An adolescent's post-divorce adjustment depends upon his or her (28) _____, (29) _____, (30) _____, (31) _____, and (32) _____. Studies show that (33) _____ children are at greater risk for long-term problems than are (34) _____ children, partly due to their (35) _____, (36) _____, and inability to use (37) _____ resources.

Custodial mothers lose about (38) _____ to _____ of their predivorce income, compared to a (39) ____ percent loss by custodial fathers. In addition, divorced mothers experience (40) _____ workloads, high rates of (41) _____ instability, and moves to (42) _____ neighborhoods with (43) _____ inferior schools.

Early adolescence is an especially difficult time for (44) _____ to occur. It takes up to (45) _____ years longer for adolescents to adjust to living in a stepfamily as opposed to a divorced family. The uncertainty in stepfamilies about family roles and responsibilities is known as (46) _____. (47) Step-_____ are more (48) _____ than (49) step-_____. Adolescents have more adjustment problems in (50) _____ stepfamilies than in (51) _____ stepfamilies.

Working (52) _____ and (53) _____ experiences generally do not have a negative effect on adolescents. However, (54) _____ and (55) _____ of parents have detrimental effects. Culture plays a large part in determining what the (56) _____ role in the family should be, the extent of (57) _____ systems, and how children should be (58) _____. Large and extended families are more common among (59) _____ than White Americans. More than (60) _____ percent of Latino families consist of five or more individuals. More African American and Latino children interact with (61) _____ than do White Americans.

The main responsibility for child-rearing still falls on the (62) _____. Mothers do (63) ___ to ___ times the amount of family work than fathers do. The father's role in the family has changed since the (64) _____, from that of mostly (65) _____, to the expectation of his being an (66) _____, (67) _____, and (68) _____ parent. In low-income African American families, children with close relationships with their fathers during adolescence were (69) ____ as likely to find a stable job or enter college, (70) ____ percent less likely to have become unwed parents, (71) _____ percent less likely to have been incarcerated, and (72) _____ less likely to have developed depression. Unfortunately, only (73) _____ percent of economically disadvantaged children have close relationships with their fathers.

Families with adolescents have been neglected in (74) _____ programs and (75) _____. The Carnegie Council on Adolescent Development has recommended that (76) _____, (77) _____, (78) _____, and (79) _____ should participate in strengthening adolescent-parent relationships.

Explorations in Adolescence
Compare and contrast the extended family structures in African-American and Mexican-American families. What positive effects do these systems have on adolescent development?

_____

_____

Adventures for the Mind
1.   Write down your ideas for how an adolescent boy or girl (you choose which one you would like to discuss) and his or her parents could engage in collaborative problem solving to set ground rules for dating.

_____

_____

2.   Talk to one of your friends or acquaintances whose parents separated when they were teenagers (or use yourself if your parents did so). When, how, and what did their parents tell them about the separation? Could they have done it in a better way? What suggestions would they give to parents of teenagers who are about to separate?

_____

_____

Adolescence in Research
Concerning Lapsley and colleagues' 1989 research on the psychological separation and adjustment of college students, state the hypothesis, the research methods (if known), the research conclusions, and the implications and applications for adolescent development.

Comprehensive Review
1.   The father and one child make up a _____ system, and the mother and the father and the child make up a _____ system.
    a.   dyadic; polyadic
    b.   dyadic; dyadic
    c.   polyadic; polyadic
    d.   polyadic; dyadic

2.   The discontinuity view of relationships might suggest that the parent-child mode would be useful in dealing with
    a.   siblings.
    b.   teachers.
    c.   peers.
    d.   only one's parents.

3.   What frequently happens between adolescents and parents?
    a.   They compete for family resources.
    b.   They violate one another's expectations.
    c.   They reject one another's personal space.
    d.   They get along well because they share similar levels of cognitive development.

4. Marital dissatisfaction is greatest when their offspring are
    a. adolescents.
    b. young children.
    c. older children.
    d. adults.

5. Typically, the transition into parenthood is accompanied by
    a. greater marital satisfaction for husband and wives.
    b. greater marital dissatisfaction for husbands and wives.
    c. greater marital satisfaction for husbands and greater marital dissatisfaction for wives.
    d. greater marital satisfaction for wives and greater marital dissatisfaction for husbands.

6. Diane Baumrind describes authoritative parents as
    a. restrictive, punitive, and allowing little verbal guide.
    b. encouraging independence and placing limits on adolescents' actions.
    c. power assertive, rejecting, unresponsive, and parent centered.
    d. undemanding, rejecting, uninvolved, and controlling.

7. Bill's parents have few rules for household conduct or academic expectations. They do not punish Bill when he violates rules, but merely accept his behavior. Bill is likely to develop
    a. social competence because his parents unconditionally accept him.
    b. anxiety about social comparisons and social inferiority feelings.
    c. self-reliance, social responsibility, and autonomy.
    d. little impulse control and disregard for rules.

8. Conflict between adolescents and parents is typically strongest in early adolescence, and may be a healthy aspect of the development of
    a. autonomy.
    b. attachment.
    c. parenting skills.
    d. dating skills.

9. You are depressed because you argue with your 10-year-old daughter almost daily, and these arguments last for several minutes. Expects on adolescents would tell you that
    a. this high level of conflict will lead to later disturbances.
    b. this type of conflict is normal and you should not worry about it.
    c. if you are arguing this much now, your arguments will increase in later adolescence.
    d. these arguments will prevent your daughter from developing an autonomous identity.

10. The most crucial transition for the development of adolescent autonomy is from
    a. school to work.
    b. high school to college.
    c. middle school to high school.
    d. virginity to sexual activity.

11. Adolescents who are securely attached to their parents
    a. cannot adequately develop autonomy.
    b. show less secure attachment to peers.
    c. have more difficulty engaging with peers and separating from parents.
    d. have higher self-esteem than insecurely attached peers.

12. Sibling conflict is often lower in adolescence than in childhood due to changes in
    a. social development.
    b. physical development.
    c. the power relationship.
    d. the way parents deal with conflict.

13. Firstborn children are
    a. more achievement-oriented than those born later.
    b. less achievement-oriented than those born later.
    c. more psychologically well adjusted than those born later.
    d. on the average, less socially responsible than those born later.

14. _____ refers to the confusion in stepfamilies regarding the membership of the family and each individual's responsibility.
    a. Family blending
    b. Boundary ambiguity
    c. Stepfamily dynamism
    d. Stepfamily individuation

15. _____ is a logical consequence of maternal employment.
    a. Increased sex-role stereotyping of children
    b. Children receiving less attention
    c. Children having greater individuation crises
    d. Child socialization for adult roles.

16. After coming home from school, Juan washes the breakfast dishes, does the laundry, and starts dinner before his parents get home at 6 PM. Juan is a
    a. hurried child.
    b. latchkey child.
    c. neglected child.
    d. Stepchild.

17. Ethnic families tend to differ from White American families in that the former
    a. are smaller.
    b. show more extended networks.
    c. encourage more autonomy among girls than boys.
    d. have more employed mothers.

18. It is a mistake to attribute the problems of adolescents to their mothers because
    a. fathers spend more time with children and adolescents than ever before.
    b. mothers and fathers are partners in parenting.
    c. behavior is determined by multiple factors.
    d. peers and siblings have more influence on adolescents than parents.

19. Fathers of adolescents who are older than most other fathers of children that age are
   a. more likely to enforce rules than younger fathers.
   b. warmer and communicate better than younger fathers.
   c. more aloof than younger fathers.
   d. more demanding than younger fathers.

20. African American and Latino adolescents are most likely to differ from White adolescents in that the former are more likely to
   a. live in extended families.
   b. live in rural areas.
   c. attend church.
   d. use drugs.

Adolescence on the Screen
- *Ordinary People* concerns parents and their teenage son's struggle to deal with the death of a younger sibling. The surviving son feels guilt and blame, leading him to suicidal depression.

- *Tumbleweeds* is the story of a displaced single mother and her teenage daughter who move from place to place and live on a shoestring, while the mother looks for a man that will give them a better life.

- *Liberty House* depicts the changing sociopolitical climate of the 1950s, including integration, interracial dating, and changing family structure and influence.

Adolescence in Books
- *Between Parent & Teenager*, by Haim Ginott (Avon, 1999), continues to be one of the most widely read and recommended books for parents who want to communicate more effectively with their teenagers.

- *Growing Up with Divorce* , by Neil Kalter (Free Press, 1990), provides divorced parents with information to help their children and youth avoid emotional problems.

- *I'm Not Mad, I Just Hate You!*, by R. Cohen-Sandler & M. Silver (Viking, 1999), deals with adolescent mother/daughter conflict.

- *The Shelter of Each Other: Rebuilding Our Families*, by Mary Pipher (Ballantine, 1996), calls for strengthening the family for the benefit of children, parents, and grandparents.

Answer Key

Key Terms
1. **reciprocal socialization** The process by which children and adolescents socialize parents, just as parents socialize them.
2. **synchrony** The carefully coordinated interaction between the parent and the child or adolescent in which, often unknowingly, they are attuned to each other's behavior.
3. **developmental construction views** Views sharing the belief that as individuals grow up, they acquire modes of relating to others. There are two main variations of this view. One emphasizes continuity and stability in relationships throughout the life span, the other emphasizes discontinuity and changes in relationships throughout the life span.
4. **continuity view** A developmental view that emphasizes the role of early parent-child relationships in constructing a basic way of relating to people throughout the life span.

5. **discontinuity view** A developmental view that emphasizes change and growth in relationships over time.

6. **authoritarian parenting** This is a restrictive, punitive style in which the parent exhorts the adolescent to follow the parent's directions and to respect work and effort. Firm limits and controls are placed on adolescents, and little verbal exchange is allowed. This style is associated with adolescents' socially incompetent behavior.

7. **authoritative parenting** This style encourages adolescents to be independent but still places limits and controls on their actions. Extensive verbal give-and-take is allowed, and parents are warm and nurturant toward the adolescent. This style is associated with adolescents' socially competent behavior.

8. **neglectful parenting** A style in which the parent is very uninvolved in the adolescent's life. It is associated with adolescents' social incompetence, especially a lack of self-control.

9. **indulgent parenting** A style in which parents are highly involved with their adolescents but place few demands or controls on them. This is associated with adolescents' social incompetence, especially a lack of self-control.

10. **emotional autonomy** The capacity to relinquish childlike dependencies on parents.

11. **insecure attachment** In this attachment pattern, infants either avoid the caregiver or show considerable resistance or ambivalence toward the caregiver. This pattern is theorized to be related to difficulties in relationships and problems in later development.

12. **secure attachment** In this attachment pattern, infants use their primary caregiver, usually the mother, as a secure base from which to explore the environment. Secure attachment is theorized to be an important foundation for psychological development later in childhood, adolescence, and adulthood.

13. **dismissing/avoidant attachment** An insecure attachment category in which individuals de-emphasize the importance of attachment. This category is associated with consistent experiences of rejection of attachment needs by caregivers.

14. **preoccupied/ambivalent attachment** An insecure attachment category in which adolescents are hypertuned to attachment experiences. This is thought to occur mainly because parents are inconsistently available to the adolescents.

15. **unresolved/disorganized attachment** An insecure category in which the adolescent has an unusually high level of fear and is disoriented. This may result from such traumatic experiences as a parent's death or abuse by parents.

16. **boundary ambiguity** The uncertainty in stepfamilies about who is on or out of the family and who is performing or responsible for certain tasks in the family system.

Key People
1. C   2. A   3. F   4. B   5. E   6. D   7. G

The Nature of Family Processes
Guided Review

1. reciprocal socialization
2. synchrony
3. generation
4. gender
5. role
6. dyadic
7. polyadic
8. polyadic
9. developmental construction
10. continuity
11. discontinuity
12. puberty
13. logical
14. idealistic
15. violated
16. schooling
17. peers
18. friendships
19. dating
20. independence
21. mothers
22. sons
23. marital
24. economic
25. career
26. health/body
27. war
28. famine
29. mass immigration
30. mobility
31. television
32. dissatisfaction/restlessness
33. cognition
34. beliefs
35. values
36. perceive
37. organize
38. understand
39. regulation
40. production
41. understanding

Parent-Adolescent Relationships
Guided Review

1. managers
2. initiate
3. manage
4. monitor
5. authoritarian
6. authoritative
7. neglectful
8. indulgent
9. authoritative
10. indulgent
11. generation
12. stereotype
13. hard work
14. achievement
15. careers
16. religion/political
17. early
18. family
19. mother
20. 20
21. childhood
22. self-direction
23. independence
24. emotional
25. childlike dependencies
26. cultures
27. parents
28. adolescents
29. college
30. attachment
31. social
32. healthy
33. secure-autonomous
34. insecure
35. dismissing/avoidant
36. preoccupied/ambivalent
37. unresolved/disorganized

Parent-Adolescent Relationships
Section Review

1. J
2. G
3. B
4. E
5. F
6. A
7. C
8. D
9. H
10. I

Sibling Relationships
Guided Review

1. 80
2. siblings
3. help
4. teach
5. share
6. play
7. emotional
8. rivals
9. communication partners
10. adolescence
11. childhood
12. change
13. time
14. power
15. Birth
16. adult
17. aggressive
18. achievers
19. positions
20. better
21. peers
22. diplomatic
23. negotiator
24. spoiled brat
25. desirable
26. achievement
27. overdramatized/overemphasized
28. temperament
29. differential

The Changing Family in a Changing Society and Social Policy
Guided Review

1. divorced
2. adjustment
3. nondivorced
4. academic
5. acting out
6. delinquency
7. anxiety
8. depression
9. socially
10. competent
11. drop out of
12. sexually active/take
13. antisocial
14. lower self-esteem
15. 20 – 25 percent
16. 10 percent
17. conflict
18. adolescents
19. harmonious
20. authoritative
21. fathers
22. criticize
23. control
24. monitor
25. warmth
26. support
27. monitoring
28. personality
29. temperament
30. developmental stages
31. gender
32. custody
33. younger
34. older
35. anxiety
36. self-blame
37. extrafamilial
38. 1/4 to 1/2
39. 10
40. greater
41. job
42. less desirable
43. inferior
44. remarriage
45. five
46. boundary ambiguity
47. fathers
48. controlling
49. mothers
50. complex
51. simple
52. mother
53. latchkey
54. relocation
55. unemployment
56. father
57. support
58. disciplined
59. ethnic minority
60. 30
61. relatives
62. mothers
63. 2/3
64. 1970s
65. breadwinner
66. active
67. nurturant
68. care giving
69. twice
70. 75
71. 80
72. 50
73. 10
74. community
75. public policy
76. schools & churches
77. professionals
78. employers
79. businesses

Explorations in Adolescence

Both ethnic groups tend to "stick together." African-American grandmothers are a great resource for mothers and infants. Mothers of adolescents who have good relationships with their mothers pass that on to their children. Family support has been directly related to adolescent school success and self-reliance. In Mexican-American families the father is the undisputed authority but the mother is the main source of affection and care. These families exist more for each other, rather than for themselves. Self-reliance is not valued as highly as it is in African-American (and White) families.

Adventures for the Mind

1. Example: Parents and adolescent should set aside a time when the teen first indicates an interest in dating to discuss only this issue. Each come to the "meeting" with a list of what they feel they "must" have and what they would "like" to have. Beginning with the "must" have list, they should discuss and negotiate, then move on to the "like" to have list. They should come up with a written agreement that both are comfortable with signing. The agreement could have a method for resolving disputes that arise about dating, such as submitting the issue to a respected and neutral party (such as an aunt or uncle).

2. Example: Parents should tell their child as soon as the separation is decided upon. Both parents should be present and should make it clear that they respect each other and love their child, and that the separation is no fault of the child's. The teenager should be consulted about which parent he or she wishes to live with and the arrangements for visiting the other parent. The teen should be given the opportunity to ask questions and express his or her feelings.

Adolescence in Research

The researchers studied 130 college freshmen and 123 college upper-classmen. The hypothesis was that freshmen would show more psychological dependency on their parents and poor social and personal adjustment than upperclassmen. The results supported the hypothesis.

Comprehensive Review

1. a	5. b	9. c	13. a	17. b
2. b	6. b	10. b	14. b	18. c
3. b	7. d	11. d	15. d	19. b
4. a	8. a	12. c	16. b	20. a

◆ Chapter 6   Peers

Learning Objectives with Key Terms and Key People in Boldface

1.0   **What is the Nature of Peer Relations?**
- A.   **Peer Group Functions**
  - 1.1   What are peers, and how are they important to adolescent social development?
  - 1.2   How do peers provide a basis for social comparison and a source of information about the world outside the family?
  - 1.3   Why are good peer relations necessary for normal social development?
  - 1.4   How can peer relations be either positive or negative?
  - 1.5   What did Jean Piaget and Harry Stack Sullivan stress about peer relations?
  - 1.6   According to Willard Hartup, in what ways do peer relations vary?
- B.   **Family-Peer Linkages**
  - 1.7   How do healthy family relations promote healthy peer relations?
  - 1.8   What parental choices influence the pool from which adolescents choose their friends?
  - 1.9   What is the main difference between the quality of adolescent's relations with their peers and parents?
- C.   **Peer Conformity**
  - 1.10   What is the difference between **conformity, nonconformity**, and **anticonformity**?
  - 1.11   At what point does conformity to antisocial peers peak?
- D.   **Peer Status**
  - 1.12   How would you describe **popular children**?
  - 1.13   What is the peer status of **neglected children**?
  - 1.14   How well do **rejected children** fare among their peers?
  - 1.15   Where do **controversial children** fit in with their peer group?
- E.   **Social Cognition**
  - 1.16   How is social knowledge associated with improved peer relations?
  - 1.17   How do good information processing skills improve peer relations?
- F.   **Conglomerate Strategies for Improving Social Skills**
  - 1.18   How do **conglomerate strategies** improve social skills?
- G.   **Bullying**
  - 1.19   What are the short-term and long-term effects of bullying on its victims?

2.0   **What is the Significance of Friendship for Adolescent Development?**
- A   **Importance of Friendship**
  - 2.1   What are the six functions that friendship play in adolescence?
- B.   **Harry Stack Sullivan's Ideas**
  - 2.2   How does research support or refute Sullivan's ideas?
- C.   **Intimacy and Similarity**
  - 2.3   What are the key aspects of friendship?
- D.   **Mixed-Age Friendships**
  - 2.4   What happens to adolescents who become close friends with other individuals?
  - 2.5   Are there gender differences in mix-group friendships and their effects on younger adolescents?

3.0   **What Are the Nature, Function, and Characteristics of Adolescent Groups?**
    A.   **Group Function and Formation**
        3.1   How do groups satisfy adolescents' personal needs, reward them, provide information, raise their self-esteem, and give them an identity?
    B.   **Children Groups and Adolescent Groups**
        3.2   What are group **norms**?
        3.3   What are group **roles**?
        3.4   What did Muzafer Sherif learn about adolescent groups?
    C.   **Ethnic and Cultural Variations**
        3.5   What are the main characteristics of children groups?
        3.6   What are the distinguishing features of adolescent groups?
        3.7   What are some features of lower-socioeconomic status groups?
        3.8   Why do ethnic minority adolescents often have two sets of peers?
        3.9   Why do ethnic minority adolescents turn to peer groups more than White adolescents?
    D.   **Cliques**
        3.10   What is the difference between a **clique** and a **crowd**?
        3.11   How many cliques are found in most secondary schools?
        3.12   With what type of cliques is membership associated with high self-esteem?
        3.13   How does the self-esteem of clique members compare with that of independents?
    E.   **Youth Organizations**
        3.14   In what way do youth organizations influence adolescent development?
        3.15   What is the mission of Boys' Clubs and Girls' Clubs?

4.0   **Dating and Romantic Relationships**
    A.   **Functions of Dating**
        4.1   What is dating and what are its functions?
    B.   **Types of Dating and Developmental Changes**
        4.2   At what age do adolescents start to hang out together in heterosexual groups?
        4.3   What is the difference between hooking up, seeing each other, and going out?
        4.4   What is cyberdating?
        4.5   With what problems is early dating associated?
        4.6   How much time do young adolescents spend thinking about the opposite sex as opposed to actually being with them?
    C.   **Culture and Dating**
        4.7   What special problems do immigrant adolescents face with their families in relationship to dating?
    D.   **Male and Female Dating Strategies**
        4.8   What are the differences between male and female **dating scripts**?
    E.   **Emotion and Romantic Relationships**
        4.9   How do romantic relationships affect an adolescent's life?
        4.10   What emotions are associated with adolescent romantic relationships?
    F.   **Romantic Love and Its Construction**
        4.1   What is the difference between **romantic love** and **affectionate love**?
        4.12   At what age do adolescents get involved with romantic love?
        4.13   When is affectionate love more prominent?
        4.14   What is the developmental construction view of romantic love?
        4.15   What role do group leaders play in dating?
        4.16   How important are peers and friends in adolescent romantic relationships?

5.0   **Explorations in Adolescent Development: Social Policy, Peers, and Youth Organizations**
        5.1   What did the 1992 Carnegie Council report on youth-oriented organizations conclude about the role of youth organizations in adolescent's lives?
        5.2   What positive impact can youth organizations have on adolescent development?

6.0   Adventures for the Mind

    6.1   How do adolescent-parent relationships affect adolescent, peer, friendship and dating relationships?

    6.2   What advice would you give to today's adolescents about dating and romantic relationships?

Key Terms

Write a sentence using each of these key terms by either defining the term or giving an example of it. For instance, you might write, "Cliques are..." or, "(give examples) is an example of a clique." Compare your definitions with those given at the end of study guide chapter, and check your examples by referring to the text. Review the text for those terms you don't know or define incorrectly.

1.   peers

_____

_____

2.   conformity

_____

_____

3.   nonconformity

_____

_____

4.   anticonformity

_____

_____

5.   popular children

_____

_____

6.   neglected children

_____

_____

7.   rejected children

_____

_____

8.   controversial children

_____

_____

9. intimacy in friendship

_____

_____

10. norms

_____

_____

11. roles

_____

_____

12. crowd

_____

_____

13. cliques

_____

_____

14. dating scripts

_____

_____

15. romantic love

_____

_____

16. affectionate love

_____

_____

Key People in the Study of Adolescence

___	1. Gary Ladd	A.	Studied conformity
___	2. Thomas Berndt	B.	Studied nature and function of adolescent and children's groups, emphasizing change in sexual make-up
___	3. John Coie & Kenneth Dodge	C.	Studied role of attachment patterns in adolescent romantic relationships
___	4. William Hartup	D.	Studied role of peers in romantic involvement
___	5. Harry Stack Sullivan	E.	Studied adolescent cliques and crowds
___	6. Muzafer Sherif	F.	Studied formation of groups and how to overcome intergroup hatred
___	7. Dexter Dunphy	G.	Psychoanalytical theorist who emphasized importance of friendship for adolescents
___	8. James Coleman	H.	Studied nature of child and adolescent friendships
___	9. Bradford Brown, Wyndol Furman, and Candice Feiring		Studied role of peer influences in child and adolescent aggression and antisocial behavior
___	10. Jennifer Connolly		Studied peer relationships and social competence

102

The Nature of Peer Relations
Guided Review

Children or adolescents who are of about the same age or maturity level are known as (1) _____. Their most important functions are to provide information about (2) _____ and give adolescents (3) _____ about their abilities. Common peer-related activities are (4) _____, (5) _____, and (6) _____. Lack of peer relations can lead to problems such as (7) _____, (8) _____, and (9) _____. (10)_____ and (11) _____ were influential theorists who believed that children and adolescents learned the (12) _____ mode of relationships. Rejection by peers can lead to feelings of (13) _____ and (14) _____, which can, in turn, lead to (15) _____ and (16) _____ problems. It is important to keep in mind that peer influences must be considered as (17) _____ conditions.

Peers are connected to (18) _____ in several ways. Their choices of (19) _____, (20) _____, (21) _____, and their own (22) _____ influence the pool from which adolescents select friends. Parents also (23) _____ or (24) _____ their adolescents in ways of relating to peers. Adolescents who have a (25) _____ attachment with their parents will generally have positive peer relations.

Adopting the behavior or attitude of others because of real or imagine pressure from them is known as (26) _____. Negative conformity behavior includes (27) _____, (28) _____, (29) _____, and (30) _____. Nonnegative conformity consists of wanting to (31) _____ and (32) _____ the group. In the (33) _____ grade conformity to peers becomes the strongest, as does (34) _____ opposition to adolescent's (35) _____. Conformity to antisocial adolescent peers decreases in (36) _____. Knowing what others are doing but not being like them is (37) _____, while deliberately not being like the main actions of the group is (38) _____. Two contemporary anticonformity groups are (39) _____ and (40) _____.

(41) _____ children are more often nominated as "best" friends and are rarely disliked by peers. These children are (42) _____, act like (43) _____, show (44) _____ and (45) _____ for others, and are (46) _____. They are also more (47) _____ and (48) _____ than nonpopular children. (49) _____ children are not disliked but are not nominated as best friends; (50) _____ children are actively disliked and not nominated as best friend, and (51) _____ children are frequently nominated both as someone's best friend and are disliked by others. Rejected children and adolescents may become (52) _____ or (53) _____, especially if they were (54) _____ in grade school. The goal of training programs with rejected children is to teach them (55) _____ skills and eliminate (56) _____ behaviors.

Children and adolescents may have difficulty in peer relations because they lack (57) _____ skills, such as having appropriate strategies for (58) _____. (59) _____ use a combination of coaching techniques to improve adolescent's social skills. Social skills training programs have been more successful with children (60) _____ of age or younger than with adolescents.

Victims of bullies often have parents who are (61) _____ and (62) _____ but low in (63) _____. Overly close and emotionally intense relationships between parents and sons may foster (64) _____ and (65) _____, _____ that are perceived as (66) _____ in male peer groups. On the other hand, bullies' parents are likely to be (67) _____, (68) _____, or (69) _____ about their child's aggression. Short-term effects of being bullied include being (70) _____, losing interest in and avoiding (71) _____. Long-term effects are (72) _____ and (73) _____. (74) _____ percent of middle-school bullies had at least (75) _____ criminal conviction by their 20s, and (76) _____ had three or more.

The Nature of Peer Relations
Section Review

1. List and give an example of five appropriate strategies for making friends.

_____

_____

2. List and give examples for three inappropriate strategies for making friends.

_____

_____

3. List four interventions that teacher can use to reduce bullying.

_____

_____

Friendships
Guided Review

Adolescent friendships serve six functions: (1) _____, (2) _____, (3) _____ support, (4) _____ support, (5) social _____, and (6) _____. (7) _____ was the most influential theorist to discuss the importance of adolescent friendship, while other theorists emphasize (8) _____-adolescent relationships. He believed that adolescents seek friends mainly to satisfy (9) _____ needs, and adolescents spend more time seeking out the companionship and assurances of worth from friends than they do from (10) _____. Teenagers with superficial or no close friends report feeling (11) _____ and more (12) _____; they have lower (13) _____. Friendship in (14) _____ adolescence is a significant predictor of (15) _____ in early adulthood. The way adolescent friends related to each other is described as a (16) _____ _____- mode, which requires that adolescents use appropriate (17) _____, provide (18) _____ support to friends, and manage (19) _____. This way of relating requires skills in (20) _____, (21) _____, and (22) _____ problem solving. Willard Hartup concluded that adolescents use friends as (23) _____ and (24) _____ resources. (25) _____ friendships are more developmentally advantageous than (26) _____ friendships. An adolescent's (27) _____ influences the nature of friendships.

Two of the most important aspects of friendship are (28) _____ and (29) _____. Intimacy in friendship involves (30) _____ or sharing of (31) _____ thoughts. Girls have more (32) _____ friendships than boys. Girls are more likely than boys to have a (33) _____ and to be a (34) _____ members. Boys and girls regard (35) _____ as very important in friends. Adolescent friends are generally similar in terms of (36) _____, (37) _____, and (38) _____. They have similar attitudes toward (39) _____ and (40) _____ orientations. They like to wear the same (41) _____ and engage in the same (42) _____ activities. Adolescents who become close friends with older individuals engage in more (43) _____ behaviors than those with same-age friends. (44) _____-maturing (45) _____ are more likely than (46) _____-maturing (47) _____ to have (48) _____ friends; they may also contribute to their (49) _____ behaviors.

Adolescent Groups
Guided Review

Groups satisfy adolescents' (1) _____ needs, provide (2) _____ and (3) _____, raise (4) _____, and contribute to their (5) _____. All groups have two things in common: (6) _____, rules that apply to all (7) _____ and (8) _____, positions in a group that are governed by (9) _____ and (10) _____. Musafer Sherif studied how groups are (11)

_____ and how they developed (12) _____ and (13) _____. In order to reduce hatred between the groups, members of both groups were required to work together to achieve (14) _____ goals. When Sherif and his colleagues observed the boys in groups, they generally (15) _____, (16) _____ and engaged in, discussed, or attended (17) _____. They also talked about (18) _____ a lot. The most common deviant behavior they engaged in involved (19) _____.

Children groups are less (20) _____, (21) _____, and (22) _____ than adolescent groups. Opposite-sex participation in groups (23) _____ during adolescence, and (24) _____-sex groups replace (25) _____-sex groups.

In many schools peer groups are strongly segregated ac cording to (26) _____ and (27) _____. African American and low-income adolescents have achieved parity or surpassed middle- and upper-income adolescents on (28)_____. White and middle-class students generally are leaders in (29) _____, (30)_____ society, and (31) _____ and _____. Ethnic minority adolescents often have different peers at (32) _____ and in the (33) _____, and they may turn to them more often than (34) _____ adolescents.

The (35) _____ is the largest, most loosely defined unit of adolescent peers. Members meet because of (36) _____ in an (37) _____. (38) _____ are smaller in size, more (39)_____ and more (40) _____ than crowds. However, they are usually (41) _____ in size and less (42) _____ than friendships. Most high schools have (43) _____ to _____ well-defined cliques. These include (44) _____, (45) _____, (46) _____, (47) _____, and (48) _____. Clique membership can be associated with (49) _____, (50) _____, and (51) _____ behavior.

More than (52) _____ youth organizations currently exist in the U.S. The largest youth organization is (53) _____, the smallest (54) _____ and (55) _____. Adolescents who join community groups are more likely to participate in (56) _____ activities in adulthood and have higher (57) _____. They are better (58) _____ and come from families with (59) _____ incomes. Reasons given for not participating in youth programs are lack of (60) _____ , (61) _____, and (62) _____ of what is available. Two organizations designed to increase membership among (63) _____ youth in low-income neighborhoods are (64) _____ and _____ Clubs. Their activities are designed to enhance (65) _____ and (66) _____ development.

Adolescent Groups
Section Review

1.   Describe what Dunphy found to be the five stages of progression of peer group relations in adolescence.

_____

_____

2   Summarize the conclusions of Bradford Brown and colleagues' most recent research on cliques.

_____

_____

Dating and Romantic Relationships
Guided Review

Serious contacts between adolescent boys and girls occur through (1) _____, a phenomenon that did not become popular until the (2) _____. This process serves at least (3) _____ functions. It can be a form of (4) _____, a source of (5) _____ and _____, part of the (6) _____ process of adolescence, the context for sexual (7) _____ and _____, provide (8) _____, contribute to (9) _____ formation, and help select a mate. Different forms of commitment are represented by (10) _____, (11) _____ each other, and (12) _____. The newest form of dating is (13) _____, dating over the Internet. Most girls in the U.S. begin dating by the age of (14) _____, with boys beginning sometime between the ages of (15) _____ and _____. By the age of 16, (16) ____ percent of teens have had at least one date. More than (17) ____ percent of high school students have one or more dates a week. Early dating is associated with (18) _____ and (19) _____ at home and school. Most dates involve going to a (20) _____, having (21) _____, (22) _____ out at (23) _____ or _____, and (24) _____ each other at their homes. Younger adolescents spend more time (25) _____ about the opposite sex than (26) _____ with them, a trend that (27) _____ in high school.

(28) _____ is a powerful influence on dating (29) _____ and (30) _____. (31) _____ and (32) _____ cultures have more conservative standards about dating than (33) _____ cultures. Males and females have different dating (34) _____, the models that individuals use to (35) _____ and (36) _____ dating interactions. Males are generally (37) _____, controlling the (38) _____ domain, while females are more often (39) _____, focusing on the (40) _____ domain. Emotions associated with dating are both (41) _____ and (42) _____. Negative emotions include feelings of (43) _____, (44) _____, (45) _____, and (46) _____.

(47) _____ love has strong sexual and (48) _____ components and characterizes most adolescent love relationships. (49) _____ love is a form of companionate love, and involves individuals desiring to be near a person and care for them. This is more characteristic of (50) _____ love. Physical (51) _____ and (52) _____ are important ingredients of dating relationships. The (53) _____ view of the developmental construction view stresses that relationships with (54) _____ influences dating relationships. The discontinuity view places the emphasis on (55) _____ relations and (56) _____ as important influences in romantic relationships. Adolescents with a (57) _____ attachment pattern may be more in control of their emotions in romantic relationships.

Dating and Romantic Relationships
Section Review
1. Go on-line and see if you can find a bulletin board where middle-school students are trying to establish virtual relationships. Compare the way boys and girls describe themselves and their interests.

_____

_____

2. a. Describe the three main activities involved in the male dating script and give an example of each.

_____

_____

b. Describe the three main activities involved in the female dating script and give an example of each.

_____

_____

3. Describe how adolescents with each attachment pattern would likely approach or behave in romantic relationships.

   a. Secure

   _____

   _____

   b. Dismissing/avoidant

   _____

   _____

   c. Preoccupied/ambivalent

   _____

   _____

Explorations in Adolescence

What did the 1992 Carnegie Council Report find that adolescents want from youth-oriented organizations?

_____

_____

Adventures for the Mind

1. How did your relationship with your parents affect your peer relationships and friendships in adolescence? How did your parents influence your choice of peers and friends? How did your parents' marital relationship affect your dating and romantic relationships?

   _____

   _____

2. Think back over your adolescent dating experiences. How were your experiences different when you were 13, 15, and 17? What would you do differently if you could begin anew today? What advice would you offer today's teenagers of those ages?

   _____

   _____

Adolescence in Research

Concerning Brown and Lohr's 1987 research dealing with the self-esteem of students in grades 7 through 12, state the hypothesis, the research methods (if known), the research conclusions, and the implications and applications for adolescent development.

_____

_____

Comprehensive Review

1. Jason is a sixth-grader who spends a lot of time with his peers. Statistically speaking, in which activity is he most likely engaging?
    a. going to stores
    b. watching television
    c. team sports
    d. girl-watching

2. A(n) _____ is a person who purposively diverges from the expectations of the group.
    a. anticonformist
    b. independent
    c. nonconformist
    d. leader

3. Participating in a newspaper drive with one's club because the club wants everyone to be involved in this activity is an example of _____ conformity.
    a. negative
    b. positive
    c. independent
    d. responsible

4. Thomas Berndt found that adolescent conformity to antisocial, peer-endorsed behavior ____ in late high school years, and _____ agreement between parents and pepers begins to occur in some areas.
    a. decreases; greater
    b. decreases; lesser
    c. increases; greater
    d. increases; lesser

5. The adolescent who does not have significant interactions with peers is likely to be
    a. handicapped.
    b. Antisocial.
    c. Neglected.
    d. mature and independent.

6. Kenneth Dodge indicates that adolescents go through five steps when processing information about their social world. Which of the following is not one of these steps?
    a response search
    b. selecting an optimal response
    c. decoding of social cues
    d. elaboration of possibilities

7. Your teenage son Jeremy has a friend who brags about his clothes and jewelry and his athletic accomplishment. Jeremy's friend
    a. is probably well liked by his peers.
    b. would probably be called an anticonformist.
    c. probably compliments others for their accomplishments.
    d. might need coaching to gain peer group acceptance.

8. Which of the following is not among the six functions of friendship?
   a. physical support
   b. skill-streaming
   c. social comparisons
   d. intimacy

9. Which theorist stressed the importance of friendship to adolescent development?
   a. Kenneth Dodge
   b. Erik Erikson
   c. Muzafer Sherif
   d. Harry Stack Sullivan

10. As the parent of an adolescent male, you are concerned about his friends who are 3–5 years older than he is. Your concern is
    a. not justified.
    b. not justified, because he will probably not drop out of school.
    c. justified because his friend is probably a drug user.
    d. justified because your son will likely engage in deviant behavior.

11. In social groups, all members are expected to
    a. assume roles.
    b. conform to norms.
    c. discriminate against outsiders.
    d. maintain secrecy about group activities.

12. Mazur Sherif learned about groups by intermingling with group members and
    a. systematic observation
    b. using interviews, surveys, and questionnaires.
    c. administering standardized tests.
    d. engaging in case studies.

13. Compared to adolescent groups, children's groups
    a. are not as formalized.
    b. include a broader array of members.
    c. have well-defined rules and regulations.
    d. are composed of large cliques.

14. In formal groups, such as athletic teams and student councils,
    a. racial and ethnic cliques predominate.
    b. socially active collegiates predominate.
    c. the greatest mixture of social class and ethnicity occurs.
    d. lower-class students have gained parity with middle-class students.

15. Sarah is 16 years old and does not want to belong to any clique. She does her own thing and is good at what she does. Her level of self-esteem is likely
    a. the same as the "jocks."
    b. lower than the "populars."
    c. lower than the "normals."
    d. the same as the "nobodies."

16. Which of the following is not a main function of adolescent dating?
    a. recreation
    b. status
    c. socialization
    d. procreation

17. What percent of adolescents have had at least one date by the time they are 16 years old?
    a. 20
    b. 50
    c. 75
    d. 90

18. In dating, boys and girls
    a. seek sexual intimacy on most dates.
    b. self-disclose at about the same rate.
    c. conform to cultural patterns and norms.
    d. want to go steady to avoid anxiety.

19. That adolescents enjoy being with people who are similar to them in values and beliefs is predicated by the principle called
    a. the matching hypothesis.
    b. identity narcissism.
    c. value matching.
    d. consensual validation.

20. In mate selection, the matching hypothesis suggests that we often pair up with someone who is like us in
    a. attractiveness
    b. intelligence.
    c. key personality factors.
    d. intimacy.

Adolescence on the Screen

- *Diner* follows a group of friends during high school and graduation.

- *Breakfast Club* depicts how students who must spend Saturday morning in detention develop into a cohesive group.

- *Trainspotting* involves a group of friends whose lives revolve around using drugs.

- *Romeo and Juliet*, a Shakespearean classic about romantic love, appeals to today's adolescents.

Adolescence in Books

- *Just Friends*, by Lillian Rubin (HarperCollins, 1985), explores the nature of friends and intimacy.

Answer Key

Key Terms

1. **peers** Children or adolescents who are of about the same age or maturity level.
2. **conformity** This occurs when individuals adopt the attitudes or behaviors of others because of real or imagined pressure from them.
3. **nonconformity** This occurs when individuals know what people around them expect but do not use these expectations to guide their behavior.
4. **anticonformity** This occurs when individuals react counter to a group's expectations and deliberately move away from the actions or beliefs the group advocates.
5. **popular children** Children who are frequently nominated as a best friend and are rarely disliked by their peers.
6. **neglected children** Children who are infrequently nominated as a best friend but are not disliked by their peers.
7. **rejected children** Children who are infrequently nominated as a best friend and are actively disliked by their peers.
8. **controversial children** Children who are frequently nominated both as a being a best friend and as being disliked.
9. **intimacy in friendship** In most research, this is defined narrowly as self-disclosure or sharing of private thoughts.
10. **norms** Rules that apply to all members of a group.
11. **roles** Certain positions in a group that are governed by rules and expectations. Roles define how adolescents should behave in those positions.
12. **crowd** The largest, most loosely defined, and least personal unit of adolescent peer society. Crowds often meet because of their mutual interest in an activity.
13. **cliques** These units are smaller, involve more intimacy, and are more cohesive than crowds. They are, however, larger and involve less intimacy than friendships.
14. **dating scripts** The cognitive models that adolescents and adults use to guide and evaluate dating interactions.
15. **romantic love** Also called passionate love or Eros, this love has strong sexual and infatuation components, and it often predominates in the early part of a love relationship.
16. **affectionate love** Also called companionate love, this love occurs when an individual wants to have another person near and has a deep, caring affection for that person.

Key People

1. J	3. I	5. G	7. B	9. C
2. A	4. H	6. F	8. E	10. D

The Nature of Peer Relations
Guided Review

1. peers
2. the world outside the family
3. feedback
4. general play
5. going places
6. socializing
7. delinquency
8. problem drinking
9. depression
10. Jean Piaget
11. Harry Stack Sullivan
12. symmetrical reciprocity
13. loneliness
14. hostility
15. mental health
16. criminal
17. "setting"
18. parents
19. neighborhoods
20. churches
21. schools
22. friends
23. model
24. coach
25. secure
26. conformity
27. using bad language
28. stealing
29. vandalizing
30. making fun of parents and teachers
31. dress like friends
32. spend time with
33. ninth
34. parental
35. independence
36. late high school
37. nonconformity
38. anticonformity
39. skinheads
40. punks
41. popular
42. happy
43. themselves
44. enthusiasm
45. concern
46. self-confident
47. physically attractive
48. brighter
49. neglected
50. rejected
51. controversial
52. delinquents
53. dropouts
54. aggressive
55. social
56. aggressive
57. social cognitive
58. making friends
59. conglomerate strategies
60. 60.10
61. intrusive
62. demanding
63. responsiveness
64. self-doubt
65. worries
66. weaknesses
67. rejecting
68. authoritarian
69. permissive
70. depressed
71. school
72. depression
73. lower self-esteem
74. sixty
75. one
76. 1/3

The Nature of Peer Relations
Section Review

1. Initiate interaction, be nice, engage in prosocial behavior, show respect for self and others, and provide social support.

_____

_____

2. Using psychological aggression, having a negative self-presentation, and engaging in antisocial behavior.

_____

_____

3. Have older peers monitor and intervene with bullying; develop school-wide rules and actions against bullying; form friendship groups for adolescents who are regularly bullied by peers, and incorporate anti-bullying messages into church, community, and school activities

_____

_____

Friendships
Guided Review

1. companionship
2. stimulation
3. physical
4. ego
5. companionship
6. intimacy/affection
7. Harry Stack Sullivan
8. parental
9. intimacy
10. parents
11. lonelier
12. depressed
13. self-esteem
14. early
15. self-worth
16. symmetrical intimate mode
17. self-disclosure
18. emotional
19. disagreements
20. perspective taking
21. empathy
22. social
23. cognitive
24. social
25. Supportive
26. coercive
27. temperament
28. intimacy
29. similarity
30. self-disclosure
31. private
32. intimate
33. best
34. clique
35. loyalty
36. age
37. sex
38. ethnicity
39. school
40. achievement
41. clothes
42. leisure
43. deviant
44. Early
45. girls
46. late
47. girls
48. older
49. problem

Adolescent Groups
Guided Review

1. personal
2. rewards
3. information
4. self-esteem
5. identity
6. norms
7. members
8. roles
9. rules
10. expectations
11. formed
12. in-groupness
13. competition
14. superordinate
15. hung out
16. talked
17. athletic events
18. cars
19. alcohol
20. formal
21. heterogeneous
22. heterosexual
23. increase
24. opposite
25. same
26. ethnic
27. socioeconomic
28. athletic
29. student counsel
30. honor
31. fraternities/sororities
32. school
33. community
34. white
35. crowd
36. mutual interest
37. activity
38. cliques
39. intimate
40. cohesive
41. larger
42. intimate
43. 3/6
44. jocks
45. brains
46. burnouts
47. populars
48. nonconformists
49. school failure
50. drug use
51. sexual
52. 400
53. 4-H
54. AS-PIRA
55. WAVE
56. community
57. self-esteem
58. educated
59. higher
60. awareness
61. transportation
62. interest
63. at-risk
64. Boys'/Girls'
65. educational
66. personal

Adolescent Groups
Section Review

1.
   a. Precrowd stage consisting of isolated, unisexual groups;
   b. beginning of the crowd; unisexual groups start group-group interaction;
   c. crowd in structural transition; unisex groups are forming mixed-sex groups;
   d. fully developed crowd; mixed-sex groups are closely associated;
   e. crowd begins to disintegration as loosely associated groups of couples pair off.

2.
   a. The influence of cliques is not entirely negative;
   b. the influence of cliques is not uniform for all adolescents; and
   c. developmental changes occur in cliques.

113

Dating and Romantic Relationships
Guided Review

1. dating
2. 1920s
3. 8
4. recreation
5. status/achievement
6. socialization
7. experimentation/exploration
8. companionship
9. identity
10. hooking up
11. seeing
12. going out
13. cyberdating
14. 14
15. 14/15
16. 90
17. 50
18. pregnancy
19. problems
20. movie
21. dinner
22. hanging
23. malls/homes
24. visiting
25. thinking
26. being
27. reverses
28. culture
29. patterns
30. mate selection
31. Latino
32. Asian/American
33. Anglo-American
34. scripts
35. guide
36. evaluate
37. proactive
38. public
39. reactive
40. private
41. positive
42. negative
43. anxiety
44. anger
45. jealousy
46. depression
47. Romantic
48. infatuation
49. affectionate
50. adult
51. attractiveness
52. sexuality
53. continuity
54. parents
55. peer
56. friendships
57. secure

Dating and Romantic Relationships
Section Review

1.   No answer provided. Individual activity.

2.   a.   (1) Initiating the date (asking for and planning it); (2) controlling the pubic domain (driving and opening doors); and (3) initiating sexual interaction (making physical contact).
      b.   (1) Concern for private domain (concern about appearance, enjoying the date); (2) participating in structure of the date (being picked up, having doors opened); and (3) responding to sexual gestures.

3.   a.   Secure—Feel comfortable and express closeness, warmth, and intimacy.
      b.   Dismissing/avoidant—Be distance and expect romantic partners to be unresponsive and unavailable.
      c.   Preoccupied/ambivalent—Be disappointed and frustrated with intimacy and closeness.

Explorations in Adolescence

Stable relationships with caring peers and adults; safe and attractive places to relax and be with their friends; opportunities to develop life skills, contribute to the communities, and feel competent.

Adventures for the Mind

No answers. Individual activity.

Adolescence in Research

Two hundred twenty-one adolescents were either associated with major cliques (jocks, populars, normals, druggies/toughs, and nobodies) or not associated with any clique. The self-esteem of the jocks and populars was the highest, while that of the nobodies was the lowest. Those involved with no clique—the independents—had self-esteem equivalent to the jocks and the populars.

Comprehensive Review

1. c	**5.** c	**9.** d	**13.** a	**17.** d
2. a	**6.** d	**10.** d	**14.** c	**18.** c
3. b	**7.** d	**11.** b	**15.** a	**19.** c
4. a	**8.** b	**12.** a	**16.** d	**20.** a

◆ Chapter 7   Schools

Learning Objectives with Key Terms and Key People in Boldface

1.0   What is the Nature of the Adolescent's Schooling?
  A.   Approaches to Educating Students
    1.1   How have secondary schools changed since the 19th century?
    1.2   What is the comprehensive high school?
    1.3   What functions of secondary schools are being debated today?
    1.4   What is the **back-to-basics movement**?
    1.5   What arguments are being made for schools to fulfill more comprehensive functions?
    1.6   What is **direct instruction approach** to student learning?
    1.7   What are **cognitive constructivist approaches** to student learning?
    1.8   What are **social constructivist approaches** to student learning?
    1.9   What is the American Psychological Association's learner centered psychological principles?
  B.   Schools Changing Social Developmental Contexts
    1.10   How do schools change to meet the developmental needs of the students?
    1.11   How do the social context of schools differ at the preschool, elementary school, and secondary school levels?

2.0   What are Transitions in Schooling?
  A.   Transition to Middle- Or Junior-High School
    2.1   What is the origin of junior high schools?
    2.2   What were the justifications for junior high schools?
    2.3   Why have middle schools become more popular?
    2.4   How are middle schools related to pubertal development?
    2.5   Why is the transition to middle- or junior-high school stressful?
    2.6   What is the **top-dog phenomenon**?
  B.   Successful Middle Schools
    2.7   According to Lipsitz, what makes a middle school successful?
    2.8   What did the Carnegie Foundation recommend about the redesign of middle schools?
  C.   Transition from High School to College
    2.9   How does the transition from high school to college parallel the transition from elementary to middle-junior high school?
    2.10   What happens to parental interaction with the transition?
    2.11   What are the effects of discontinuity between high school and college?
  D.   High School Dropouts and Noncollege Youth
    2.12   What educational deficiencies do students who dropout experience in adulthood?
    2.13   What are the extent and characteristics of ethnic minority students who drop out?
    2.14   What factors are associated with dropping out?
    2.15   How can the dropout rate be reduced?

3.0   **What are the Processes and Related Ideas Associated with Schools, Classrooms, Teachers, and Parents?**

    A.   **Size and Climate**

        3.1   What are the most desirable classroom and school size?

        3.2   What are some of the drawbacks of large schools?

        3.3   Which class size best benefits student learning?

        3.4   What are the components of a positive classroom climate?

        3.5   What is the **authoritative strategy of classroom management**?

        3.6   What is the **authoritarian strategy of classroom management**?

        3.7   What is the **permissive strategy of classroom management**?

        3.8   To what variables are classroom climate generally linked?

        3.9   What is the effect of school climate on student achievement?

    B.   **Person-Environment Fit and Aptitude-Treatment Interaction**

        3.10   What happens when the schools do not meet the adolescent's needs?

        3.11   What is meant by aptitude-treatment interaction?

    C.   **Teachers and Parents**

        3.12   Can we compile a profile of a competent teacher?

        3.13   How does parental involvement with schools change as students move into adolescence?

        3.14   Why is greater collaboration between schools, families, and communities needed?

4.0   **What are the Effects of Socioeconomic Status and Ethnicity in Schools?**

    A   **Socioeconomic Status and Ethnicity in Schools**

        4.1   What is the effect of poverty on student learning?

        4.2   What are the characteristics of schools in low-income neighborhoods?

    B.   **Ethnicity**

        4.3   How does ethnicity impact on school experiences?

        4.4   What is the role of teacher's positive expectations of ethnic students?

        4.5   What are some effective teaching strategies for improving relations with ethnically diverse students?

        4.6   What is a **jigsaw** classroom?

    C.   **Social Policy and the Education of Adolescents**

        4.7   What are some social policy recommendations for improving schools for adolescents?

5.0   **What Are the Issues Associated with Adolescents Who Are Exceptional?**

    A.   **Who Are Adolescents with Disabilities?**

        5.1   How many U.S. students receive special education services?

        5.2   What percentage of students receiving special education has **learning disabilities**?

    B.   **Learning Disabilities**

        5.3   How are learning disabilities defined?

        5.4   What is the most common problem for students with a learning disability?

    C.   **Attention Deficit/Hyperactivity Disorder (ADHD)**

        5.5   How is **ADHD** defined?

        5.6   What interventions are recommended for children and adolescents with ADHD?

    D.   **Educational Issues Involving Adolescents with a Disability**

        5.7   What is Public Law 92–142?

        5.8   What is The Individuals with Disabilities Act (IDEA)?

        5.9   What does least restrictive environment (LRE) mean?

        5.10   What is meant by inclusion?

    E.   **Adolescents Who Are Gifted**

        5.11   What are the criteria for giftedness?

        5.12   What are some characteristics that characterize **gifted adolescents**?

6.0   Explorations in Adolescence
   6.1   What are the differences in secondary schools in Australia, Brazil, Germany, Japan, Russia, and the United States?

7.0   Adventures for the Mind
   7.1   If you could redesign the middle school you attended in order to improve student's socioemotional development, what changes would you make?
   7.2   Do schools provide learning disabled students with the services they need?

Key Terms

Write a sentence using each of these key terms by either defining the term or giving an example of it. For instance, you might write, "A jigsaw classroom..." or, "(give examples) is an example of a jigsaw classroom." Compare your definitions with those given at the end of study guide chapter; and check your examples by referring to the text. Review the text for those terms you don't know or define incorrectly.

1.   back-to-basics movement

_____

_____

2.   direct instruction approach

_____

_____

3.   cognitive constructivist approach

_____

_____

4.   social constructivist approach

_____

_____

5.   top-dog phenomenon

_____

_____

6.   authoritative strategy of classroom management

_____

_____

7.   authoritarian strategy of classroom management

_____

_____

8.   permissive strategy of classroom management

_____

_____

9.   aptitude-treatment interaction (ATI)

_____

_____

10.   jigsaw classroom

_____

_____

11.   learning disability

_____

_____

12.   attention deficit/hyperactivity disorder (ADHD)

_____

_____

13.   Public Law 94–142

_____

_____

14.   Individuals with Disabilities Act (IDEA)

_____

_____

15.   least restrictive environment

_____

_____

16.   inclusion

_____

_____

17.   adolescents who are gifted

_____

_____

Key People
Match the person with the concept of adolescent development with which they are associated.

___	1.	Joan Lipsitz	A.	Believed teachers should help students achieve industry
___	2.	Jacqueline Eccles	B.	Pioneered research on the jigsaw classroom
___	3.	Erik Erikson	C.	Studied how developmentally appropriate school environments could meet students' needs
___	4.	Joyce Epstein	D.	Conducted research into what makes a good middle school
___	5.	Jonathan Kozol	E.	Believes that parents needs to be more involved in schools
___	6.	John Ogbu	F.	Anthropologist who says American schools exploit minority students
___	7.	Eliot Aronson	G.	Author of *Savage Inequities*
___	8.	James Banks	H.	Believes that a community, team approach is the best way to educate students
___	9.	James Comer	I.	Conducted research about gifted children
___	10.	Ellen Winner	J.	Studied the needs of exceptional children
___	11.	Daniel Hallahan	K.	A proponent of multicultural education

The Nature of Adolescent's Schooling
Guided Review

Between (1) _____ and _____ states developed compulsory education laws. But schools were mainly for the (2) _____, and they emphasized (3) _____ courses. By the 1920s, educators added (4) _____ education, (5) _____, and (6) _____ education courses. By the middle of the 20th century, schools became more (7)_____, designed to train adolescents (8) _____, (9) _____, and (10) _____.

Expert panels in the 1970s agreed that high schools were contributing to adolescent (11) _____ and that schools had become teenage (12) _____. As a result some states lowered the mandatory age for staying in school from (13) _____ to _____. In the 1980s, the (14) _____ movement gained momentum. It stressed that schools should be concerned only with (15) _____, not with adolescents' (16) _____ and (17) _____ lives. This movement was partly in response to the (18) _____ approach that was based on the British system, one that allowed adolescents to learn and develop at their own pace. Today, the modern high school often resembles a (19) _____, due to its wide range of courses. The (20) _____ about what schools should do changes, much as a (21) _____ swings.

The back-to-basics movement believes in the (22) _____ instruction approach to learning. This method is (23) _____-centered and characterized by (24) _____ control, mastery of (25) _____ skills, high expectation for students' (26) _____, and maximum time spent on (27) _____ tasks. The cognitive constructivist approaches emphasize the adolescent's (28) _____, _____ construction of (29) _____ and _____. (30) _____ theory is an example of this approach. (31) _____ theory is represented in the (32) _____ approach, one that relies on (33) _____ with others to produce (34) _____ and _____. The direct approach may produce more (35) _____ learners and not adequately challenge and prepare students to think in (36) _____ and _____ ways.

APA's (37) _____ principles address (38) _____ and _____ factors, (39) _____ and _____ factors, (40) _____ and _____ factors, and (41) _____ difference factors.

The (42) _____ contexts of schools vary at each level. Preschool children interact with peers in (43) _____ relationships or in (44) _____ groups. The elementary school class is more like a social (45) _____. The (46) _____ become the learning community. In middle or junior high schools the social field is the (47) _____ as a whole. Students have many (48) _____ and interact with (49) _____, (50) _____, and the (51) _____. Secondary students are more aware of the entire school as a (52) _____.

The Nature of Adolescent's Schooling
Section Review
Match the APA Learner-Centered Psychological Principle with its description.

Cognitive and Metacognitive Factors

____   1. nature of the learning process   A. Successful learners can create a repertoire of thinking and reasoning strategies to achieve complex goals.

____   2. goals of the learning process   B. Successful learners can create meaningful, coherent representations of knowledge.

____   3. construction of knowledge   C. Higher order strategies for selecting and monitoring mental operations facilitate creative and critical thinking.

____   4. strategic thinking   D. The learning of complex subject matter is more effective when it is an intentional process of constructing meaning and experience.

____   5. thinking about thinking   E. Successful learners can link new information with existing knowledge in meaningful ways.

____   6. context of learning   F. Learning is influenced by environmental factors, including culture, technology, and instructional practices.

Motivational, Instructional, Developmental, Social, and Individual Difference Factors

____   1. motivational and emotional influences on learning   A. The learner's creativity, higher order thinking, and natural curiosity all contribute to motivation to learn.

____   2. intrinsic motivation to learn   B. Acquiring complex knowledge and skills requires extended learner effort and guided practice. Without learners' motivation to learn, the willingness to exert this effort is unlikely without coercion.

____   3. effects of motivation on effort   C. What and how much is learned is influenced by the learner's motivation, which, in turn, is influenced by the learner's emotional states, beliefs, interests, goals, and habits of thinking.

____   4. developmental influences on learning   D. Setting appropriately high and challenging standards and assessing the learner and learning progress are integral aspect of the learning experience.

____   5. social influences on learning   E. Learning is influenced by social interactions, interpersonal relations, and communication with others.

____   6. individual differences in learning   F. Learners have different strategies, approaches, and capabilities for learning that are a function of prior experience and heredity.

____   7. learning and diversity   G. Learning is most effective when differential development within and across physical, cognitive, and socioemotional domains is taken into account.

____   8. standards and assessment   H. Learning is most effective when differences in learner's linguistic, cultural, and social backgrounds are considered.

Transitions in Schooling
Guided Review

Junior high school emerged in the 1920s and 1930s in order to meet the (1) _____, (2) _____, and (3) _____- needs of adolescents and in response to the (4) _____ student population. The modern system of public schooling is based on a (5) _____ model, with elementary school the (6) _____ to _____ grades, junior high the (7) _____ to _____ grades, and high school, (8) _____ to _____ grades. Gradually, (9) ____ grade has been returned to the (10) _____, and grades (11) _____ and _____ make up the middle schools. Middle schools were created as a result of the (12) _____ of puberty in adolescence. Some say that middle schools are just a (13) _____ version of high schools. The transition to middle school or junior high school is both (14) _____ and (15) _____ for most children. Stress results from the many (16) _____, (17) _____, and (18) _____ changes children are going through, as well as their move from a (19) _____ to a (20) _____ position. The older two-tier system of schooling, the (21) _____ arrangement, is best for minimizing school transition stress, because

122

students only have to change schools (22) _____ times. Elementary to middle school or junior high school adjustment stress can be lessened if schools provide more (23) _____ and _____, and less (24) _____ and _____. Parents who are attune to their adolescents' (25) _____ needs and who support their (26) _____ also lessen transition stress.

The best middle schools are those who are willing to adapt their school practices to (27) _____ differences in (28) _____, (29) _____, and (30) _____ development of the students. In addition, the most effective middle schools provide a positive environment for the adolescent's (31) _____ and (32) _____ development. Middle schools who have followed the 1989 Carnegie Council's (33) _____ recommendations have shown positive results in improving students' (34) _____, (35) _____, and (36) _____.

Transition from high school to college involves going from (37) _____ to _____ and from being the oldest and most (38) _____ to being the youngest and least (39) _____. One of the major changes is (40) _____ with parents. There is a great (41) _____- between high school and college. High schools need to make the transition (42) _____ by assisting students in (43) _____ colleges. Today's college students appear to be experiencing more (44) _____ and (45) _____ than in the past, which many say is the result of (46) _____ of _____.

Today the overall high-school drop out rate is approximately (47) _____ percent. The highest dropout rate is among (48) _____ students. (49) _____ percent of 20- to 21-year-old Latinos dropped out of school. Fewer than (50) _____ of Native Americans graduate from high school. In some inner city areas, the drop out rate for minority students is as high as (51) _____ percent. Dropout rates of African Americans are similar to that of (52) _____. One study showed that (53) _____ percent of the dropouts occurred for school-related reasons. Other reasons are related to (54) _____, (55) _____, (56) _____., and (57) _____ problems One of the main family factors in dropout is (58) _____. Approximately (59) _____ of girls who drop out do so as a result of (60) _____ or (61) _____. Dropout rates can be reduced by (62) _____ the (63) _____ between school and (64) _____ . An effective dropout prevention program is the (65) _____ Foundation, which involves (66) _____ sponsors in school (67) _____.

Transitions in Schooling
Section Review

1. What six recommendations did the Carnegie Council report recommend for improving middle schools?

_____

_____

_____

_____

_____

_____

2. What six approaches can schools and community institutions use to break down the barriers between work and school?

_____

_____

_____

_____

_____

_____

Schools, Classrooms, Teachers, and Parents
Guided Review

Increased size of secondary schools in the U.S. is the result of increasing (1) _____, decreasing (2) _____, and increased (3) _____. Larger schools, those more than (4) _____ to _____ students may not be as effective as smaller schools. Smaller schools may be more (5) _____ and have less (6) _____- behavior. Smaller class size, (7) _____ or less students, provides the greatest achievement gains. Three categories of classroom management strategies are derived from (8) _____ parenting styles. The authoritative strategy of classroom management encourages students to be (9) _____ thinkers, but teachers still (10) _____ students, engage them in (11) _____ give-and-take and show a (12) _____ attitude. The (13) _____ strategy is restrictive and punitive. The focus is on (14) _____ order in the classroom, rather than on (15) _____ and _____. The permissive strategy offers students (16) _____, but provides them with little (17) _____ for developing (18) _____ or managing their own (19)_____. The (20) _____ strategy will benefit students the most and help students become (21) _____, _____- _____ learners. To function smoothly, classrooms need clearly defined (22) _____ and (23) _____. Rules should be (24) _____ and _____ and consistent with (25) _____ and (26) _____ goals. Classroom climate is often linked to a teacher's (27) _____ and (28) _____. School climates are important as well. Those with a climate of (29) _____ and (30) _____ for students' success benefit student (31) _____ and (32) _____.

Researcher Jacqueline Eccles found that often a (33) _____ -_____ mismatch harms adolescent development. Considering the characteristics and motivation of the adolescent in determining what is developmentally appropriate education is known as (34) _____-_____ _____, or (35) _____, and it stresses the importance of the adolescent's characteristics and their school experiences. (36) _____ refers to the academic potential and personality characteristics of the individual students; while (37) _____ refers to educational techniques.

Erik Erikson believed that good teachers produce a sense of (38) _____, rather than (39) _____ in their students. Stephen Feeney stresses that meaningful learning takes place when (40)_____ has been established and when adolescents feel free to (41) _____, to (42) _____, and to make (43) _____. Student-teacher relationships begin to deteriorate after the transition to (44) _____ school. Parents are key factors in schooling at all grade levels, yet parental involvement is (45) _____ in elementary and even (46) _____ in high schools. (47) _____ _____ has provided a framework for parental involvement in schools. She believed that parent involvement in (48)_____ and home (49) _____ activities needs to be increased.

Schools, Classrooms, Teachers, and Parents
Section Review

1. List three things teachers can do to improve the likelihood that students will cooperate with them in the classroom.

_____

_____

2. List eight teacher traits that are associated with positive student outcomes.

_____

_____

3. According to Joyce Epstein, what are the six factors that form a framework for improving parental involvement in adolescent's schooling.

_____

_____

Socioeconomic Status, Ethnicity, Schools, and Social Policy
Guided Review

Adolescents from low-income, (1) _____ _____ backgrounds have (2) _____ difficulties in school than their (3) _____ counterparts. These adolescents in poverty face problems at (4) _____ and in (5) _____ that present barriers to learning. They often attend schools that have (6) _____. Students in these schools have lower (7) _____ and (8) _____ rates. The schools often encourage (9) _____ learning instead of (10) _____.

(11) _____ wrote about problems adolescents in poverty face in their neighborhoods and schools in the book (12) _____. School (13) _____ is still a factor in education. Almost (14) _____ of African-American and Latino students attend schools in which (15) ____ percent or more students are from ethnic minority groups. African American and Latino students are much less likely than (16) _____ or _____ students to be enrolled in academic, college preparatory programs, and more likely to be enrolled in (17) _____ and (18) _____ programs. Ethnic minorities of color constitute the majority in (19) _____ of the _____ largest school district in the United States; however (20) ____ percent of the teachers are (21) _____. American Anthropologist (22) _____ proposed that the American educational system (23) _____ ethnic minority students. Margaret Beale Spencer says that a form of (24) _____ racism permeates many American schools, and that teachers fail to (25) _____ students of color, accepting a (26) _____ of performance. John Santrock has proposed several strategies for (27) _____ between ethnically diverse students. A particularly effective strategy is use of the (28) _____ classroom, a concept developed by (29) _____, in which students from different cultural backgrounds work in (30) _____ groups. In *Turning Points*, the (31) _____ issued a set of (32) _____ principles for transforming adolescents' education. These principles can form the core of (33) _____ initiatives.

Socioeconomic Status, Ethnicity, Schools, and Social Policy
Section Review

1. What five home factors present learning barriers to adolescents who live in poverty?

_____

_____

2. Describe the neighborhood and school conditions that Jonathan Kozol found in one inner city East St. Louis school district. .

_____

_____

3. Give an example of how a teacher might apply each of John Santrock's six strategies for improving relations between ethnically diverse students.

_____

_____

4. List the eight principles for transforming adolescent education propounded in the Carnegie Council's *Turning Points* report.

_____

_____

Adolescents Who Are Exceptional
Guided Review

An estimated (1) _____ percent of all students receive special education or related services. Within this group, a little more than (2) _____ have a (3) _____ disability. (4) _____ percent have speech or language impairment, (5) _____ percent mental retardation, and (6) ____ percent have emotional disturbances. Children with a learning disability are of (7) _____ or above intelligence, have difficulties in at least one (8) _____ area, and their difficulty cannot be attributed to any other (9) _____, such as (10) _____. Learning disabilities are manifest in problems with (11) _____, (12) _____, (13) _____, and (14) _____. About (15) ___ times as many boys as girls have learning disabilities, a figure partially attributable to (16) _____ vulnerability of boys as well as (17) _____ bias.

By definition, adolescents do not have a learning disability unless they have an (18) _____ problem. Among the most common academic problem areas are (19) _____, (20) _____, and (21) _____. About (22) ____ percent of the total school age population receive special education services because of a learning disability.

Attention deficit/hyperactivity disorder, or (23) _____, is shown by characteristics of (24) _____, (25) _____, and (26) _____. Children and adolescents with ADHD comprise more than (27) _____ of the child and adolescent recipients of special education services. The disorder occurs as much as (28) ___ to _____ times more in boys than girls. Controversy about the increased diagnosis of ADHD includes belief that there is an (29) _____ of the disorder, as well as concerns that it is being (30) _____. ADHD only decreases in about (31) _____ of all adolescents. The causes of ADHD are not definitely known, but there is evidence that (32) _____, prenatal and postnatal (33) _____, and (34) _____ toxins may be factors. (35) ___ - _____ percent of children and adolescents with ADHD have a (36) _____ or _____ with the disorder. About (37) ____ - _____ percent of students with ADHD are taking the drug (38) _____ to control their behavior. Many experts recommend a combination of (39) _____, (40) _____, and (41) _____ interventions for students with ADHD.

(42) _____, the Education for All Handicapped Children Act, requires that all students with disabilities be given a (43) _____, _____, and _____ education. In 1983, the law was renamed (44) _____. It requires an individualized evaluation and program, known as an (45) _____, and mandates that interventions occur in the (46) _____. This used to be described as (47) _____; however, that term has been replaced with the term (48) _____, which means educating a child or adolescent with special needs in a (49) _____ program.

Adolescents with an IQ above 120 and/or with superior talents are considered to be (50) _____. Changing conceptions of (51) _____ are moving educators to move towards more towards specific (52) _____ and away from specific (53) _____ scores in determining giftedness. (54) _____, an expert on giftedness, describes gifted adolescents as being (55) _____, (56) _____, and having a (57) _____ to master their domain. They also appear to excel in (58) _____. Gifted adolescents who are not challenged may become (59) _____, (60) _____ classes, and lose (61) _____- in achieving. Gifted adolescents may be (62) _____ isolated, (63) _____ by their peers, and labeled as (64) _____ or _____. Ellen Winner recommends that underchallenged gifted students be allowed to attend (65) _____ classes in their area of (66) _____, including taking (67) _____ courses.

Adolescents Who Are Exceptional

Section Review

Rank in order, from 1 to 12 (with 1 being the highest number and 12 being the lowest number), these disabilities experienced by American school children in the 1994–1995 school year: deaf-blindness, visual impairments, hearing impairments, orthopedic impairments, serious emotional disturbance, mental retardation, speech or language impairments, specific learning disabilities, other health impairments, autism, traumatic brain injury, multiple disabilities.

_____

_____

_____

_____

_____

_____

_____

_____

_____

_____

_____

_____

_____

Explorations in Adolescent Development

Compare and contrast the following aspects of secondary schools in Australia, Brazil, Germany, Japan, Russia, and the United States: (a) mandatory age: (b) number of levels; (c) role of sports; (d) entrance and exit exams; (e) content and philosophy; and (f) foreign language education.

_____

_____

Adventures for the Mind

1. If you could do just two things to redesign your middle or junior high school in order to improve students' socioemotional development, what would you do?

_____

_____

2. Think back on your high school classmates that were of diverse ethnic, religious, and socioeconomic background. How well did your school meet the social and educational needs of these students? Knowing what you know now, how would you have responded to the needs of these students if you had been a teacher at the school?

_____

_____

Comprehensive Review

1. In the 1970s, three independent panels that examined the benefits of secondary school for adolescents concluded that high schools
   a. increase adolescents' exposure to adults.
   b. restrict the transition to adulthood.
   c. decrease adolescents' sense of alienation.
   d. increase employment opportunities for adolescents.

2. According to the back-to-basics movement, the main function of schools should be to
   a. provide extracurricular activities.
   b. enhance the social and emotional development of adolescents.
   c. be comprehensive and provide a multifaceted curriculum.
   d. develop an intellectually mature person by emphasizing training in basic subject.

3. The major rationale for the establishment of junior high schools in the 1920s—19390s was that
   a. early adolescents experience many changes at this time and need to be segregated.
   b. the poor economic conditions put pressure upon the schools to provide more "baby-sitting" space.
   c. too many older adolescents were fighting with the young adolescents.
   d. high schools were "upgraded" and reorganized to encourage students to go on to college or university.

4. The top-dog phenomenon refers to
   a. the superior formal operational reasoning of high school students compared to junior high students.
   b. the dating advantage that junior high school girls have over junior high school boys.
   c. the self-perceptions of junior high school students who attend supportive and stable schools.
   d. the lowered status experienced by students when they move from elementary to junior high school.

5. Darren has been complaining about not being able to make good grades. He says he used to feel good in school, but now feels like a little fish in a big pond. Darren
   a. probably have the same school crises as girls of his age.
   b. is struggling with the transition to junior high school.
   c. is becoming self-conscious because of the emergence of formal operational thought.
   d. probably has developed the underdog adjustment disorder associated with junior high entry.

6. Effective schools for young adolescents have all of the following characteristics except
   a. similar methods of grouping students.
   b. emphasis on the school context as a community.
   c. curricula emphasizing self-exploration and definition.
   d. responsiveness to their community political milieus.

7. The report from the Carnegie Commission encourages
   a. disbanding middle schools in favor of a longer stay in elementary school.
   b. eliminating high schools land moving from junior high directly to college prep schools.
   c. arranging middle school students in smaller groups.
   d. eliminating middle schools in favor of junior high schools.

8. The students least likely to complete high school are
   a. African American.
   b. from single-parent homes.
   c. Native Americans.
   d. Urban Hispanics.

9. About 50 percent of the dropouts do so for school-related reasons, whereas another 20 percent drop out of high school
   a. for economic reasons.
   b. because they are unable to read and write well.
   c. because they are in trouble with law-enforcement authorities.
   d. are Native Americans.

10. Small schools are more likely to
    a. be associated with prosocial behavior than large schools.
    b. provide fewer opportunities for school participation than large schools.
    c. promote better academic achievement than large schools.
    d. promote more antisocial behavior than large schools.

11. The _____ classroom is characterized by teachers who serve as facilitators of student learning rather than teaching in the traditional manner.
    a. open
    b. new wave
    c. multi-dimensional
    d. California

12. Young adolescents appear to respond well to teachers who
    a. let the students set the limits in the classroom.
    b. are pals.
    c. are insensitive to student criticism.
    d. use natural authority.

13. A teacher says to a student, "Thank you for being quiet in class today for a change." With which type of student is this more likely to occur?
    a. a "trouble-maker"
    b. a White American student
    c. an African American student
    d. the "best" student in the class

14. Among minority youth who stay in school, poor academic performance is linked to
    a. the refusal of other students to study with them.
    b. the unwillingness to engage in cooperative learning.
    c. the language barriers.
    d. coming from a poor, single-parent family.

15. The Education for All Handicapped Children Act mandated that all states do which of the following for all handicapped children?
    a. provide free health care
    b. provide educational programs for their parents
    c. provide free testing programs
    d. provided individualized educational programs

16. Mainstreaming or inclusion refers to
    a. teaching handicapped children in public schools.
    b. assigning handicapped children to regular classrooms.
    c. giving handicapped children a high educational priority.
    d. assuring handicapped children interact with nonhandicapped children whenever possible.

17. Shawna, a second grader, has no trouble with math, science, or art, but she cannot spell, read, or write. It is likely that Shawna has a(n)
    a. visual impairment.
    b. speech handicaps.
    c. learning disability.
    d. attention deficit.

18. Timothy is suffering from attention-deficit hyperactivity disorder. He is most likely to be experiencing all but which of the following symptoms?
    a. short attention span.
    b. easily distracted.
    c. below-normal intelligence.
    d. high levels of physical activity.

19. What type of drug is used to control attention-deficit hyperactivity disorder?
    a. stimulants
    b. depressant
    c. tranquilizers
    d. relaxants

20. _____ is the only country in the world that has high school athletics and sports as an integral part of the educational system.
    a. South Africa
    b. Japan
    c. Italy
    d. The United States

Adolescence on the Screen

- *To Sir, With Love* is the story of a black engineer who takes a job in a rough London school.

- *The Breakfast Club* portrays how students in a Saturday detention class coalesce as a group.

- *Dangerous Minds* depicts a female teacher struggling to deal with tough inner city teenagers.

- *Dead Poet's Society* stars Robin Williams playing an English teacher who tries to change the way students learn literature.

Adolescence in Books

- *Adolescence in the 1990s,* edited by Ruby Takanishi (Teachers College Press, 1993), features a number of experts on adolescence addressing the risks and opportunities for adolescents in today's world. Many chapters focus on improving the quality of schooling for adolescents.

- *Successful Schools for Young Adolescents*, by Joan Lipsitz (Transaction Books, 1984), is a classic resource for people involved in middle school education.

Adolescence in Research

Concerning Simmons and Blyth's 1987 study comparing school systems with a 6–3–3 arrangement and those with an 8–4 arrangement, state the hypothesis, the research methods (if known), the research conclusions, and the implications and applications for adolescent development.

Answer Key

Key Terms

1. **back-to-basics movement** This philosophy stresses that the function of schools should be the rigorous training of intellectual skills through such subjects as English, mathematics, and science.

2. **direct instruction approach** A teacher-centered approach that is characterized by teacher direction and control, mastery of academic skills, high expectations for students' progress, and maximum time spent on learning tasks.

3. **cognitive constructivist approaches** Emphasize the adolescent's active, cognitive construction of knowledge and understanding; an example of these approaches is Piaget's theory.

4. **social constructivist approach** Focus on collaboration with others to produce knowledge and understanding; an example of this approach is Vygotsky's theory.

5. **top-dog phenomenon** The circumstance of moving from the top position (in elementary school, the oldest, biggest, and most powerful students) to the lowest position (in middle or junior high school, the youngest, smallest, and least powerful).

6. **authoritative strategy of classroom management** Encourages students to be independent thinkers and doers but still involves effective monitoring. Authoritative teachers engage students in considerable verbal give-and-take and show a caring attitude toward them. However, they still declare limits when necessary.

7. **authoritarian strategy of classroom management** Is restrictive and punitive. The focus is mainly on keeping order in the classroom rather than on instruction and learning.

8. **permissive strategy of classroom management** Offers students considerable autonomy but provides them with little support for developing learning skills or managing their behavior.

9. **aptitude-treatment interaction (ATI)** This interaction stresses the importance of both the attitudes and the characteristics of the adolescent, such as academic potential or personality traits, and the treatments or experiences, such as the educational techniques that the adolescent receives. *Aptitude* refers to such characteristics as the academic potential and personality characteristics on which students differ; *treatment* refers to educational techniques, such as structured versus flexible classrooms.

10. **jigsaw classroom** Students from different cultural backgrounds are placed in a cooperative group in which they have to construct different parts of a project to reach a common goal.

11. **learning disability** Describes individuals who 1) are of normal intelligence or above, 2) have difficulties in a least one academic area and usually several, and 3) their difficulties cannot be attributed to any other diagnosed problem or disorder, such as mental retardation.

12. **attention deficit/hyperactivity disorder (ADHD)** Is a disability in which children and adolescents show one or more of the following characteristics over a period of time: 1) inattention, 2) hyperactivity, and 3) impulsivity.

13. **Public Law 94–142** The Education for All Handicapped Children Act, which requires all students with disabilities to be given a free, appropriate education and provides the funding to help implement this education.

14. **Individuals with Disabilities Act (IDEA)** This spells out broad mandates for services to all children and adolescents with disabilities. These include evaluation and eligibility determination, appropriate education and the Individualized Education Program (IEP), and least restrictive environment.

15. **least restrictive environment** A setting that is as similar as possible to the one in which the children, or adolescents without a disability are educated; under the Individuals with Disabilities Act, the child or adolescent must be educated in this setting.

16. **inclusion** Educating a child or adolescent with special education needs full-time in a general school program.

17. **adolescents who are gifted** They are characterized by having above average intelligence (usually defined as an IQ of 120 or higher) and/or superior talent in some domain such as art, music, or mathematics.

Key People

1. D	3. A	5. G	7. B	9. H	11. J
2. C	4. E	6. F	8. K	10. I	

The Nature of Adolescents' Schooling
Guided Review

1. 1890/1920
2. elite
3. liberal arts
4. general education
5. college prepatory
6. vocational education
7. comprehensive
8. intellectually
9. vocationally
10. Socially
11. alienation
12. warehouses
13. 16/14
14. back-to-basics
15. imparting knowledge
16. social
17. emotional
18. open
19. shopping mall
20. debate
21. pendulum
22. direct
23. teacher
24. teacher
25. academic
26. progress
27. learning
28. active/cognitive
29. knowledge/understanding
30. Piaget's
31. Vygotsky's
32. social constructivist
33. collaboration
34. knowledge/understanding
35. passive
36. critical/creative
37. Learner-centered
38. cognitive/metacognitive
39. motivational/affective
40. developmental/social
41. individual
42. social
43. dyadic
44. small
45. unit
46. peer
47. school
48. teachers
49. extracurricular activities
50. clubs
51. community
52. system

The Nature of Adolescent's Schooling
Section Review
Cognitive and Metacognitive Factors

1. D   2. B   3. E   4. A   5. C   6. F

Motivational, Instructional, Developmental, Social, and Individual Difference Factors
1. C   2. a   3. B   4. G   5. E   6. F   7. H   8. D

Transitions in Schooling
Guided Review

1. physical
2. cognitive
3. social
4. growing
5. 6–3–3
6. 1–6
7. 7th–9th
8. 10–12
9. 9th
10. high schools
11. 7/8
12. earlier onset
13. watered-down
14. normative
15. stressful
16. physical
17. cognitive

18. socioemotional
19. top-dog
20. bottom-dog
21. 8–4
22. 2
23. support/stability
24. anonymity/complexity
25. developmental
26. autonomy
27. individual
28. physical
29. cognitive
30. social
31. social
32. emotional
33. Turning Points

34. reading
35. math
36. language
37. top dog/bottom dog
38. powerful
39. powerful
40. reduced contact
41. discontinuity
42. smoother
43. choosing
44. stress
45. depression
46. fear/failure
47. 15
48. ethnic minority
49. 35
50. 10

51. 50
52. whites
53. 50
54. economic
55. family
56. peer
57. personal
58. socioeconomic status
59. 1/3
60. pregnancy
61. marriage
62. bridging
63. gap
64. work
65. I Have a Dream
66. personal
67. improvement

Transitions in Schooling
Section Review

1. a. Develop smaller "communities" or "houses" within schools to make them less impersonal.
   b. Lower student-to-counselor ratios to 10–1.
   c. Involve parents and community leaders in schools.
   d. Develop curriculum that produces students who are literate, understand the sciences, and have some knowledge of health, ethics, and citizenship.
   e. Encourage team-teaching and curriculum blocks.
   f. Have more in-school health and fitness programs.

2. a. Monitor work experiences through cooperative education, apprenticeships, internships, preemployment training, and youth-operated enterprises.
   b. Utilize community and neighborhood services, including voluntary service and youth-guided services.
   c. Redirect vocational education to provide basic skills needed in a wide range of work.
   d. Provide continuing education, employment, and training in conjunction with mentoring programs.
   e. Provide career information and counseling.
   f. Use school volunteer programs so students can have adult mentors and friends.

Schools, Classrooms, Teachers, and Parents
Guided Review

1. urban enrollments
2. budgets
3. academic stimulation
4. 500/600
5. prosocial
6. antisocial
7. 20
8. Diana Baumrind
9. independent
10. monitor
11. verbal
12. caring
13. authoritarian
14. keeping
15. instruction/learning
16. autonomy
17. support
18. learning skills
19. behavior
20. authoritative
21. active/self-regulated
22. rules
23. routines
24. reasonable/necessary
25. instructional
26. learning
27. beliefs
28. practices
29. self-efficacy
30. positive expectations
31. learning
32. achievement
33. person-environment
34. aptitude-treatment interaction
35. ATI
36. Aptitude
37. treatment
38. industry
39. inferiority
40. trust
41. explore
42. experiment
43. mistakes
44. junior high
45. minimal
46. less
47. Joyce Epstein
48. school
49. learning

Schools, Classrooms, Teachers, and Parents
Section Review

1.
   a. develop a positive relationship with students.
   b. get students to share and assume responsibility.
   c. reward appropriate behavior.

2.
   a. enthusiasm
   b. ability to plan
   c. poise
   d. adaptability
   e. warmth
   f. flexibility
   g. awareness of individual differences
   h. positive teacher expectations

3.
   a. Parents need to be knowledgeable about adolescent health and safety issues.
   b. Schools need to communicate with families about school programs and the individual progress of the adolescents.
   c. Parents need to be more involved in schools assisting teachers, teaching special skills, and providing clerical or supervisory assistance.
   d. Parents need to be involved in their children's homework.
   e. Parents need to be involved in decision making at school.
   f. Schools need to collaborate with community organizations.

Socioeconomic Status and Ethnicity in Schools
Guided Review

1. ethnic minority
2. more
3. middle socioeconomic status
4. home
5. school
6. fewer resources
7. achievement test scores
8. graduation rates
9. rote
10. thinking skills
11. Jonathan Kozol
12. Savage Inequities

13. segregation
14. 1/3
15. 90
16. non-Latino white/Asian-Americans
17. remedial
18. special education
19. 23/25
20. 90
21. non-Latino
22. John Ogbu
23. exploits

24. institution
25. challenge
26. low-level
27. improving relations
28. jigsaw
29. Eliot Aronson
30. cooperative
31. Carnegie
32. eight
33. social policy

Socioeconomic Status, Ethnicity, Schools, and Social Policy
Section Review

1.
   a. Parents don't set high educational standards.
   b. Parents can't help them with their homework.
   c. Parents don't have money for educational materials and experiences.
   d. They may be poorly nourished.
   e. They may live in neighborhoods where crime and violence are a way of life.

2.
   a. 98 percent of the residents were African American
   b. no obstetric services
   c. no regular trash collection
   d. few jobs
   e. 1/3 of families living on less than $7,500 a year
   f. 75 percent of population living on welfare
   g. blocks of dilapidated housing
   h. chemical pollution and raw sewage
   i. malnutrition
   j. violence
   k. schools old, unattractive, unhealthy, and unsafe
   l. lack of supplies like chalk and paper
   m. old science labs
   n. poor heating system
   o. lack of books

3.
   a. The jigsaw classroom and give each group a part of a project to work on. Group members from each group will then try to teach their part of the task to the rest of the group.
   b. Encourage students to get to know each other by sharing their worries, success, failures, and interests. They then see each other as individuals rather than as members of a stereotyped cultural group.
   c. Encourage students to "step into the shoes" of students who are culturally different from them.
   d. Encourage students to think about the ways in which they are prejudiced and how that makes others feel hurt and angry.
   e. Involve parents and community groups in a team approach to education.
   f. Teachers should learn about different ethnic groups and be sensitive to students' varying ethnic attitudes.

4.   a.   Create communities for learning.
     b.   Teach a core of common knowledge.
     c.   Provide opportunity for all students to succeed.
     d.   Strengthen teachers and principals.
     e.   Prepare teachers for the idle grades.
     f.   Improve academic performance through better health and fitness.
     g.   Engage families in the education of adolescents.
     h.   Connect schools with communities.

Adolescents Who Are Exceptional
Guided Review

1. 10
2. half
3. learning
4. 21
5. 12
6. 9
7. normal
8. academic
9. disorder
10. mental retardation
11. listening
12. concentrating
13. speaking
14. thinking
15. 3
16. biological
17. referral
18. academic
19. reading
20. written language
21. math
22. 4
23. ADHD
24. inattention
25. hyperactivity
26. impulsivity
27. half
28. 4/9
29. increase
30. misdiagnosed
31. 1/3
32. brain chemicals
33. abnormalities
34. environmental
35. 30/50
36. sibling/parent
37. 85/90
38. Ritalin
39. academic
40. behavioral
41. medical
42. Public Law 94–142
43. free/appropriate/public
44. Individuals with Disabilities Act (IDEA)
45. IEP
46. least restrictive environment
47. mainstreaming
48. inclusive
49. general
50. gifted
51. intelligence
52. talents
53. I!
54. Ellen Winner
55. precocious
56. marching to their own drummer
57. passion
58. information processing skills
59. disruptive
60. skip
61. interest
62. socially
63. ostracized
64. "geeks"/"nerds"
65. advanced
66. exceptional ability
67. college

Adolescents Who Are Exceptional
Section Review

1. specific learning disabilities
2. speech or language impairments
3. mental retardation
4. serious emotional disturbance
5. multiple disabilities
6. hearing impairments
7. orthopedic impairments
8. other health impairments
9. visual impairments
10. autism
11. deaf-blindness
12. traumatic brain injury

Explorations in Adolescent Development
1. Brazil—14; Russia—17; Germany, Japan, Australia, and U.S.—15 to 16.
2. Most schools have two or more levels (elementary, junior/middle, and high school), but Germany has three ability tracks.
3. U.S. is the only country in the world that has integrated sports into the public school system. Private schools in other countries may have organized sports.
4. Japanese secondary schools have entrance exam, but other five countries do not; only Australia and Germany have exit exams.
5. Russia emphasizes preparation for work, but gifted students attend special schools; Brazil requires that students take four foreign languages, due to the country's international characters; Australian students take courses in sheep husbandry and weaving, activities important to the country's economics and culture; Japanese students take courses in Western languages, literature, physical education, and art.

Adventures for the Mind
1. No answer provided. Individual activity.
2. No answer provided. Individual activity.

Adolescence in Research
The adolescents in the 8–4 arrangement had higher self-esteem and participated more in extracurricular activities than the adolescents in the 6–3–3 arrangement, who had to change schools twice. The researchers concluded that the earlier the school transitions occur in adolescence, the more difficult it likely is for students.

Comprehensive Review

1. b	6. a	11. a	16. b
2. d	7. c	12. d	17. c
3. a	8. c	13. c	18. c
4. d	9. a	14. d	19. a
5. b	10. a	15. d	20. d

◆ Chapter 8   Culture

Learning Objectives with Key Terms and Key People in Boldface

1.0   **What is the Relationship between Culture and Adolescence?**
    A.   **The Nature of Culture**
        1.1   What is the nature of culture?
    B.   **The Relevance of Culture to the Study of Adolescence**
        1.2   What is the relevance of culture to the study of adolescence in the 21st century?
    C.   **Cross-Cultural Comparisons**
        1.3   What is the nature of cross-cultural studies of adolescence?
        1.4   In what context did the study of adolescence emerge?
    D.   **Models of Cultural Change**
        1.5   What models have been used to understand cultural changes within and between cultures?
        1.6   What is **assimilation**?
        1.7   What is **acculturation** ?
        1.8   What is **alternation model**?
        1.9   What is the multiculturalism?
        1.10   What is the advantage of using the **multicultural model**?
    E.   **Rites of Passage**
        1.11   What is mean by **rites of passage**?
        1.12   How are rites of passage different for American and primitive cultures?
2.0   **How Do Socioeconomic Status (SES) and Poverty Affect Adolescent Development?**
    A.   **The Nature of Socioeconomic Status**
        1.13   What is meant by socioeconomic status?
        1.14   What is the significance of socioeconomic status for adolescent development?
    B.   **Socioeconomic Variations in Families, Neighborhoods, and Schools**
        1.15   How does socioeconomic status affects the families, neighborhoods, and schools of adolescents?
        1.16   What effect do socioeconomic variables in families, neighborhoods, and schools affect adolescent development?
        1.17   How do low-socioeconomic parents differ from their middle-SES counterparts?
    C.   **Poverty**
        1.18   What is poverty?
        1.19   What percentage of U.S. children lives in poverty?
        1.20   What is the nature of the subculture of the poor?
        1.21   What is meant by the **feminization of poverty**?
        1.22   What effects do persistent and long-lasting poverty have on development?
3.0   **What is the Effect of Ethnicity on Adolescent Development?**
    A.   **Domains and Issues**
        3.1   What is the difference between socioeconomic status and ethnicity?
        3.2   How do history, the economic, and social experiences produce legitimate differences between ethnic minority groups and between ethnic minority groups and the White majority?

Key Terms

Write a sentence using each of these key terms by either defining the term or giving an example of it. For instance, you might write, "Ethnocentrism is..." or, "(give example) is an example of a ethnocentrism." Compare your definitions with those given at the end of study guide chapter, and check your examples by referring to the text. Review the text for those terms you don't know or define incorrectly.

1. culture

_____

_____

2. socioeconomic status (SES)

_____

_____

3. ethnicity

_____

_____

4. ethnocentrism

_____

_____

5. cross-cultural studies

_____

_____

6. assimilation

_____

_____

7. acculturation

_____

_____

8. alternation model

_____

_____

9. multicultural model

_____

_____

10. rites of passage

_____

_____

11. feminization of poverty

_____

_____

12. prejudice

_____

_____

13. Chicano

_____

_____

14. experience sampling method

_____

_____

15. Internet

_____

_____

16. E-mail

_____

_____

Key People

Match the person with the concept of adolescent development with which they are associated.

_____	1.	Richard Brislin	A. One of the two persons who used the experience sampling method to learn about how adolescents spend their time.
_____	2.	Teresa Lafromboise	B. The other person who used the experience sampling method to learn about how adolescents spend their time.
_____	3.	Vonnie McLoyd	C. A cross-cultural psychologist who argues that intimate contact reduces conflict between individuals from different ethnic backgrounds.
_____	4.	Stanley Sue	D. Psychologist who observed that one function of education is to rearrange prejudice.
_____	5.	James Jones	E. Studied the effect on children of ethnic minority mothers' poverty and stress.
_____	6.	Howard Stevenson	F. Studies the psychological impact of biculturalism.
_____	7.	Mihalyi Csikszentmihalyi	G. Studies the role of the technological revolution in adolescent development.
_____	8.	Reed Larson	H. Asian American researcher who studies prejudice and discrimination.
_____	9.	Sandra Calvert	I. Researcher who studies mathematics achievement of American students.

Culture and Adolescence
Guided Review

The behavior, patterns, and beliefs of groups of people passed on from generation to generation is known as (1) _____. Three important cultural settings of adolescent development discussed in earlier chapters are (2) _____, (3) _____, and (4) _____. Two additional important dimensions of culture in adolescents' lives are (5) _____ and (6) _____. When we refer to a group of people with similar occupational, educational, and economic characteristics we are talking about their (7) _____. Ethnicity is based on (8) _____, (9) _____, (10) _____, (11) _____, and (12) _____. For the most part, the study of adolescents has been (13) _____, emphasizing White, middle-class, and male American values. Early in this century, researchers made (14) _____ about the universal aspects of adolescents of any given culture. (15) _____ studies involves comparison of culture with each other, to ascertain how much adolescent development is (16) _____ across cultures or the degree to which it is (17) _____.

Anglo-American adolescents are more (18) _____ oriented than (19) _____ young people, but not as achievement oriented as (20) _____ and (21) _____ adolescents. American adolescents have a more (22) _____ attitude toward sexuality than that of the (23) _____, but not as liberal as sexual behavior of the (24) _____. The cultural diversity of adolescent sexual behavior is testimony to the power of (25) _____ experiences in determining sexuality.

(26) _____ occurs when individuals relinquish their cultural identity and move into the larger society. (27) _____ is the change that results from continuous, firsthand contact between two distinctive cultural groups. The (28) _____ model of cultural change assumes that it is possible for an individual to maintain positive relationships with both cultures. The (29) _____ model promotes a pluralistic approach to understanding two or more cultures.

Rituals that mark an individual's transition into adulthood and other changes of status are known as (30) _____. Rites of passage are very common and important in (31) _____ cultures. The closest thing to a nationwide rite of passage in the United States is (32) _____.

Culture and Adolescence
Section Test
1. List the seven features of culture, according to Richard Brislin (1993).

_____

_____

2. List five common features of ethnocentrism present in all cultures.

_____

_____

Socioeconomic Status and Poverty
Guided Review

Socioeconomic status carries with it inequalities in (1) _____, (2) _____, (3) _____ resources, and (4) _____. Though there are as many as (5) _____ categories of socioeconomic status, two categories, (6) _____ and (7) _____, are usually used. Adolescents' (8) _____, (9) _____, and (10) _____ reflect socioeconomic characteristics. Adolescents who live in isolated neighborhoods where crime is prevalent may have (11) _____ and (12) _____ distress. Socioeconomic status affects child-rearing. Low-income parents often place a high value on (13) _____ characteristics, such as (14) _____ and (15) _____. Middle and upper SES parents place more value on (16) _____ characteristics, such as (17) _____ and (18) _____ of gratification. Low-income parents are more likely to use (19) _____ punishment and (20)

_____ their children. Students from lower SES families (21) _____ less and (22) _____ more. Children from lower SES families are at high risk for (23) _____ problems.

Poverty is defined by (24) _____ hardship, and its most common marker is the (25) _____ threshold, originally based on the estimated cost of (26) _____ multiplied by the number (27) _____. About (28) _____ percent of children under the age of 18 live in families below the poverty threshold, (29) _____ the number of those in other industrialized nations. The long-term effects of persistent poverty include lower (30) _____ and more (31) _____ behavior problems than never-poor children. More than (32) _____ of single mothers live in poverty, compared to only (33) _____ percent of single fathers. This factor is referred to as the (34) _____ of poverty. A recent trend in anti-poverty programs involves (35) _____ interventions, providing services for (36) _____ and their (37) _____. (38) _____ benefits are the most likely grain to children in such problems. Two programs that have been beneficial for children and adolescents living in poverty are (39)_____ and (40) _____.

Socioeconomic Status and Poverty
Section Review

1. According to Richards and colleagues (1994), what three negative experiences are worse for adolescents living in poverty than their middle-class counterparts?

_____

_____

2. Compare the poverty rate of adolescents in the United States to those living in Canada and Sweden.

_____

_____

3. Compare the poverty rate of African American and Latino adolescents with the overall adolescent poverty rate in the United States.

_____

_____

4. Give three explanations for why poverty is so high among American youth?

_____

_____

Ethnicity
Guided Review

Ethnicity refers to the (1) _____, (2) _____ characteristics, (3) _____, (4) _____, and (5) _____ of individuals. Much of the research on ethnic minority adolescents has failed to distinguish between the influences of (6) _____ and that of (7) _____, thus they fail to take into account developments that are based more on (8) _____ than on (9) _____. Minority group members suffer from (10) _____, (11) _____, and (12) _____. For many, (13) _____ contributes to stressful life experiences.

Legitimate differences between various ethnic minority groups are the result of (14) _____, (15) _____, and (16) _____ experiences. Their behaviors that differ from the white majority are (17) _____ for them. Currently, more emphasis is being placed on the (18) _____ of various ethnic minority groups, when for too long the differences have been seen as (19) _____. Further, ethnic minority groups are not (20) _____; they have different (21) _____, (22) _____, and (23) _____ backgrounds. There are (24) _____ different Native American tribes, each with (25) _____ values and characteristics. Asian Americans include the (26) _____, (27) _____, (28) _____, (29) _____, and (30) _____, each group having distinct (31) _____ and (32) _____. Failure to recognize diversity and individual variations results in the (33) _____ of an ethnic minority group.

An unjustified negative attitude toward an individual because of the individual's membership in a group is known as (34) _____. Ethnic minority adolescents are hindered by (35) _____ stereotypes. Discrimination and prejudice are present in the (36) _____, (37) _____-interactions, and daily (38) _____. Whites have a long-standing sense of (39) _____ and (40) _____. Today, children of immigrants are less likely to (41) _____ their parents' values or to strive for cultural (42) _____.

Adolescence is a special juncture for ethnic minority students because they are aware of negative (43) _____ of themselves, (44) _____ values, and restricted (45) _____. Many lack successful ethnic minority (46) _____ and some try to (47) _____ to middle-class White values. The largest group of ethnic minority adolescents in the United States is (48) _____. A substantial proportion of African American adolescents are growing up in (49) _____- SES families and share middle-class values with (50) _____ middle-SES adolescents. A number also still live in (51) _____. (52) _____ percent of the total U.S. population is Latino. They trace their roots to (53) _____, (54) _____, (55) _____, (56) _____ and _____ American countries, and the (57)_____. The largest group of Latino adolescents is of (58) _____ origin. (59) _____ is the name they give themselves, reflecting the combination of their (60) _____-_____-_____ heritage and (61) _____ influences. (62) _____ adolescents are the fastest-growing segment of the American adolescent population. Since the 1970s there has been rapid growth in groups from (63) _____, the Pacific islands of (64) _____ and _____ and (65) _____. Japanese and Chinese children are generally raised in a subculture where (66) _____ loyalty and (67) _____ are powerful and they tend to maintain their separate (68) _____. Asian adolescents take considerable advantage of (69) _____ opportunities.

Native American adolescents have experienced an inordinate amount of (70) _____ . Native Americans were the victims of terrible (71) _____ and _____. They have the lowest (72) _____, the highest (73) _____ rate, the highest (74) _____ rate, and the highest school (75) _____ rate of any ethic group in the United States.

Ethnicity
Section Review

1.   Fill in the blanks with the characteristics of African American adolescents.

a.   African American male adolescents are _____ times more likely to be a homicide victim.

b.   An African American female teenager is more than _____ as likely to have a baby than her White peer.

c.   An African American teenager is more than _____ as likely as a White teenager to be enrolled in a remedial math class.

d.   An African American high school graduate is only _____ as likely as a White graduate to receive a bachelor's degree 4 years after high school.

e.   One in _____ African American teenagers live with only one parent.

f.   One in _____ African American teenagers live with a parent who did not graduate from high school.

g.   One in _____ African American teenagers live with an unemployed parent.

2. Fill in the blanks with characteristics of Latino adolescents.

    a. A Latino teenager is _____ as likely as a White teenager to have no health insurance.

    b. Sixteen and 17-year-old Latina girls are _____ times more likely than their White peers to be behind in school.

    c. Male Latino 18 and 19-year-olds are _____ times more likely than their White peers to be behind in school.

    d. Latino 18- and 19-year-olds are more than _____ as likely as their White peers to be school dropouts.

    e. One in every ____ Latino teenager lives with a parent who did not graduate from high school.

    f. One in every ____ Latino teenager lives with an unemployed parent.

Television and Other Media
Guided Review

Media serve six functions for adolescents: (1) _____, (2) _____, (3) _____, (4) _____, (5) _____ modeling, and (6) _____ identification. Adolescents spend (7) _____ of their waking hours with some form of mass media. Time spent (8) _____ is declining; the use of (9) _____ media is increasing. As adolescents get older, (10) _____ increases. Newspaper reading often begins at about (11) _____ to _____ years of age; (12) _____ to _____ percent of adolescents report some newspaper reading. (13) _____, (14) _____, (15) _____, (16) _____ status, and (17) _____ are all related to the type, extent, and purpose of media used.

A special concern of television is the portrayal of (18) _____. They have been historically (19) _____ and (20) _____ on television. Their characters are often presented as less (21) _____ and (22) _____ that White characters. Another major concern about television is (23) _____. Studies have related (24) _____ acts and (25) _____ behavior to long-term exposure to television violence. However, since these investigations are (26) _____, we can't say that television (27) _____ violence, only that it is (28) _____ with it. Watching television can influence teens' attitudes towards (29) _____. This is a particular problem because (30) _____ and _____ generally don't feel comfortable discussing (31) _____ with young people.

Music meets a number of (32) _____ and (33) _____ needs for adolescents. The most important personal needs are (34) _____ control and (35) _____ filling. Very few consider the (36) _____ important. Social functions of music include providing a (37) _____ atmosphere and expressing (38) _____ against authority. Associations have been found between a preference for (39) _____ music and (40) _____ or _____ behavior. No research data has linked (41) _____ or (42) _____ to (43) _____ or (44) _____ music.

The (45) _____ revolution will demand that adolescents make (46) _____ an integral part of their lives. However, non-technological competencies like good (47) _____ skills, the ability to (48) _____, think (49) _____ and _____, and have (50) _____ attitudes will continue to be important. (51) _____ is the core of computer-mediated instruction. By 1998, (52) _____ of public schools had been connected to the Internet. By 2002, more than (53) _____ percent of adolescents are expected to be on-line. (54) _____ is another way in which adolescents use the Internet. Issues surrounding increased use of technology in homes and schools involve concern about the widening (55) _____ between rich and poor and male and female students. In 1996, less than (56) _____ of schools with a majority of low-income students had Internet access, while (57) _____ of schools with students from higher-SES backgrounds had Internet access. In addition, computers are too often used for (58) _____ and _____ activities rather than (59) _____ learning. Many teachers do not have adequate (60) _____ in computers.

The (61) _____ has made recommendations about social policy initiatives concerning the media and young people. (62) _____ is an organization that is developing an (63) _____ curriculum on violence to be used to train students who hope to become (64) _____.

Television and Other Media
Section Review

1. List three general negative effects (unrelated to sex and violence) that television viewing can have on adolescents.

_____

_____

2. What three harmful effects stem from long-term exposure to television violence?

_____

_____

3. Fill in the percent of American adolescents who engage in each on-line activity.

Activity	Percent
E-mail	
Search engine	
Music sites	
General research	
Games	
TV/movie sites	
Chat room	
Using their own Web page	
Sports sites	

4. List the five social policy initiative concerning the media and adolescents recommended by the Carnegie Council on Adolescent Development (1995).

_____

_____

Explorations in Adolescent Development

1. What is El Puente?

_____

_____

2. a. What mixture of cultures comprised Canada up to the late 19th century?

_____

_____

   b. Immigrants from what countries have come to Canada in the latter part of the 19th and 20th centuries?

_____

_____

3. List four ways that the Internet can be effectively used in classrooms.

_____

_____

Adventures for the Mind

1. What classroom strategy that you learned about in another chapter might help White students overcome prejudices about ethnic minority students? Why is this method effective?

_____

_____

2. If you have access to MTV, watch it for two hours one evening and make a list of sexist behaviors such as degrading comments about females, provocative sexist lyrics, and any other examples that are apparent. Evaluate the results of your findings. Do they support the claim that MTV is sexist?

_____

_____

Adolescence in Research

Concerning the evaluation of the Quantum Opportunities Program, comparing mentored students with a nonmentored control group, state the hypothesis, the research methods (if known), the research conclusions, and the implications and applications for adolescent development.

_____

_____

Comprehensive Review

1. The learning and shared behavioral patterns, beliefs, and values of a group of people that are passed on from one generation to the next is known as
   a. culture.
   b. minority.
   c. ethnicity.
   d. socioeconomic status.

2. Family income is a good measure of
   a. ethnicity.
   b. social class.
   c. culture.
   d. ethnocentrism.

3. In comparison to adolescents from other cultures, American adolescents are often described as more
   a. passive.
   b. Rebellious.
   c. achievement-oriented.
   d. mentally healthy.

4. The melting pot belief in the United States assumes which process of cultural change?
   a. assimilation
   b. acculturation
   c. accommodation
   d. cultural schema shifting

5. Rituals such as bar mitzvah and confirmation are examples of
   a. rites of passage.
   b. cultural transitions of sexuality.
   c. evidence of ethnocentrism.
   d. family traditions.

6. The most common rite of passage for American adolescents is probably
   a. a religious ceremony.
   b. going off to college.
   c. graduating from high school.
   d. buying the first car.

7. ___ percent of the children in the United States live in poverty.
   a. Eleven
   b. Thirty-three
   c. Sixteen
   d. Twenty

8. The adolescent raised in a single-parent, female-headed household is more likely than not to be
   a. sexually active.
   b. promiscuous.
   c. in trouble with the law.
   d. poor.

9. When an adolescent has a negative attitude about another individual because that individual belongs to a particular group, the adolescent is exhibiting
   a. values
   b. an opinion
   c. prejudice
   d. cognitive narrowing.

10. El Puente is a social program for _____ Latinos.
    a. low-income
    b. female
    c. Protestant
    d. English-speaking

11. Which ethnic minority adolescent group has the highest suicide rate in the United States?
    a. African American
    b. Hispanic
    c. Native American
    d. Asian

12. Compared to the United States, the ethnic subcultures of Canadian adolescents tend to be organized along the lines of
    a. economic power.
    b. political affiliation.
    c. religious participation.
    d. gender differences.

13. Adolescents spend approximately _____ of their waking hours with some form of mass media.
    a. one-eighth
    b. one-third
    c. one-half
    d. two-thirds

14. Television has been criticized for all of the following except
    a. teaching adolescents that problems are easily resolved.
    b. declining national achievement test scores.
    c. increasing the leisure activities of adolescents.
    d. creating passive learners.

15. Which is the most accurate conclusion about the long-term effects of watching television violence?
    a. Watching television violence causes crime
    b. Watching television violence has no relationship to crime
    c. Watching television violence may be associated with violence in some young people
    d. Watching television violence makes young people less afraid of being a victim.

Adolescence on the Screen
- *Saturday Night Fever* highlights the disco era.

- *Pulp Fiction* is a parody of drug-use, violence, and down-and-out diner bandits.

- *Woodstock* captures the drug and rock culture of the 1960s.

Adolescence in Books
- *The Adolescent & Young Adult Fact Book*, by Janet Simons, Belva Finlay, and Alice Yang (Children's Defense Fund, 1991), describes the role of poverty and ethnicity in adolescent development.

- *Children's Journey Through the Information Age*, by Sandra Calvert (McGraw-Hill, 1999), covers topics related to the information age, including television and computers.

- *Understanding Culture's Influence on Behavior*, by Richard Brislin (Harcourt Brace, 1993), details the role of culture in behavior and development.

Answer Key

Key Terms
1. **culture** The behavior, patterns, beliefs, and all other products of a particular group of people that are passed on from generation to generation.
2. **socioeconomic status (SES)** A grouping of people with similar occupational, educational, and economic characteristics.
3. **ethnicity** A dimension of culture based on cultural heritage, nationality, race, religion, and language.
4. **ethnocentrism** A tendency to favor one's own group over other groups.
5. **cross-cultural studies** Studies that compare a culture with one or more other cultures. Such studies provide information about the degree to which adolescent development is similar, or universal, across cultures or about the degree to which it is culture specific.
6. **assimilation** The absorption of ethnic minority groups into the dominant group, which often means the loss of some or virtually all of the behavior and values of the ethnic minority group.

7. **acculturation** Cultural change that results from continuous, first-hand contact between two distinctive cultural groups.

8. **alternation model** This model assumes that it is possible for an individual to know and understand two different cultures. It also assumes that individuals can alter their behavior to fit a particular social context.

9. **multicultural model** This model promotes a pluralistic approach to understanding two or more cultures. It argues that people can maintain their distinctive identities while working with others from different cultures to meet common national or economic needs.

10. **rites of passage** Ceremonies or rituals that mark an individual's transition from one status to another, especially into adulthood.

11. **feminization of poverty** The fact that far more women than men live in poverty. Likely causes are women's low income, divorce, and the resolution of divorce cases by the judicial system, which leaves women with less money than they and their children need to adequately function.

12. **prejudice** An unjustified negative attitude toward an individual because of her or his membership in a group.

13. **Chicano** The name politically conscious Mexican American adolescents give themselves, reflecting the combination of their Spanish-Mexican-Indian heritage and Anglo influence.

14. **experience sampling method** A research method in which participants carry electronic pagers, usually for a week, and provide reports on their activities when signaled by the pagers at random times.

15. **Internet** The core of computer-mediated communication. The Internet is worldwide and connects thousands of computer networks, providing an incredible array of information adolescents can access.

16. **E-mail** Stands for electronic mail and is a valuable way the Internet can be used. Written messages can be sent to and received by individuals as well as large numbers of people.

Key People
1. C
2. F
3. E

4. H
5. D
6. I

7. A or B
8. A or B
9. G

Culture and Adolescence
Guided Review
1. culture
2. family
3. peers
4. school
5. social class
6. ethnicity
7. social class
8. cultural heritage

9. nationality characteristics
10. race
11. religion
12. language
13. ethnocentric
14. overgeneralizations
15. cross-cultural
16. universal

17. culture-specific
18. achievement
19. Mexican
20. Japanese
21. Chinese
22. Asian American
23. Ines Beag
24. Mangaians
25. environmental

26. Assimilation
27. Acculturation
28. alternation
29. multicultural
30. rites of passage
31. African
32. high school graduation

Culture and Adolescence
Section Test
1.
   a. Culture is made up of ideals, values, and assumptions about life that guide people's behaviors.
   b. Culture is made by people.
   c. Culture is transmitted from generation to generation.
   d. Culture's influence is noticed most in well-meaning clashes between people from very different cultural backgrounds.
   e. Despite compromises, cultural values still remain.

f.   People react emotionally when their cultural values are violated or when their cultural expectations are ignored.

g.   People accept a cultural value at one point in their life and reject it at another.

2.   a.   People believe that what happens in their culture is natural and correct and that what happens in other cultures is unnatural and incorrect.

     b.   People perceive their cultural customs as universally valid, that is, good for everyone.

     c.   People behave in ways that favor their own cultural group.

     d.   People feel proud of their cultural group.

     e.   People feel hostile toward other cultural groups.

Socioeconomic Status and Poverty
Guided Review

1. occupations	12. psychological	23. psychological	34. feminization
2. education	13. external	24. economic	35. two-generation
3. economic	14. obedience	25. federal poverty	36. children
4. power	15. neatness	26. food	37. parents
5. five	16. internal	27. 3	38. Health
6. low	17. self-control	28. 20	39. Quantum
7. middle	18. delay	29. twice	Opportunities
8. families	19. physical	30. 1Q	Program
9. neighborhoods	20. criticize	31. internalized	40. El Puente
10. schools	21. read	32. one-third	
11. low self-esteem	22. watch television	33. 10	

Socioeconomic Status and Poverty
Section Review

1.   a.   physical punishment and lack of structure at home

     b.   violence in the neighborhood

     c.   domestic violence in their homes

2.   The overall poverty rate for American adolescents is 20 percent. In Canada it is 9 percent, while in Sweden it is only 2 percent.

3.   The overall poverty rate is 20 percent. The poverty rate for African American adolescents is 50 percent; for Latino adolescents, it is 40 percent.

4.   a.   Economic changes have eliminated many blue-collar jobs that paid reasonably well.

     b.   Increase in the percentage of youth living in single-parent families headed by the mother.

     c.   Reduction of government benefits during the 1970s and 1980s.

Ethnicity
Guided Review

1. cultural heritage
2. national
3. race
4. religion
5. language
6. ethnicity (or socioeconomic status)
7. socioeconomic status (or ethnicity)
8. socioeconomic status
9. ethnicity
10. prejudice
11. discrimination
12. bias
13. poverty
14. historical
15. economic
16. social
17. functional
18. strengths
19. deficits
20. homogenous
21. social
22. historical
23. economic
24. 511
25. differing
26. Chinese
27. Japanese
28. Phillipinos
29. Koreans
30. Southeast Asians
31. ancestries
32. languages
33. stereotyping
34. prejudice
35. negative
36. media
37. interpersonal
38. conversations
39. entitlement
40. superiority
41. reject
42. assimilation
43. appraisals
44. conflicting
45. occupational opportunities
46. role models
47. conform
48. African Americans
49. middle-SES
50. White
51. poverty
52. Fifteen
53. Mexico
54. Puerto Rico
55. Cuba
56. Central/South
57. Caribbean
58. Mexican
59. Chicano
60. Spanish-Mexican-Indian
61. Anglo
62. Asian Americans
63. Korea
64. Guam/Samoa
65. Vietnam
66. family
67. influence
68. subcultures
69. education
70. discrimination
71. physical abuse/punishment
72. standard of living
73. teenage-pregnancy
74. suicide
75. dropout

Ethnicity
Section Review

1.
   a. nine
   b. twice
   c. twice
   d. half
   e. two
   f. three
   g. three

2.
   a. twice
   b. four
   c. five
   d. twice
   e. two
   f. four

Television and Other Media
Guided Review

1. entertainment
2. information
3. sensation
4. coping
5. gender-role
6. youth culture
7. one-third
8. watching television
9. music
10. newspaper reading
11. 11/12
12. 60/80
13. gender
14. age
15. ethnicity
16. socioeconomic
17. intelligence
18. minority groups
19. underrepresented
20. misrepresented
21. dignified
22. positive
23. violence
24. criminal
25. aggressive
26. correlational
27. causes
28. associated
29. sex
30. parents/education
31. sex
32. personal
33. social
34. mood
35. silence
36. lyrics
37. party
38. rebellion
39. heavy metal
40. reckless/antisocial
41. depression
42. suicide
43. heavy metal
44. rap
45. technological
46. computers
47. communication
48. solve problems
49. deeply/creatively
50. positive
51. The Internet
52. 89
53. 70
54. E-mail
55. gap
56. one-third
57. two-thirds
58. drill/practice
59. constructive
60. training
61. Carnegie Council on Adolescent Development
62. Mediascope
63. ethics
64. filmmakers

Television and Other Media
Section Review

1. a. Take adolescents away from the printed media and books.
    b. Train them to become passive learners.
    c. Train them in a passive lifestyle.

2. a. Learn aggressive attitudes and behaviors.
    b. Become desensitized to the seriousness of violence.
    c. Feel frightened of becoming a victim of real-life violence.

3.

Activity	Percent
E-mail	83
Search engine	78
Music sites	59
General research	58
Games	51
TV/movie sites	43
Chat room	42
Using their own Web page	38
Sports sites	35

4. a. Encourage socially responsible programming.
   b. Support public efforts to make the media more adolescent friendly.
   c. Encourage media literacy programs as part of school curricula, youth and community organizations, and family life.
   d. Increase media presentations of health promotions.
   e. Expand opportunities for adolescents' views to appear in the media.

Explorations in Adolescent Development

1. El Puente is a program for Latinos in New York City. Young people develop a 4-month plan that includes health, education, achievement, personal growth, and social growth programs.

2. a. Up to the late 19th century Canadian culture included native people, Canada's original inhabitants and French and British settlers.
   b. In the late 19th century, immigrants came from Asia, various European countries, Latin American, the Caribbean, Asia, Africa, India, the former Soviet Union, and the Middle East.

3. a. Help students navigate and integrate knowledge.
   b. Foster collaborative learning.
   c. Allow e-mail that can aid in electronic mentoring.
   d. Improve teacher's knowledge and understanding.

Adventures for the Mind

1. The jigsaw classroom concept involving cooperative learning was discussed in Chapter 7. This method is effective in neutralizing prejudice because students must depend upon each other to learn the assigned material.

2. No answer provided. Individual activity

Adolescence in Research

An evaluation of the Quantum project compared the mentored students with a nonmentored control group. The methods were experimental. The hypothesis was that the features of the Quantum project would help overcome the intergenerational transmission of poverty and its negative outcomes. The mentored students were involved in academic-related activities, community service projects, and cultural enrichment and personal development activities. Students also received financial incentives for participating, including bonuses for every 100 hours of education. Sixty-three percent of the mentored students graduated from high school, but only 42 percent of the control group did. Forty-two percent of the mentored group are currently enrolled in college, but only 16 percent of the control group. The control-group students were twice as likely as mentored students to receive food stamps or be on welfare and they had more arrests. The conclusions is that programs like the Quantum project have the potential to help overcome the intergenerational transmission of poverty and its negative outcomes.

Comprehensive Review

1. a
2. b
3. c
4. a

5. a
6. c
7. d
8. d

9. c
10. a
11. c
12. a

13. b
14. c
15. c

◆ Chapter 9 The Self and Identity

Learning Objectives with Key Terms and Key People in Boldface

1.0   **What is Self-Understanding?**
    A.   **The Definition of Self-Understanding**
        1.1   How is self-understanding defined?
        1.2   What is the link between self-understanding and an adolescent's identity?
    B.   **The Dimensions of Adolescents' Self-Understanding**
        1.3   What are the dimensions of adolescents' **self-understanding**?
        1.4   What is the difference between the real and ideal self, and the true and false self?
        1.5   What is mean by **possible self**?
        1.6   What is social comparison?
        1.7   What does it mean to be self-conscious and self-protective?
        1.8   What is self-integration?

2.0   **What Are Self-Esteem and Self-Concept?**
    A.   **Self-Esteem and Self-Concept**
        2.1   What is **self-esteem**?
        2.2   What is **self-concept**?
    B.   **Measuring Self-Esteem**
        2.3   How do you measure an adolescent's self-esteem?
        2.4   What is Harter's Self-Perception Profile for Adolescents?
        2.5   What additional assessments are used to measure self-esteem?
    C.   **Are Some Domains More Salient than Others to the Adolescent's Self Esteem?**
        2.6   How important is perceived physical appearance to an adolescent's self-esteem?
        2.7   What role does peer acceptance play in the self-esteem of adolescents?
    D.   **Parental and Peer Influences**
        2.8   What parental influences and behaviors are associated with adolescent self-esteem?
        2.9   What role do peer judgments play in self-esteem?
        2.10   Is classmate support more strongly linked to self-esteem than best-friend support?
    E.   **Consequence of Low Self-Esteem**
        2.11   What is the consequence of low self-esteem for most adolescents?
        2.12   What are the ramifications for some adolescents when low self-esteem persists?
    F.   **Increasing Adolescents' Self-Esteem**
        2.13   What are some strategies for increasing adolescent self-esteem?

3.0   **What is Identity?**
    A.   **Erikson's Ideas on Identity**
        3.1   What is the meaning and significance of Erikson's 5th stage, **identity versus identity confusion**?
        3.2   What is **psychosocial moratorium** as it relates to identity development?
        3.3   According to Erikson, what do personality and role exploration have to do with identity development?

Key Terms

Write a sentence using each of these key terms by either defining the term or giving an example of it. For instance, you might write, "Self-understanding is..." or, "(give example) is an example of self-understanding." Compare your definitions with those given at the end of study guide chapter, and check your examples by referring to the text. Review the text for those terms you don't know or define incorrectly.

1. self-understanding

    _____

    _____

2. possible self

    _____

    _____

3. self-esteem

    _____

    _____

4. self-concept

    _____

    _____

5. identity versus identity confusion

    _____

    _____

6. psychosocial moratorium

    _____

    _____

7. crisis

    _____

    _____

8. commitment

    _____

    _____

9. identity diffusion

    _____

    _____

10. identity foreclosure

    _____

    _____

11.   identity moratorium

_____

_____

12.   identity achievement

_____

_____

13.   individuality

_____

_____

14.   connectedness

_____

_____

15.   ethnic identity

_____

_____

16.   intimacy versus isolation

_____

_____

17.   intimate style

_____

_____

18.   preintimate style

_____

_____

19.   stereotyped style

_____

_____

20.   pseudointimate style

_____

_____

21.   isolated style

_____

_____

22. self-focused level

_____

_____

23. role-focused level

_____

_____

24. individuated-connected level

_____

_____

25. emotional isolation

_____

_____

26. social isolation

_____

_____

Key People
Match the person with the concept of adolescent development with which they are associated.

___	1.	Susan Harter	A.	Most famous for his theory of identity development
___	2.	Hazel Markus	B.	Developed an assessment for adolescent self-esteem
___	3.	Erik Erikson	C.	Expanded on Erikson's identity development theory
___	4.	James Marcia	D.	Distinguished two forms of loneliness
___	5.	Alan Waterman	E.	Developed a model of relationship maturity
___	6.	Catherine Cooper	F.	Conducted research on ethnic identity
___	7.	Stuart Hauser	G.	Believes that ethnic minority youth must bridge multiple worlds in constructing identity
___	8.	Jean Phinney	H.	Developed a classification of five styles of intimate interaction
___	9.	Jacob Orlofsky	I.	Illuminated family processes that promote adolescent identity development
___	10.	Kathleen White	J.	Conducted research on timing of identity achievement
___	11.	Robert Weiss	K.	Believes that the self-system is the basis of cultural-specific identity

The Self
Guided Review
The adolescent's cognitive representation of the self is known as (1) _____. It provides rational (2) _____ for personal identity. Adolescents begin to think of themselves in more (3) _____ and (4) _____ ways than they did as children. Their self-understanding becomes increasingly (5) _____. Their self (6) _____ across situations and self. Sometimes they experience (7) _____ within their differentiated selves. They begin to recognize a discrepancy between their (8) _____ and _____ selves, and they have an image of a (9) _____ self. Adolescents are more likely to show their (10) _____ sense of self in a dating situation, but are least likely to show it with (11) _____. Adolescents may be more likely to use (12) _____ to evaluate themselves in the context of others. They are more likely to be (13) _____ about and (14) _____- with their self-understanding. Adolescents use more mechanisms to (15) _____ the self. Self-understanding involves

greater recognition that the self includes (16) _____, as well as conscious, components. In adolescence, self-understanding becomes more (17) _____. James Marcia believes that changes in the self in adolescence can be divided into three phases: (18) _____, (19) _____, and (20) _____.

The Self
Section Review
List and give an example or explanation for the five ways an adolescent's sense of self differs from that of a child.

_____

_____

_____

_____

_____

Self-Esteem and Self-Concept
Guided Review
     (1)_____ is the global evaluative dimension of the self. It is also referred to as (2) _____ or (3) _____. (4) _____ refers to the domain-specific evaluations of the self. It is not easy to (5) _____ self-esteem. Susan Harter developed a measure for adolescents, the (6) _____. A combination of (7) _____ should be used to measure self-esteem. One of the most powerful contributors to adolescent self-esteem is (8) _____. In the most extensive investigation of parent-child relationships and self-esteem, Coopersmith found that several (9) _____ attributes were associated with children's self-esteem. (10) _____ judgments gain increasing importance among older children and adolescents. Two types of peer support, (11) _____ and _____ support become more important than parenting support for late adolescents.

    For most adolescents, low-esteem results in only (12) _____ emotional discomfort. But in some cases it can translated into problems like (13) _____, (14) _____, (15) _____, (16) _____, and other (17) _____ problems. Self-esteem programs encouraged to make young people simply feel good about themselves have been deemed (18) _____ for improving self-esteem. This is because to improve self-esteem, one needs to address the (19) _____ of low self-esteem.

(20) _____ support and social (21) _____ powerfully influence adolescents' self-esteem. When children have low levels of support at home, programs like Big (22) _____ and Big _____ have been useful. (23) _____ can lead to enhancement of self-esteem, a factor that is related to Bandura's (24) _____ concept of (25) _____. Self-esteem is increased when adolescents try to (26) _____ a problem rather than (27) _____ it. On the other hand, (28) _____, (29) _____, and (30) _____ can lead to unfavorable self-evaluation.

Self-Esteem and Self-Concept
Section Review
Complete the chart by filling in the positive and negative behavioral indicators of self-esteem

Positive Indicators	Negative Indicators

Identity
Guided Review

Erikson's fifth developmental stage is known as (1) _____ vs. _____. At this time, adolescents examine (2) _____, what (3) _____, and (4) _____. The gap between childhood security and adult autonomy is, according to Erikson, a (5) _____. Adolescents who do not resolve their identity crisis suffer what Erikson calls (6) _____, in which individuals either (7) _____ from the family and peers or (8) _____ themselves in their peers and lose their identity in the (9) _____. Erikson wrote about the identity crises of two famous men, (10) _____ and (11) _____. Two core ingredients of Erikson's theory of identity development are (12) _____ and role (13) _____. Erikson believes that by late adolescence (14) _____ roles are central to identity development. Identity is a (15) _____ composed of many pieces. Erikson believed that identity was very complex and involved at least (16) _____ dimensions. More contemporary views hold that identity development is less (17) _____- than Erikson implied and extends beyond (18) _____. Identity is not necessarily (19) _____ throughout one's life. A healthy identity is (20) _____ and (21) _____, open to changes in (22) _____, (23) _____, and in (24) _____.

James Marcia believes that Erikson's theory of identity development contains (25) _____ status of identity, or ways of (26) _____ the identity crisis. They are identity (27) _____, (28) _____, (29) _____, and (30) _____. Marcia calls the period of time when one is choosing among identity alternatives a time of (31) _____. When adolescents show a personal investment in what they are going to do, they indicate a (32) _____ to identity. If they have not yet experienced a crisis or made a commitment, Marcia says that they are in a state of identity (33) _____. Adolescents who are in the midst of a crisis but who have not made a commitment are in a state of identity (34) _____. Once an adolescent has undergone a crisis and made a commitment, they are in a state of identity (35) _____.

According to Marcia, the three aspects of development that are important in identity formation are an adolescent's confidence that he or she has (36) _____; possession of a sense of (37) _____, and able to adopt a (38) _____ stance toward the future. Some researchers think that more important identity changes take place in (39) _____ rather than adolescence. Many identity status researchers believe that a common pattern of individuals who develop positive identity is the (40) _____ cycle of (41) _____-(42) _____-(43) _____-(44) _____.

The presence of a family atmosphere that promotes both (45) _____ and (46) _____ are important for adolescent identity development. Individuality consists of two dimensions: (47) _____ and (48) _____. Connectedness consists of two dimensions: (49) _____ and (50) _____. Hauser and colleagues (1990, 1984) found that parents who use (51) _____ behaviors facilitate the adolescent's identity development more than do parents who use (52) _____ behaviors.

The aspect of the self that includes a sense of membership in an ethnic group is known as (53) _____ identity. Many ethnic minority adolescents have (54) _____ identities. Many ethnic minority adolescents have to confront issues of (55) _____ and (56) _____. Many also live in pockets of (57) _____, and are exposed to (58) _____, (59) _____, and (60) _____ activity.

(61) _____ difference sin identity development seem to be disappearing, although males and females may go through Erikson's stages in (62) _____ order. Females tend to be more concerned with (63) _____ and (64) _____ bonds, while males are more concerned with (65) _____ and _____. In addition, females may tend to establish identities in more (66) _____ than males do because options for females have (67) _____.

Identity
Section Review
1.   Fill in the table by giving an example or explanation for each component of one's identity.

Component	Example
Vocational/career	
Political identity	
Religious identity	
Relationship identity	
Achievement identity	
Sexual identity	
Ethnic and cultural identity	
Interest identity	
Personality identity	
Physical identity	

2.   List the seven dimensions of Erikson's theory of identity development.

_____

_____

_____

_____

_____

_____

_____

Identity and Intimacy
Guided Review
Erikson's sixth developmental stage is (1) _____vs. _____, which individuals experience during early (2) _____. At this time individuals face the task of forming (3) _____ relationships with others. (4) A strong _____ is important in forming intimate connections. Males tend to display greater (5) _____ and females more (6) _____. Inability to develop meaningful relationships with others leads individuals to (7) _____, (8) _____, or (9) _____ those who frustrate them. Jacob Orlofsky developed (10) _____ styles of intimate interaction. The individual who forms and maintains one or more long-lasting love relationships has an (11)_____ style. Someone who has mixed emotions about commitment has a (12)

_____ style. Superficial relationships dominated by same-sex friendships is the hallmark of the (13) _____ style. Those who withdraw from social encounters have an (14) _____ style. Kathleen White and her colleagues developed a model of relationship maturity that involved progression through three levels: (15) _____-focused, (16) _____-focused, and (17) _____-_____.

The highest levels of loneliness often appear during (18) _____ adolescence. Loneliness is associated with an individual's (19) _____, (20) _____ history, (21) _____, and (22) _____ skills. A lack of time spent with (23) _____ is associated with loneliness in (24) _____ and _____. Loneliness may first develop when someone leaves for (25) _____.According to Robert Weiss, loneliness is a response to the (26) _____ of some type of (27) _____. He distinguished two forms of loneliness: (28) _____ isolation, arising from a lack of an (29) _____ attachment relationship, and (30) _____ isolation, arising from a lack of integrated involvement. Lack of group and community involvement can lead one to feel (31) _____, (32) _____, and (33) _____. Individuals can reduce their loneliness by either changing their social (34) _____ or changing their social (35) _____ and _____.

Explorations in Adolescent Development

1. Why do some ethnic minority young people develop multiple selves?

_____

_____

2. What successful programs have been linked to enhancing adolescents' ability to develop a healthy identity?

_____

_____

3. What conditions create special challenges for Native American young people's identity development?

_____

_____

Adventures for the Mind

1. Think about what your future selves might be. Which of your prospective selves do you think will make you the happiest? Which of your prospective selves might have negative possibilities?

_____

_____

2.   What is your identity status? Think about your exploration and commitment in the areas listed below. For each area, check whether your identity status is diffused, foreclosed, moratorium, or achieved. If you check "diffused" or "foreclosed" for any areas, take some time to think about what you need to do to move into a moratorium identity status in those areas.

Identity Component	Diffused	Foreclosed	Moratorium	Achieved
Vocational (career)				
Political				
Religious				
Relationship				
Achievement				
Sexual				
Gender				
Ethnic/Cultural				
Interests				
Personality				
Physical				

Adolescence in Research

Concerning the research about boys' self-esteem by Coopersmith (1967), state the hypothesis, the research methods (if known), the research conclusions, and the implications and applications for adolescent development.

Comprehensive Review

1.   Bernie describes himself as in control, masculine, and intelligent when he is with his girlfriend; but when he is with his buddies, he describes himself as fun loving and spontaneous. Bernie is
   a.   two-faced.
   b.   differentiated.
   c.   schizophrenic.
   d.   lacking an identity.

2.   Joyce is on a date with someone she wants to impress. She uses large words that she does not normally use and exaggerates her intellectual ability. She is exhibiting her
   a.   negative possible self
   b.   positive possible self.
   c.   ideal self.
   d.   false self.

3.   Adolescents understand that there may be an unconscious aspect of the self because they have
   a.   formal operations.
   b.   concrete knowledge of the unconscious.
   c.   better education about unconscious influences.
   d.   a broad world-view.

4.   An adolescent who starts to admit inconsistencies in his behavior is achieving
   a.   his ideal self.
   b.   egocentrism.
   c.   self-reference
   d.   self-integration.

5. Using two instruments to measure self-esteem is considered by developmental psychologists as
    a. likely to lead to confusion.
    b. likely to give inconsistent results.
    c. likely to reflect the richness of the self.
    d. unethical.

6. Which of the following parental characteristics is associated with self-esteem in children?
    a. expression of affection
    b. setting permissive rules
    c. conflicted family environments
    d. parental intelligence

7. Rodney's parents don't set any limits on his behavior. The family seems to always be in a state of chaos. Research indicates that Rodney's self-esteem will likely be
    a. low.
    b. high.
    c. unconscious.
    d. differentiated.

8. Programs that emphasize both academic and social skills are likely to enhance
    a. identity achievement.
    b. patience.
    c. self-esteem.
    d. harmonious family relationships.

9. Which is the most accurate statement of Erikson's views on identity development?
    a. Losing your identity in a crowd is a form of identity confusion.
    b. Running away and dropping out of school indicates moratorium.
    c. The identity crisis is unrelated to earlier psychosocial stages.
    d. Experimenting with different roles and personalities indicates a negative identity.

10. According to James Marcia and others, identity formation
    a. is a lifetime activity.
    b. should occur after intimacy.
    c. is much easier than Erikson made it out to be.
    d. does not require advanced thinking skills.

11. Karen, who is in a state of identity foreclosure,
    a. has not experienced any crisis or made any commitment.
    b. has made a commitment but has not experienced a crisis.
    c. is in the midst of a crisis.
    d. has undergone a crisis and made a commitment.

12. Jackson came home with green spiked hair. Which is the least adequate explanation for his behavior?
    a. identity moratorium
    b. negative identity
    c. identity confusion
    d. identity foreclosure

13. According to Cooper and her colleagues, the two dimensions of connectedness are
    a. bonding and respect.
    b. mutuality and sensitivity.
    c. self- and other-connectedness.
    d. mutuality and permeability

14. Adolescence may be a particularly difficult time for minority individuals because this is the time they
    a. are subject to the most intense discrimination.
    b. also confront their own ethnicity.
    c. have the fewest resources to achieve identity.
    d. become aware of other people's resources.

15. Gender differences in identity formation
    a. are a backlash against the women's movement.
    b. are greater now because of the New Age movement.
    c. have decreased in the last twenty years.
    d. are the same as they have always been.

16. Erikson believed that intimacy should come after one has established
    a. identity.
    b. trust.
    c. generativity.
    d. Industry.

17. Jacob Orlofsky discovered that college students who had a stable sense of identity were more likely to achieve _____ status.
    a. stereotyped
    b. preintimacy
    c. pseudointimacy
    d. intimacy

18. _____-focused is the first level of relationship maturity.
    a. Role
    b. Image
    c. Self
    d. Parent

19. Robert Weiss distinguished between
    a. emotional and social isolation.
    b. individuation and connectedness.
    c. intimate and isolated relationships.
    d. situational and chronic loneliness.

20. The Boston Compact Youth Incentive Program provides troubled adolescents with
    a. good-paying jobs.
    b. birth control counseling.
    c. day care centers.
    d. food stamps.

Adolescence on the Screen

■ *The Cider House Rules* A young boy born raised in an orphanage breaks away from the his surrogate-father who runs the orphanage and charts his own course in life..

■ *King Gimp* Two University of Maryland professors won the Academy Award in 2000 for best documentary short subject with this film spanning the adolescence and young adulthood of Dan Keplinger, a young man suffering from a highly disabling form of cerebral palsy, as he searches for identity in a world that shuns him.

■ *Shine* Based on the true story of Australian pianist David Helfgott, the movie chronicles Helfgott's search for an identity. He has to overcome an abusive childhood, loss of his family in concentration camps, and mental illness before he finds himself as a concert pianist.

■ *Simon Birch* Simon Birch, age 12, believes that God made him for a special purpose. The movie presents his quest to fulfill the destiny he believes in

Adolescence in Books

■ *Gandhi*, by Erik Erikson (Norton, 1966), the Pulitzer Prize-winning biography of Mahatma Gandhi, emphasizes Gandhi's identity crisis.

■ *Identity's Architect: A Biography of Erik H. Erikson*, by Lawrence J. Friedman (Scribner, 1999), traces Erik Erikson's own identity crises, which contributed to the development of his psychosocial theory.

■ *Intimate Connections*, by David D. Burns (William Morrow, 1985), presents a program for overcoming loneliness.

Answer Key

Key Terms
1. **self-understanding** The adolescent's cognitive representation of the self, the substance and content of the adolescent's self-conceptions.
2. **possible self** What individuals might become, what they would like to become, and what they are afraid of becoming.
3. **self-esteem** The global evaluative dimension of the self. Self-esteem is also referred to as self-worth or self-image.
4. **self-concept** Domain-specific evaluations of the self.
5. **identity versus identity confusion** Erikson's fifth developmental stage, which individuals experience during the adolescent years. At this time, individuals are faced with finding out who they are, what they are all about, and where they are going in life.
6. **psychosocial moratorium** Erikson's term for the gap between childhood security and adult autonomy that adolescents experience as part of their identity exploration.
7. **crisis** A period of identity development during which the adolescent is choosing among meaningful alternatives.
8. **commitment** The part of identity development in which adolescents show a personal investment in what they are going to do.
9. **identity diffusion** Marcia's term for the state adolescents are in when they have not yet experienced a crisis or made any commitments.
10. **identity foreclosure** Marcia's term for the state adolescents are in when they have made a commitment but have not experienced a crisis.

11. **identity moratorium** Marcia's term for the state of adolescents who are in the midst of a crisis, but whose commitments are either absent or are only vaguely defined.

12. **identity achievement** Marcia's term for having undergone an crisis and made a commitment.

13. **individuality** An important element in adolescent identity development. It consists of two dimensions: self-assertion, the ability to have and communicate a point of view; and separateness, the use of communication patterns to express how one is different from others.

14. **connectedness** An important element in adolescent identity development. It consists of two dimensions: mutuality, sensitivity to and respect for others' views; and permeability, openness to others' views.

15. **ethnic identity** An enduring, basic aspect of the self that includes a sense of membership in an ethnic group and the attitudes and feelings related to that membership.

16. **intimacy versus isolation** Erikson's sixth developmental stage, which individuals experience during the early adulthood years. At this time, individuals face the developmental task of forming intimate relationships with others.

17. **intimate style** The individual forms and maintains one or more deep and long-lasting love relationships.

18. **preintimate style** The individual shows mixed emotions about commitment, an ambivalence reflected in the strategy of offering love without obligations.

19. **stereotyped style** The individual has superficial relationships that tend to be dominated by friendship ties with same-sex rather than opposite-sex individuals.

20. **pseudointimate style** The individual maintains a long-lasting sexual attachment with little or no depth or closeness.

21. **isolated style** The individual withdraws from social encounters and has little or no attachment to same or opposite-sex individuals.

22. **self-focused level** The first level of relationship maturity, at which one's perspective of another or of a relationship is concerned only with how it affects oneself.

23. **role-focused level** The second or intermediate level of relationship maturity, at which perceiving others as individuals in their own right begins to develop. However, at this level the perspective is stereotypical and emphasizes social acceptability.

24. **individuated-connected level** The highest level of relationship maturity, at which there is evidence of an understanding of oneself, as well as consideration of others' motivations and anticipation of their needs. Concern and caring involve emotional support and individualized expression of interest.

25. **emotional isolation** A type of loneliness that arises when a person lacks an intimate attachment relationships; single, divorced, and widowed adults often experience this type of loneliness.

26. **social isolation** A type of loneliness that occurs when a person lacks of sense of integrated involvement. Being deprived of participation in a group or community involving companionship, shared interests, organized activities, and meaningful roles causes a person to feel alienated, bored, and uneasy.

Key People

1. B	3. A	5. J	7. I	9. H	11. D
2. K	4. C	6. G	8. F	10. E	

The Self
Guided Review

1. self-understanding	6. fluctuates	11. close friends	16. unconscious
2. underpinnings	7. contradictions	12. social comparison	17. integrative
3. abstract	8. real/ideal	13. self-conscious	18. deconstruction
4. idealistic	9. false	14. preoccupied	19. reconstruction
5. differentiated	10. false	15. protect	20. consolidation

The Self
Section Review
Individual answers may vary.

Abstract and idealistic: A teenager is more apt to describe themselves in abstract terms, such as saying that they are compassionate and caring.

Differentiated: An adolescent is likely to describe themselves as having one set of characteristics in relationship to their families and another in relationship to their peers and friends.

Fluctuating: Adolescents' sense of themselves changes over short periods of time. They can be self-confident one moment, and anxious the next.

Contradictions within the self: Adolescents' self-descriptions show contradictions. They may think of themselves as both attractive and unattractive.

Real and ideal selves: Depression and self-doubt can arise when an adolescent feels that they are not living up to their idea sense of self.

Self-Esteem and Self-Concept
Guided Review

1. Self-esteem
2. self-worth
3. self-image
4. Self-concept
5. measure
6. Self-Perception Profile for Adolescents
7. methods
8. physical appearance
9. parenting
10. Peer
11. classmate/close friend
12. temporary
13. depression
14. suicide
15. anorexia nervosa
16. delinquency
17. adjustment
18. ineffective
19. causes
20. emotional
21. approval
22. Brother/Sister
23. Achievement
24. social cognition
25. self-efficacy
26. cope with
27. avoid
28. denial
29. deception
30. avoidance

Self-Esteem and Self-Concept
Section Review

Positive Indicators	Negative Indicators
Gives others directives or commands	Puts down others by teasing, name-calling, or gossiping
Uses voice quality appropriate for situation	Uses gestures that are dramatic or out of context
Expresses opinions	Engages in inappropriate touching or avoids physical contact
Sits with others during social activities	Gives excuses for failures
Works cooperatively in a group	Glances around to monitor others
Faces others when speaking or being spoken to	Brags excessively about achievements, skills, appearance
Maintains eye contact during conversation	Verbally puts self down; self-deprecation
Initiates friendly contact with others	Speaks too loudly, abruptly, or in a dogmatic tone
Maintains comfortable space between self and others	Does not express views or opinions, especially when asked
Little hesitation in speech, speaks fluently	Assumes a submissive stance

Identity
Guided Review

1. identity/identity confusion
2. who they are
3. what they are about
4. where they are going
5. psychosocial moratorium
6. confusion
7. withdraw
8. immerse
9. crowd
10. Luther
11. Gandhi
12. personality
13. experimentation
14. vocational
15. self-portrait
16. seven
17. cataclysmic
18. adolescence
19. stable
20. flexible
21. adaptive
22. society
23. relationships
24. careers
25. four
26. resolving
27. diffusion
28. foreclosure
29. moratorium
30. achievement
31. crisis
32. commitment
33. diffusion
34. moratorium
35. achievement
36. parental support
37. industry
38. self-reflective
39. youth
40. MAMA
41. moratorium
42. achievement
43. moratorium
44. achievement
45. individuality
46. connectedness
47. self-assertion
48. separateness
49. mutuality
50. permeability
51. enabling
52. constraining
53. ethnic
54. multiple
55. prejudice
56. discrimination
57. poverty
58. drugs
59. gangs
60. criminal
61. Gender
62. different
63. relationships
64. emotional
65. autonomy/achievement
66. domains
67. increased

Identity
Section Review

1.

Component	Example
Vocational/career	Career or work interests
Political identity	Conservative, liberal, or middle-of-the road
Religious identity	Spiritual beliefs
Relationship identity	Single, married, divorced
Achievement identity	Motivation to achieve
Sexual identity	Heterosexual, homosexual, bisexual
Ethnic and cultural identity	What country one is from; identification with cultural heritage
Interest identity	Sports, hobbies, music
Personality identity	Introverted or extraverted; anxious or calm; friendly or hostile
Physical identity	Body image

2. Genetic, adaptive, structural, dynamic, subjective or experiential, psychosocial reciprocity, and existential status.

Identity and Intimacy
Guided Review

1. intimacy/isolation
2. adulthood
3. intimate
4. sense of self
5. superficiality
6. dependency
7. repudiate
8. ignore
9. attack
10. five
11. intimate
12. preintimate
13. stereotyped
14. isolated
15. self
16. role
17. individuated
18. late
19. sex
20. attachment
21. self-esteem
22. social
23. females
24. men/women
25. college
26. absence
27. relationship
28. emotional
29. intimate
30. social
31. alienated
32. bored
33. uneasy
34. relations
35. needs/desires

Explorations in Adolescent Development

1. The multiple selves of ethnic minority youths reflect their efforts to bridge multiple worlds. Many move in multiple contexts, some of them populated by members of their own ethnic group, and others populated by the majority culture. Some move smoothly between these different worlds, while others adopt strong bi- or multi-cultural selves.

2. Programs that promote the active and realistic exploration of broad identity goals, like educational and occupational choice. Those that strengthen the link between school and work, such as the Boston Compact Youth Incentive Program, are especially successful because they let adolescents choose their work and educational opportunities.

3. Substandard living conditions, poverty, chronic unemployment, and the negative image of Native Americans that has been perpetuated by the majority White American culture.

Adventures for the Mind

1. No answers provided. Individual activity

2. No answers provided. Individual activity.

Adolescence in Research

The hypothesis was that relationships with parents and peers contribute to adolescents' self-esteem. Coopersmith administered a self-esteem assessment to boy, and also interview boys and their mothers about their family relationships. The methods were assessment instrument and interviews. The study was correlational. The conclusions were that the following parenting attributes were associated with high self esteem: expression of affection, concern about the boys' problems, harmony in the home, participation in joint family activities, giving boys competent, organized help when needed, setting and abiding by clear and fair rules, and allowing boys freedom within prescribed limits. The research is important because it establishes parenting factors that may be related to self-esteem.

Comprehensive Review

1. b	5. c	9. a	13. d	17. d
2. d	6. a	10. a	14. b	18. c
3. a	7. a	11. b	15. c	19. a
4. d	8. c	12. d	16. a	20. a

◆ Chapter 10   Gender

Learning Objectives with Key Terms and Key People in Boldface

1.0   **What is the Nature of Gender and Its Biological, Social, and Cognitive Influences?**
    A.   **What is Gender?**
        1.1   What is the nature of gender?
        1.2   What is meant by one's **gender role**?
    B.   **Biological, Social, and Cognitive Influences**
        1.3   What are the biological influences on gender?
        1.4   What is the role of sexuality in adolescent gender development?
        1.5   How do Freud and Erikson's ideas promote the premise that anatomy is destiny?
        1.6   How do today's developmentalists believe that biological and environmental influences affect gender?
        1.7   What is the evolutionary psychology view of gender development?
        1.8   What is the social roles view of gender development?
        1.9   What roles do gender hierarchy and sexual division of labor play in sex-differentiated behavior?
        1.10   According to identification theory and social cognitive theory, what role do parents play in the development of gender-appropriate behavior?
        1.11   How do peers reward gender-appropriate behavior?
        1.12   Does gender inequity still exist in education?
        1.13   How does television portray men as opposed to women?
        1.14   What was Kohlberg's theory of gender development?
        1.15   What does the **gender schema theory** state about individual gender development?

2.0   **What are Women's and Men's Issues Concerning Developmental Changes and Junctures?**
    A.   **Developmental Changes and Junctures**
        2.1   What is the gender intensification hypothesis?
        2.2   Is early adolescence a critical juncture for females?
        2.3   What is Gilligan's belief about the critical juncture for adolescent females?
        2.4   What are some criticisms about Gilligan's beliefs about male and female differences in intimacy and connectedness?
    B.   **Women's and Men's Issues**
        2.5   What are feminist scholars' perspectives on girls' and women's experiences and development?
        2.6   What are the goals of those with the feminist perspective?
        2.7   What is the evidence that male roles involve considerable strain?
        2.8   Can we make any general conclusions about the "male experience"?

3.0   **What Is Gender Role Classification?**
    A.   **Traditional Gender Roles**
        3.1   According to past tradition, what were the characteristics of a well-adjusted male?
        3.2   According to past tradition, what were the characteristics of a well-adjusted female?
        3.3   What has been the relative merit placed on masculine versus feminine traits?

Key Terms

Write a sentence using each of these key terms by either defining the term or giving an example of it. For instance, you might write, "Gender role is..." or, "(give example) is an example of a gender role." Compare your definitions with those given at the end of study guide chapter, and check your examples by referring to the text. Review the text for those terms you don't know or define incorrectly.

1.   gender

_____

_____

2.   gender role

_____

_____

3. cognitive developmental theory of gender

_____

_____

4. social learning theory of gender

_____

_____

5. schema

_____

_____

6. gender schema

_____

_____

7. gender schema theory

_____

_____

8. sexism

_____

_____

9. androgyny

_____

_____

10. gender stereotypes

_____

_____

11. gender-role transcendence

_____

_____

12. gender intensification hypothesis

_____

_____

Key People
Match the person with the concept of adolescent development with which they are associated.

___	1.	Sigmund Freud	A.	An evolutionary psychologist
___	2.	Erik Erikson	B.	Wrote *The Dance of Intimacy*
___	3.	Alice Eagly	C.	Developed an assessment instrument for androgyny
___	4.	Eleanor Maccoby	D.	Believes that males and females have a different style of "talk"
___	5.	Myra Sadker and David Sadker	E.	Wrote *Toward a New Psychology of Women*
___	6.	Lawrence Kohlberg	F.	Believes that women have a different "voice"
___	7.	Carol Jacklin	G.	Believed that male and female psychological differences are related to genital structure
___	8.	Janet Shibley Hyde	H.	Believed that gender and sexual behavior are unlearned and instinctual
___	9.	Deborah Tannen	I.	Proponent of the male role-strain perspective
___	10.	David Buss	J.	Studied gender discrimination in schools
___	11.	Sandra Bem	K.	Says that psychological sex differences arise from social roles of men and women
___	12.	Joseph Pleck	L.	Believes that cognitive differences between females and males have been exaggerated
___	13.	Carol Gilligan	M.	Now believes that differences in male and female verbal ability have virtually disappeared
___	14.	Jean Baker Miller	N.	Worked with Eleanor Maccoby and concluded that males have better math and visuospatial abilities
___	15.	Harriet Lerner	O.	Proposed the cognitive developmental theory of gender

The Nature of Gender
Guided Review

Biology's influence on gender behavior includes (1) _____ changes, which incorporates (2) _____ into the gender attitudes and behaviors of adolescents. This leads to boys and girls expressing (3) _____ male and female behaviors. Female adolescents may behave in an (4) _____, (5) _____, (6) _____, and (7)_____ manner. Male adolescents might behave in an (8) _____, (9) _____, (10) _____, and (11) _____ way. At least in boys, sexual behavior is related to (12) _____ changes, particularly rising (13) _____ levels. Girls' sexual activity is more influenced by the type of (14) _____- than by their hormone levels. Just how sexuality becomes a part of gender is determined by such (15) _____ influences as (16) _____ standards for (17) _____ and (18) _____ norms for dating.

Sigmund Freud and Erik Erikson argued that an individual's (19) _____ influence his or her gender behavior and, therefore, that (20) _____ is destiny. Critics of this view believe that (21) _____ is not given enough credit. Erikson modified his view and said that females today are (22) _____ their biological heritage. The evolutionary psychology view emphasizes that evolutionary (23) _____ produced (24) _____ sex differences. They believe that sexual (25) _____ that led to competition for (26) _____ males, supports this view. In the contemporary vie of evolutionary psychology, (27) _____ compete with (28) _____ for access to (29) _____, and thus women developed preferences for (30) _____, _____ men.

Many social scientists locate the cause of psychological sex differences in the contrasting (31) _____ of men and women in society. In contemporary society, women have less (32) _____ and _____ than men, and thus show more (33) _____ and less (34) _____ profiles than men.

Parents influence their children's and adolescents' gender development by allowing boys more (35) _____ than girls. They have different (36) _____ expectations for their sons and daughters, especially in (37) _____ and _____. The social cognitive theory of gender emphasizes that gender development occurs through (38) _____ and _____ of gender behavior, and through (39) _____ and

_____ they experience for gender-appropriate and (40) _____ behavior. In recent years, the increasing number of (41) _____ has changed gender-role models for women.

(42) _____ approval or (43) _____ is a powerful influence on gender attitude and behavior. (44) _____ from peer norms leads to (45) _____ peer acceptance. Educators influence gender behavior in (46) _____ ways. Some believe that middle and junior high schools are better suited to the learning style of the average adolescent (47) _____ than _____. This trend continues in (48) _____, where women feel they don't fit in (49) _____ classes. (50) _____ women have reportedly felt particularly uncomfortable in predominantly (51) _____ institutions.

(52) _____ messages are an important influence on adolescents' gender development. Television portrays adolescents in (53) _____ manners. (54) _____ are highly stereotyped and slanted toward a male audience. Early adolescents have a (55) _____ sensitivity to television messages about gender roles. Males are (56) _____ and females are (57) _____. Men and women typically engage in (58) _____-typed roles. Researchers have concluded that television carries (59) _____ messages.

According to the cognitive developmental theory, children's gender typing occurs when they begin to (60) _____ of themselves as male or female and (61) _____ their world on the basis of gender. By Piaget's (62) _____ stage, children understand gender (63) _____. When adolescent's reach Piaget's (64) _____ stage, they can decide what they want their gender (65) _____ to be. As females have developed stronger (66) _____ interests, sex differences are turning into (67) _____. However adolescent females often show a greater interest in (68) _____ and (69) _____ bonds than males do.

A (70) _____ is a cognitive structure that guides an individual's (71) _____. (72) _____ theory states that an individual's gender behavior is guided by an (73) _____ motivation to conform to sociocultural gender stereotypes, causing (74) _____. This theory accepts that (75) _____ determine which schemas are important. Most cultures have a sprawling (76) _____ of gender-linked associations.

The Nature of Gender
Section Review
List the four examples Sadker & Sadker (1994) found of gender inequality in education.

_____

_____

_____

_____

Gender Stereotypes, Similarities, and Differences
Guided Review
The broad categories that reflect or impressions and beliefs about males and females are known as gender (1) _____, which all refer to an (2) _____ of what the typical male or female should be. Stereotypes are a way of (3) _____ the complexity of life. Male and female stereotyping is (4) _____. According to a large study of college students, males are believed to be (5) _____, (6) _____ and _____, (7) _____ oriented, and (8) _____, while females are believed to be (9) _____, (10) _____, less (11) _____, and more (12) _____. However, as sexual equality increases, stereotypes may (13) _____ and the sexes be seen as more (14) _____ than (15) _____. Stereotypes are often (16) _____ and involve (17) _____ and (18) _____. There has been a long history of prejudice against (19) _____. Old-fashioned (20) _____ is characterized by endorsement of traditional gender roles. Modern sexism is characterized by (21) _____ that there is (22) _____.

Most gender researches believe that sex differences have been (23) _____. What difference there are appear to be due primarily to (24) _____ and (25) _____ factors. There are many physical differences between males and females. Females are less likely than males to (26) _____ or to develop (27) _____ or _____ disorders. (28) _____ strengthens the immune system and also helps produce more good (29) _____. Testosterone triggers the production of (30) _____, which (31) _____ the blood vessels. The brain metabolism of males and females are (32) _____.

Some gender experts believe that the cognitive differences in males and females have been (33) _____. Recent evidence suggests that verbal abilities are almost (34) _____, but there still may be some lap in (35) _____ and _____ skills. Gender researchers have studied four areas of socioemotional development: (36) _____, (37) _____, (38) _____, and (39) _____. (40) _____ talk is the language of conversation and establishing (41) _____, while (41) _____ talk is talk that gives (42) _____. Males enjoy (43) _____ talk more, while females more enjoy (44) _____ talk.

Boys are more (45) _____ aggressive than girls. However, there are fewer differences in (46) _____ aggression. Males show less (47) _____ than females, and this can lead to (48) _____ problems.

Not all psychologists agree that gender differences are small. A large body of research reveals that behavior is (49) _____ differentiated to varying extents. Evolutionary psychologist David Buss argues that men and women differ (50) _____ in domains in which they have faced different (51) _____ problems. Otherwise he believes they are psychologically (52) _____. The (53) _____ in which males and females are (54) _____, _____, and _____ should be taken into account when thinking about gender differences and similarities.

Gender Stereotypes, Similarities, and Differences
Section Review

1. Complete the table by listing five beliefs that constitute old-fashioned sexism and five beliefs that constitute modern sexism.

Old-fashioned sexism	Modern sexism

2. Complete the table by listing five differences in male and female physical and biological characteristics.

Males are/have	Females are/have

3. Describe Tannen's findings about the differences in boys' and girls' play.

_____

_____

4.   Compare and contrast male and female helping behavior and display of emotions.

_____

_____

Gender-Role Classification
Guided Review

Today, (1) _____ characterizes gender roles. In the past, the well-adjusted male was expected to be (2) _____, (3) _____, and (4) _____-oriented. The well-adjusted female was expected to be (5) _____, (6) _____, and (7) _____ in power. A study conducted by Broverman and colleagues (1972) found that college students labeled characteristic male traits as (8) _____, and traits associated with females as (9) _____. This perception is unfair to females because the male traits are more (10) _____. In the late 1970s, the concept of (11) _____ was explored. A person with this trait has a high degree of (12) _____ and (13) _____ characteristics. One of the most widely used measure of androgyny is the (14)_____ Inventory, which classifies people, based upon their responses, as having one of four gender-role orientations: (15) _____, (16) _____, (17) _____, and (18) _____. An androgynous individual is simply one who has a high degree of both (19) _____ and _____ traits. An (20) _____ individual is not high on either masculine or feminine traits. Androgynous individuals are described as more (21) _____ and more (22) _____ than either masculine or feminine individuals. Individuals who are (23) _____ are the least competent. Increasing numbers of children in (24) _____ and (25) _____ are being raised to be androgynous.

An increasing number of gender researchers believe that there is a (26) _____ side to masculinity. Pleck and his colleagues found that the more masculine boys are, the more they engage in (27) _____, (28) _____ and _____, and participate in (29) _____ activities. The concept of androgyny has turned out not to be the (30) _____ that many proponents hoped for. Some believe that the concept should be replaced with one known as gender-role (31) _____, meaning that competence should not be conceptualized on the basis of (32) _____, (33) _____, or (34) _____ but on a (35) _____ basis.

Gender Role Classification
Section Review

How well do you know the measures of the Bem Sex-Role Inventory? Label the traits based upon the scoring of the Bem Sex-Role Inventory. Put an "F" for the traits that are coded on the femininity scale and an "M" for the traits that are coded on the masculinity scale. Be sure to take the test yourself. You can use the form in the book, or take it on-line at the address given at the end of the chapter under "Taking It to the Web."

_____1. self-sufficient
_____2. compassionate
_____3. willing to take a stand
_____4. acts like a teacher
_____5. gentle
_____6. understanding
_____7. analytical
_____8. athletic
_____9. cheerful
_____10. makes decisions easily

_____11. self-reliant
_____12. shy
_____13. loyal
_____14. unpredictable
_____15. forceful
_____16. willing to take risks
_____17. defends own beliefs
_____18. sympathetic
_____19. individualistic
_____20. flatterable

Developmental Changes and Junctures
Guided Review

That psychological and behavioral changes during early adolescence are due to increased social pressures to conform to traditional gender roles is known as the (1) _____ hypothesis. The (2) _____ context strongly influences gender intensification. (3) _____ believes that (4) _____ experience life differently than (5) _____ do. She says that they come to a (6) _____ in their development when they reach adolescence because they become aware that their interest in (7) _____ is not prized by the male culture. She says that girls have a (8) _____ and they begin to (9) _____ it, leading to (10) _____ and (11) _____ disorders. Research indicates that (12) _____ influence whether adolescent girls silence their "voice." (13) _____ girls have a strong voice in all contexts. Critical argue that Gilligan and her colleagues (14) _____ differences in gender. But Gilligan and her colleagues, known as (15) _____ or _____, say that their work provides a way to (16) _____ females and (17) _____ society.

Many feminist scholars believe that psychology has portrayed human behavior with a (18) _____ theme. (19) _____ has been an important voice in stimulating the examination of psychological issues from a (20) _____ perspective. According to Joseph Pleck's (21) _____ view, men experience (22) _____ when they violate expected male (23) _____, causing problems with (24) _____, (25) _____ - _____ relationships, and (26) _____- _____ relationships.

Ron Levant has offered ideas about how males can (27) _____ their masculinity in (28) _____ ways.

Developmental Changes and Junctures
Section Review

1.   What message do feminist psychologists have for men?

_____
_____

2.   What are Ron Levant's (1995) recommendations for how men can reconstruct masculinity in positive ways?

_____
_____

Explorations in Adolescence
Discuss the gender roles existing in Egypt and China today.

_____
_____
_____
_____

Adventures for the Mind

1. Make up a list of words that you associated with masculinity and femininity. Identify those words that have negative connotations for males and/or females. Then replace them with words that have more positive connotations.

_____

_____

2. How will you attempt to raise your children, in terms of gender roles. Will you try to raise gender-neutral children? Or will you encourage more traditional gender distinctions?

_____

_____

Comprehensive Review

1. _____ refers to a set of expectations about sex-appropriate behavior.
   a. Stereotype
   b. Gender role
   c. Gender intensification
   d. Sexism

2. Erik Erickson and Sigmund Feud believed that the differences between males and females
   a. was the result of females' ability and males' inability to articulate their feelings
   b. resulted from prenatal hormonal influences.
   c. resulted from anatomical differences.
   d. were gender stereotypes rather than gender differences.

3. An adolescent mother can reduce the sex-role stereotypes of her children by
   a. dressing them all the same.
   b. withholding praise for their physical appearance.
   c. holding a job outside the home.
   d. divorcing their father.

4. On the playground, girls teach girls and boys teach boys about their gender behaviors. This is known as
   a. gender socialization.
   b. gender intensification.
   c. peer socialization.
   d. peer generalization.

5. School curriculum planners decide in which grades algebra, history, and science are to be taught. These decisions are based mainly upon the
   a. cognitive developmental norms for children.
   b. social-emotional developmental norms for children.
   c. developmental norms for males.
   d. developmental norms for females.

6. Adolescent females watching television are likely to find
   a. fewer role models than their brothers will.
   b. accurate representations of women's roles.
   c. important lessons on managing relationships.
   d. little to identify with in terms of sexual intimacy.

7. A boy recognizes that he is a male and then starts doing "male" things. This description is consistent with the _____ theory of gender.
   a. socialization
   b. genderization
   c. cognitive-developmental
   d. intensification

8. Gender schema theory predicts that adolescents are drawn to sources of information that enable them to
   a. conform to stereotypes.
   b. learn about sexuality.
   c. learn about relationships.
   d. think idealistically.

9. On which of the following tasks is an adolescent girl likely to outperform an adolescent boy?
   a. spelling the word commitment
   b. calculating the area of a triangle
   c. selecting a picture from among six others than matches a standard
   d. finding a hidden object in a picture

10. Pat gets embarrassed when making a mistake in public and experiences episodes of jealousy and passion. What gender is Pat likely to be?
    a. male
    b. female
    c. equally likely to be male or female
    d. There is no research on which to base an answer.

11. According to the Bem Sex-Role Inventory, an adolescent is androgynous if she scores
    a. high on masculinity and high on femininity.
    b. high on masculinity and low on femininity.
    c. low on femininity and low on masculinity.
    d. half-way between masculinity and femininity.

12. The concept of _____ involves the notion that an individual's competence should not be conceptualized along the lines of gender orientation, but rather, the emphasis should be on the individual.
    a. gender-neutrality
    b. humanism
    c. gender-role transcendence
    d. critical feminism

13. The gender intensification hypothesis indicates that behavioral differences between males and females become greater during adolescence as a result of
    a. hormones.
    b. pressures to conform to stereotypes.
    c. television commercials.
    d. the development of a new schema.

14. The concept of ____ refers to the fact that the amount, timing, and intensity of gender socialization are different for girls and boys.
    a. gender intensification
    b. asymmetric gender socialization
    c. gender role transcendence
    d. sex difference

15. Carol Gilligan has suggested that girls
    a. are better than boys.
    b. are equal to boys.
    c. are different than boys.
    d. are none of the above.

16. According to many studies, adolescent girls are likely to suffer from declines in
    a. intelligence.
    b. self-esteem.
    c. verbal fluency.
    d. social skills.

Adolescence in Research

Concerning Pleck and colleagues' 1994 National Survey of Adolescent Males, state the hypothesis, the research methods (if known), the research conclusions, and the implications and applications for adolescent development.

_____

_____

Adolescence on the Screen

- *Boys Don't Cry* Hilary Swank won an academy award for her portrayal of the true story of a boy with gender identity disorder who was murdered when the his biological sex was revealed.

- *The Crying Game* A shocking ending reveals that one of the main characters is a transsexual.

- *Mr. and Mrs. Bridges* Joanne Woodward and Paul Newman as an upper-class couple in the American Midwest of the 1940s who embody the male and female stereotypical roles of the time.

- *Ma Vie En Rose (My Life in Pink)* A French movie (with English subtitles) about a boy with gender identity disorder who dresses and lives as a girl.

Adolescence in Books

- *A New Psychology of Men*, by Ronald Levant and William Pollack (Basic Books, 1995), is a collection of essays on men's issues and male gender roles.

- *As Nature Made Him*, by John Colapinto (HarperCollins, 2000), is the true story of one of identical twins whose penis was accidentally severed during circumcision and who was given female hormones and raised as a girl until his parents revealed the accident. He then had penile reconstructive surgery and hormone treatments and resumed life as a man.

- *Stiffed: The Betrayal of the American Man*, by Susan Faludi (William Morrow, 1999), examines the problems of men in modern life, emphasizing the stress and strain of male sex roles.

- *You Just Don't Understand*, by Deborah Tannen (Ballentine, 1990), explores the differences in male and female communication styles.

Answer Key

Key Terms

1. **gender** The sociocultural dimension of being male or female.
2. **gender role** A set of expectations that prescribes how females and males should think, act, and feel.
3. **cognitive developmental theory of gender** In this view, children's gender-typing occurs after they have developed a concept of gender. Once they begin to consistently conceive of themselves as male or female, children often organize their world on the basis of gender.
4. **social learning theory of gender** This theory emphasizes that children's and adolescents' gender development occurs through observation and imitation of gender behavior, and through rewards and punishments they experience for gender-appropriate and -inappropriate behavior.
5. **schema** A cognitive structure of network of associations that organizes and guides an individual's perception.
6. **gender schema** A cognitive structure that organizes the world in terms of male and female.
7. **gender schema theory** According to this theory, an individual's attention and behavior are guided by an internal motivation to conform to gender-based sociocultural standards and stereotypes.
8. **sexism** Prejudice and discrimination against an individual because of his or her sex.
9. **androgyny** The presence of a high degree of desirable feminine and masculine characteristics in the same individual.
10. **gender stereotypes** Broad categories that reflect our impressions and beliefs about females and males.
11. **gender-role transcendence** The belief that, when an individual's competence is at issue, it should be conceptualized not on the basis of masculinity, femininity, or androgyny but, rather, on a person basis.
12. **gender intensification hypothesis** This hypothesis states that psychological and behavioral differences between boys and girls become greater during early adolescence because of increased socialization pressures to conform to masculine and feminine gender roles

Key People

1. H	4. M	7. N	10. A	13. F
2. G	5. J	8. L	11. C	14. E
3. K	6. O	9. D	12. I	15. B

The Nature of Gender
Guided Review

1. pubertal
2. sexually
3. stereotypical
4. affectionate
5. sensitive
6. charming
7. soft-spoken
8. assertive
9. cocky
10. cynical
11. forceful
12. hormonal
13. androgen
14. friends
15. social
16. cultural
17. sex
18. peer group
19. genitals
20. biology
21. experience
22. transcending
23. adaptation
24. psychological
25. selection
26. dominant
27. men
28. men
29. women
30. successful/ambitious
31. positions
32. power/status
33. cooperative
34. dominant
35. independence
36. academic
37. math/science
38. observation/ imitation
39. rewards/punishment
40. inappropriate
41. working mothers
42. Peer
43. disapproval
44. Deviance
45. low
46. subtle
47. male/female
48. college
49. science
50. Latina
51. Anglo
52. Media
53. extreme
54. Rock music videos
55. heightened
56. overrepresented
57. television
58. sex
59. sexist
60. think
61. organize
62. concrete operational
63. constancy
64. formal operational
65. identity
66. vocational
67. similarities
68. relationships
69. emotional
70. schema
71. behavior
72. Gender schema
73. internal
74. gender-typing
75. societies
76. network

The Nature of Gender
Section Review

Sadker & Sadker (1994) found that girls' learning problems are not identified as often as boys' are; boys are given more attention in school; girls start out testing higher than boys in but end up with lower SAT scores; and boys get more pressure to achieve than girls do.

Gender Stereotypes, Similarities, and Differences
Guided Review

1. stereotypes
2. image
3. simplifying
4. pervasive
5. dominant
6. independent/ aggressive
7. achievement
8. enduring
9. nurturant
10. affiliative
11. esteemed
12. helpful
13. diminish
14. similar
15. different
16. negative
17. prejudice
18. discrimination
19. women
20. sexism
21. denial
22. discrimination
23. exaggerated
24. biological
25. sociocultural
26. die
27. physical/mental
28. Estrogen
29. cholesterol
30. lipoprotein
31. clogs
32. similar
33. exaggerated
34. identical
35. math/visuospatial
36. relationships
37. aggression
38. emotion
39. achievement
40. Rapport
41. Report
42. information
43. report
44. rapport
45. physically
46. verbal
47. self-control
48. behavioral
49. sex
50. psychologically
51. adaptive
52. similar
53. contexts
54. thinking/ feeling/behaving

Gender Stereotypes, Similarities, and Differences
Section Review
1.   Suggested answers

Old-fashioned sexism	Modern sexism
Women are not as smart as men.	Discrimination is no longer a problem in the U.S.
I would not be as comfortable with a woman for as boss as I would be having a man for a boss.	Women rarely miss out on good jobs because of discrimination.
It is more important to encourage boys to be involved in athletics than it is to encourage girls.	It is rare to see a woman treated in a sexist manner on television.
Women are not as capable as men of thinking logically.	On the average, people in our society treat husbands and wives equally.
When both parents are employed and their child gets sick at school, the school should call the mother rather than the fathers.	Men and women have equal opportunities for achievement in today's society.

2.   Suggested answers

Males are/have	Females are/have
Testosterone	Estrogen
Twice the risk of coronary disease	Twice the body fat
Body fat concentrated at abdomen	Body fat concentrated around breasts and hips
Ten percent taller than females	Brain areas involved in emotional and physical expression more active in females
Male hormones promote growth of long bones	Female hormones stop bone growth at puberty

3.   Boys play in large, hierarchically structured groups with a leader. Boys' games have winners and losers. Boys boast of their skill and argue who is best at what. Girls play in small groups or pairs. Girls have a best friend. Intimacy is pervasive. Girls take turns more. Girls like to sit and talk with each other.

4.   Males are more likely to help in contexts in which a perceived danger is present and they feel competent to help. Females are more likely to help when a child or personal problem is involved. Males are more likely to show anger toward strangers and other males and are more likely to turn their anger into aggressive action. Females are more likely than males to discuss emotion in terms of interpersonal relationships and to express fear and sadness.

Gender Role Classification
Guided Review
1. diversity
2. independent
3. aggressive
4. power
5. dependent
6. nurturant
7. uninterested
8. instrumental
9. expressive
10. valued
11. androgyny
12. masculine
13. feminine
14. Bem Sex-Role
15. masculine
16. feminine
17. androgynous
18. undifferentiated
19. masculine/feminine
20. undifferentiated
21. flexible
22. mentally healthy
23. undifferentiated
24. the United States
25. Sweden
26. negative
27. premarital sex
28. drink alcohol/take
    drugs
29. delinquent
30. panacea
31. transcendence
32. masculinity
33. femininity
34. androgyny
35. person

Gender Role Classification
Section Review

1. M	**6.** F	**11.** M	**16.** M
2. F	**7.** M	**12.** F	**17.** M
3. M	**8.** M	**13.** F	**18.** F
4. F	**9.** F	**14.** F	**19.** M
5. F	**10.** M	**15.** M	**20.** F

Developmental Changes and Junctures
Guided Review

1. gender intensification

2. family

3. Carol Gilligan

4. women

5. men

6. critical juncture

7. intimacy

8. different voice

9. silence

10. depression

11. eating

12. contextual variations

13. Androgynous

14. exaggerate

15. revisionists (or feminists)

16. liberate

17. transform

18. male-dominant

19. Jean Baker Miller

20. female

21. role-strain

22. stress

23. roles

24. health

25. male-female

26. male-male

27. reconstruct

28. positive

Developmental Changes and Junctures
Section Review

1. Feminists hope that men will become more conscious of gender issues, of male and female roles, and of fairness and sensitivity in interactions and relationships between females and males.

2. Levant believes men should (1) reexamine their beliefs about manhood, (2) separate out the valuable aspects of the male role, and (3) get rid of the part of the masculine role that are destructive.

Explorations in Adolescence

In Egypt, there is a dramatic division of labor between males and females. Males work in the public sphere; women work in the home and raise children. The Islamic religion dictates that men provide for their families and women care for the family and household. In China, women have more economic freedom and more-equal status in marital relationships than they did before the Chinese revolution, but they still make less money than men in comparable positions. In the countryside, males still dominate.

Adolescence in Research

Pleck and colleagues' hypothesized was that problem behaviors in adolescent males are associated with their attitudes toward masculinity. They also examined the risk and protective influences for problem behaviors. They studied 1,680 15- to 19-year-old males. Their findings supported their hypothesis. Males who had traditional beliefs about masculinity were more likely to have difficulty in school, use drugs and alcohol, be sexually active, and participate in delinquent activities. Risk factors for problem behaviors included low parental education, being the son of a teenage mother, living in a mother-headed household or having no nonmaterial family member in the home, lenient family rules, and infrequent church attendance. Protective factors included strict family rules and frequent church attendance.

Adventures for the Mind

No answers provided. Individual activity.

Comprehensive Review

1.	b	5.	a	9.	a	13.	b
2.	c	6.	a	10.	c	14.	a
3.	c	7.	c	11.	a	15.	c
4.	c	8.	a	12.	a	16.	b

◆ Chapter 11   Sexuality

Learning Objectives with Key Terms and Key People in Boldface

1.0   **What is Adolescent Sexuality?**
    A.   **An Aspect of Normal Development**
        1.1   What negative stereotypes exist about adolescent sexuality?
        1.2   Are sexual interests a normal part of adolescent development?
        1.3   What is the role of sexual development in adolescent development?
        1.4   What other chapters in the text serve as a backdrop for understanding adolescent sexuality?

    B.   **The Sexual Culture**
        1.5   What is the nature of adolescent sexuality in today's culture?
        1.6   What it the dichotomy between adolescent exposure to sexual culture and many adults' feelings about sex?

    C.   **Developing a Sexual Identity**
        1.7   What is involved in forming a sexual identity?
        1.8   What is an adolescent's sexual preference?
        1.9   What are the characteristics of the naïve sexual style, unassured sexual style, competent sexual style, adventurous sexual style, and driven sexual style?

    D.   **Obtaining Information about Adolescent Sexuality**
        1.10   Why is it difficult to obtain valid information about adolescent sexuality?

2.0   **What are the Prevailing Sexual Attitudes and Behaviors?**
    A.   **Heterosexual Attitudes and Behaviors**
        2.1   What is the progression of sexual behaviors?
        2.2   How many adolescents are having sexual intercourse?
        2.3   Have the number of females engaging in intercourse increased more rapidly than that of males?
        2.4   Are there ethnic and racial differences in sexual activity?
        2.5   What are the common male and female adolescent **sexual scripts**?
        2.6   What are the risk factors for sexual problems?

    B.   **Homosexual Attitudes and Behavior**
        2.7   What is the attitude today about sexual orientation?
        2.8   What do we know about adolescent's same-sex attractions?
        2.9   What causes an individual's sexual orientation?
        2.10   What does it mean to be **bisexual**?

    C.   **Self-Stimulation**
        2.11   What is the nature of sexual self-stimulation?

    D.   **Contraceptive Use**
        2.12   How many adolescents are using contraceptives?
        2.13   Which adolescents are least likely to use contraceptives?

3.0 **What Are the Incidence, Nature, and Consequences of Adolescent Pregnancy?**
- **A.** **Incidence and Nature of Adolescent Pregnancy**
  - 3.1 How many American adolescents become pregnant each year?
  - 3.2 How many adolescent births are unintended?
  - 3.3 Is adolescent pregnancy increasing or decreasing?
  - 3.4 What cultural changes have taken place in the last forty years regarding adolescent sexuality and pregnancy?
- **B.** **Consequences of Adolescent Pregnancy**
  - 3.5 What are the health risks for mother and offspring?
  - 3.6 How does adolescent pregnancy affect a mother's school and work opportunities?
  - 3.7 What else besides the pregnancy places adolescent mothers at risk?
- **C.** **Cognitive Factors in Adolescent Pregnancy**
  - 3.8 How does the personal fable impact on pregnancy prevention efforts?
- **D.** **Adolescents as Parents**
  - 3.9 What infant risks are associated with being born to an adolescent mother?
  - 3.10 What kind of mothers do adolescents make?
  - 3.11 What is the nature of adolescent fatherhood?
- **E.** **Reducing Adolescent Pregnancy**
  - 3.12 What are some recommendations for reducing adolescent pregnancy?
  - 3.13 What programs have worked to reduce adolescent pregnancy?

4.0 **What Are the Incidence, Nature, and Consequences of Sexually Transmitted Diseases (STDs)?**
- **A.** **Types**
  - 4.1 What are sexually transmitted diseases (STDs)?
  - 4.2 How are STDs contracted?
  - 4.3 What is gonorrhea?
  - 4.4 What is syphilis?
  - 4.5 What is chlamydia?
  - 4.6 What is genital herpes?
- **B.** **AIDS**
  - 4.7 What is **AIDS?**
  - 4.8 What is the rate of AIDS in adolescence?
  - 4.9 How does the long incubation period affect adolescents who may have been infected with the AIDS virus as teenagers?
  - 4.10 How is AIDS transmitted?
  - 4.11 How is AIDS prevented?

5.0 **What Are the Processes and Characteristics Related to Sexual Knowledge and Sexual Education?**
- **A.** **Sexual Knowledge and Sex Education**
  - 5.1 How much do American adolescents and adults know about sex?
  - 5.2 What is the nature of most sex information?
  - 5.3 What are the sources of sex information?
  - 5.4 What is the incidence and nature of sex education in the schools?
  - 5.5 Why do some experts believe that school-linked sex education tied to community health centers is a promising strategy?
- **B.** **Forcible Sexual Behavior and Sexual Harassment**
  - 5.6 What is the nature and incidence of **rape**?
  - 5.7 What is **date, or acquaintance, rape**?
  - 5.8 What is sexual harassment?
  - 5.9 How prevalent is adolescent sexual harassment?
  - 5.10 What is **quid pro quo sexual harassment**?
  - 5.11 What is the nature of **hostile environment sexual harassment**?

6.0 **What Is the Current Status of Social Policy As It Relates to the Sexual Well-Being of Adolescents?**
    A.   **Sexual Well-Being and Development Transitions**
        6.1   What are the five issues related to adolescent sexuality that need examination?
    B.   **Social Policy and Adolescent Sexuality**
        6.2   What social policy initiatives do we need concerning sex education?
        6.3   What initiatives are needed to reduce adolescent pregnancy?

7.0 **Explorations in Adolescence**
        7.1   What contraceptive health programs have been effective in decreasing adolescent pregnancy and reducing the rate of sexually transmitted diseases?
        7.2   What is the nature of adolescent sexuality in Holland and Sweden?

8.0 **Adventures for the Mind**
        8.1   Should a girl tell her intended sexual partner that she has genital herpes?
        8.2   How do you think sex education should be addressed?

Key Terms

Write a sentence using each of these key terms by either defining the term or giving an example of it. For instance, you might write, "A sexual script is..." or, "(give example) is an example of a sexual script." Compare your definitions with those given at the end of study guide chapter, or check your examples by referring to the text. Review the text for those terms you don't know or define incorrectly.

1.   sexual script

_____

_____

2.   bisexual

_____

_____

3.   sexually transmitted diseases (STDs)

_____

_____

4.   gonorrhea

_____

_____

5.   syphilis

_____

_____

6.   genital herpes

_____

_____

7.   AIDS

_____

_____

8.	rape

_____

_____

9.	date, or acquaintance, rape

_____

_____

10.	quid pro quo sexual harassment

_____

_____

11.	hostile environment sexual harassment

_____

_____

Key People
Match the person with the concept of adolescent development with which they are associated.

___	1.	Shirley Feldman	A.	Director of Kinsey Institute for Sex, Gender, and Reproduction
___	2.	Alfred Kinsey	B.	Views sexuality as a normal aspect of adolescent development
___	3.	Richard Savin-Williams	C.	Studies developmental issues in adolescent sexuality
___	4.	Simon LeVay	D.	Early and famous sex researcher
___	5.	P. Lindsay Chase-Lansdale	E.	Studied the brains of gay men for clues to causes of homosexuality
___	6.	June Reinisch	F.	Researched the pattern of gay and lesbian adolescents' disclosure of sexual orientation
___	7.	Jeanne Brooks-Gunn	G.	Studies contraceptive patterns in American adolescents and adolescents in foreign countries

Thinking About Adolescent Sexuality
Guided Review

Sexual development and interest are (1) _____ aspects of adolescent development. The majority of adolescents have (2) _____ sexual attitudes. Adolescence is a bridge between the (3) _____ child and the (4) _____ adult. Other chapters in the text that have been a backdrop for understanding adolescent sexual attitudes and behavior are Chapters (5) ___, _____, ____, ____, _____, _____, _____, and ____.

Many Americans are (6) _____ about sex. Sex is used to (7) _____ almost everything and sex is explicitly portrayed in (8) _____, (9) _____, (10) _____, (11) _____ of popular music, (12) _____, and the (13) _____. Sexual identity is (14) _____. It involves learning to (15) _____ sexual feelings, developing new forms of (16) _____, and learning skills to (17) _____ sexual behavior. Sexual identities emerge in the context of (18) _____, (19) _____, and (20) _____ factors. An adolescent's sexual identity involves an indication of sexual (21) _____ as either (22) _____ (23) _____, or (24) _____. It also involves a matter of developing one of five sexual styles: sexually (25) _____, (26) _____, (27) _____, (28) _____, and (29) _____. It is not easy to get information about sexual attitudes because people are (30) _____ to answer questions candidly.

Thinking About Adolescent Sexuality
Section Review
Complete the table by listing one concept from each chapter that provides a foundation for understanding adolescent sexuality.

Chapter	Concept
3: Biological Differences	
4: Cognitive Differences	
5: Families	
6: Peers	
7: Schools	
8: Culture	
9: The Self and Identity	
10: Gender	

Sexual Attitudes and Behavior
Guided Review

The progression of sexual behaviors is typically (1) _____, (2) _____, (3) _____, and (4) _____ sex. The number of adolescents reporting having had sexual intercourse (5)_____ in the 20th century, with the number of (6) _____ increasing more rapidly than the number of (7) _____. More than (8) _____ of adolescents today have had sexual intercourse by age (9) _____. This number varies by (10) _____, (11) _____, and (12) _____. The highest sexual activity is found among (13) _____ _____, who live in an (14) _____.

Adolescents have sexual (15) _____. A common one involves the (16) _____ being sexually (17) _____ and the (18) _____ setting (19) _____ on sexual activities. Females link (20) _____ with (21) _____ more than males do.

Risk factors for developing sexual problems include (22) _____ sexual activity, having (23) _____ partners, not (24) _____, and other factors like heavy (25) _____ and _____, living in (26) a _____, and one's (27) _____.

The three choices for sexual orientation are (28) _____, (29) _____, and (30) _____. Today these orientations are viewed as existing along a (31) _____. Sexual orientation is likely caused by a mix of (32) _____, (33) _____, (34) _____, and (35) _____ factors. (36) _____ is a part of adolescent sexual activity. Adolescents are increasing their use of (37) _____, but younger adolescents from (38) _____ backgrounds are less likely to use them than their (39) _____, (40)_____-income counterparts.

Sexual Attitudes and Behaviors
Section Review
1. State the four most common reasons that teenagers give for having sex, according to the Kaiser Family Foundation study (1996).

_____

_____

2. What four conclusions did Savin-Williams (1998) make about adolescents who disclose their gay or lesbian identity?

_____

_____

Adolescent Pregnancy
Guided Review

More than (1) _____ American adolescents become pregnant every year. Of these, (2) _____ of _____ are (3) _____. The rate, however, is (4) _____. American's adolescent pregnancy rate is the (5) _____ in the Western world. Adolescent pregnancy increases (6) _____ risks for both the (7) _____ and the children. Adolescent mothers are more likely to (8) _____ and have (9) _____ jobs as adults. In addition, adolescent mothers often come from (10) _____-income circumstances and were not doing (11) _____ in school. The (12) _____ makes pregnancy prevention difficult. Infants of adolescent mothers are at-risk (13) _____ and (14) _____. Adolescent mothers are less effective in (15) _____ their children and adolescent fathers do not have a (16) _____ relationship with the baby and mother. Recommendations to reduce adolescent pregnancy include (17) _____ education and (18) _____, access to (19) _____, more life (20) _____, (21) _____ involvement and (22) _____, and (23) _____.

Adolescent Pregnancy
Section Review

1. Using information about early adolescent development, America's sexual ambivalence, and adolescents' vulnerability to economic forces, list 10 specific factors that lead to adolescent pregnancy.

_____

_____

_____

_____

_____

_____

_____

_____

_____

_____

2. Complete the table by providing a brief description of each program aimed at reducing adolescent pregnancy.

Program	Description
Teen Outreach Program (TOP)	
Girls, Inc.	
Growing Together	
Will Power/Won't Power	
Taking Care of Business	
Health Bridge	

Sexually Transmitted Diseases
Guided Review

Sexually transmitted diseases, also called (1) _____, are contracted primarily through (2) _____, and not just (3) _____ but also (4) _____-_____ and (5) _____-_____ contact. Gonorrhea, commonly called (6) _____ or _____ is one of the most (7) _____ STDS in the U.S. (8) _____ is caused by the bacterium Treponema pallidum. Chlamydia is the (9) _____ of all sexually transmitted diseases. Genital herpes is caused by a family of (10) _____ with different (11) _____. There is no known (12) _____. AIDS is caused by the (13) _____ virus, which destroys the body's (14) _____ system. The rate of AIDS in adolescence is relatively (15) _____. The incubation period for AIDS means that many young adults were infected with they were (16) _____. AIDS can be transmitted through (17) _____, the sharing of (18) _____, and (19) _____.

Sexually Transmitted Diseases
Section Review

1. List five differences between AIDS in adolescents and AIDS in adults.

_____

_____

_____

_____

_____

2. List six risky behaviors associated with increased chances of coming into contact with the AIDS virus.

_____

_____

_____

_____

_____

_____

3. Live five safe sex behaviors.

_____

_____

_____

_____

_____

Sexual Knowledge and Sex Education: Forcible Sexual Behavior and Sexual Harassment
Guided Review

Sex information is abundant but often is (1) _____. Adolescents get the most sex information from (2) _____, followed by (3) _____, (4) _____, (5) _____, and (6) _____. Less than (7) ___ percent of adolescents' sex education comes from fathers. A (8) _____ of American parents support (9) _____ education in the schools. This has increased since the increase in (10) _____, especially (11) _____. Some experts believe that (12) _____-_____ sex education that ties in with (13) _____ is a promising strategy.

Forcible sexual intercourse without a person's consent is called (14) _____, Approximately (15) _____ percent of rapes are committed by males. (16) _____ rape is an increasing concern. (17) _____ is a form of power of one person over another. It is (18) _____ in adolescence. Its two forms are (19) _____ and (20) _____.

Sexual Knowledge and Sex Education: Forcible Sexual Behavior and Sexual Harassment
Section Review
1.   Describe some of the behaviors associated with the trauma of rape.

_____

_____

2.   Define and give an example of quid pro quo sexual harassment and hostile environment sexual harassment that involves something other than school.

_____

_____

Sexual Well-Being, Social Policy, and Adolescents
Guided Review
Five issues related to sexual well-being need to be considered: the (1) _____ of adolescent (2) _____ behaviors; the (3) _____ of sexual behaviors and other (4) _____-related behaviors; the (5) _____ of sexual behavior; the (6) _____ at which transitions take place; and (7) _____. Social policy needs to encourage (8) _____ sex education (9) _____ adolescents engage in sex. Studies indicate that healthy sexual pathways include practicing (10) _____, engaging in sexual (11) _____ rather than intercourse, engaging in sex and only in the context of a (12) _____ relationship. _____, and participating in (13) _____ behaviors in early adolescence. We need initiatives to reduce adolescent (14) _____ and educate adolescents about (15) _____. These programs should target (16) _____ members, as well as the adolescent mother and child.

Sexual Well-Being, Social Policy, and Adolescents
Section Review
Complete the table by listing the specific concerns involved in the five developmental issues related to the study of adolescent development.

Developmental Issue	Specific Concerns
Timing of Sexual Behaviors	
Co-Occurrence of Health-Related Behaviors	
Contexts of Sexual Behavior	
Timing of Sexual Experiences	
Gender and Sexuality	

Explorations in Adolescent Development

1. Briefly discuss three contraceptive health programs developed for adolescents.

    _____

    _____

2. What are the attitudes of young people in Holland and Sweden about sex and how to they learn about sex?

    _____

    _____

Adventures for the Mind

1. Caroline contracted genital herpes from an old boyfriend. When she started dating Charles, she told him she had the herpes infection and he broke up with her. Now she is dating Jeff and she is afraid to tell him about the herpes because she thinks he will also break up with her. She thought maybe she should just tell him to use a condom so she won't get pregnant, and then she won't need to mention the herpes. What do you think Caroline should do?

    _____

    _____

2. Based upon how you learned about sexuality, how do you expect to teach your children about sex? How do you want the schools to be involved in sex education for your children? Who other than parents and schools do you think should be involved in sex education?

    _____

    _____

Adolescence in Research

Concerning Whitman and colleagues' (1993) investigation of homosexual orientation in twins, state the hypothesis, the research methods (if known), the research conclusions, and the implications and applications for adolescent development.

_____

_____

Comprehensive Review

1. Sexual behaviors usually progress in the following order:
    a. kissing, oral sex, necking.
    b. petting, necking, kissing.
    c. intercourse, sexual adventure, oral sex.
    d. necking, petting, intercourse.

2. A _____ is a pattern involving stereotyped role prescriptions for how individuals should behave sexually.
    a. sexual bias
    b. sexual schema
    c. sexual role
    d. sexual script

3. Irresponsible sexual behavior such as unprotected intercourse is probably a reflection of
   a. cognitive immaturity.
   b. hostility against parental limits.
   c. vulnerability.
   d. parental stress or divorce.

4. An individual sexually attracted to both females and males is
   a. bisexual.
   b. homosexual.
   c. heterosexual.
   d. transsexual.

5. The most frequent sexual outlet for an adolescent is
   a. oral sex.
   b. sexual fantasy.
   c. masturbation.
   d. sexual intercourse.

6. As a drug store clerk, you are not at all surprised to find that condom sales are made most often to
   a. older adolescents.
   b. female adolescents.
   c. younger adolescents.
   d. sexually inactive adolescents.

7. Compared to those who wait to have children until they are in their mid- to late twenties, adolescent parents
   a. have a better chance of staying married.
   b. are less lonely.
   c. have fewer children throughout their adult lives.
   d. have lower incomes.

8. Infants born to adolescent mothers are more likely to
   a. be overweight.
   b. have an average survival rate.
   c. bond with their mothers.
   d. have low birth weights.

9. Sexually transmitted diseases are defined as those contracted through
   a. vaginal intercourse.
   b. vaginal intercourse and oral-genital contact.
   c. oral-genital and anal-genital contact.
   d. oral-genital and anal-genital contact and vaginal intercourse.

10. The most fatal sexually transmitted disease caused by a bacterium is
    a. syphilis.
    b. herpes.
    c. AIDS.
    d. gonorrhea.

11. The most common sexually transmitted disease among adolescents is
    a. chlamydeous.
    b. herpes.
    c. syphilis.
    d. gonorrhea.

12. If you come into intimate sexual contact with an infected person, your risk of contracting the disease is greatest for
    a. gonorrhea.
    b. syphilis.
    c. herpes.
    d. AIDS.

13. According to comparative studies, the rate of AIDS among adolescents are
    a. higher than adult rates.
    b. about the same as adult rates.
    c. lower than adult rates.
    d. not directly compared with adult rates.

14. According to the text, the average time between contracting the HIV infection and development of illness is
    a. six months.
    b. ten years.
    c. five to seven years.
    d. three years.

15. _____ are usually the main source of an adolescent's sexual information.
    a. Parents
    b. Schools
    c. Peers
    d. Literature

16. Which of the following statements concerning sex education in the schools is accurate?
    a. The majority of adults in the United States do not approve of sex education in the schools.
    b. Sex education programs are more likely to appear in high schools and junior high schools than elementary schools.
    c. The emphasis in sex education classes is on contraception and variations in sexual behavior.
    d. Most sex education programs consist of full-semester courses on human sexuality.

17. Belinda's boyfriend used a variety of psychological ploys and physical behaviors to coerce her into having sex, even though she had said no to him. This is referred to as _____ rape.
    a. power
    b. sexual
    c. controlling
    d. acquaintance

18. The factor that is most important in facilitating the recovery from rape is
    a. physical health.
    b. retaliation against the rapist.
    c. resumption of consensual sexual relations.
    d. social support.

19. The Young Men's Sexuality Awareness program seeks to encourage
    a. affection without intercourse.
    b. intercourse with affection.
    c. funding raising for elective abortions.
    d. adolescent males to marry their sex partners.

20. The purpose of sex education programs in such countries as Holland and Sweden is to _____ the experience of adolescent sexuality.
    a. promote
    b. discourage
    c. demystify
    d. simplify

Adolescence on the Screen
- *Chasing Amy* A young man is attracted to a girl who tells him that she is a lesbian. Actually she has had a wild heterosexual past and is manipulating the boy's attraction for her.

- *Taxi Driver* A New York City taxi driver tries to save a child prostitute.

- *The Summer of '42* A young boy has his first sexual experience with a kind, older women on whom he has a crush.

Adolescence in Books
- *Boys and Sex*, by Wardell Pomery (Delacorte Press, 1991), was written for adolescent boys and stresses the responsibility that comes with sexual maturity.

- *Girls and Sex*, by Wardell Pomery (Delacorte Press, 1991), poses a number of questions that young girls often ask about sex and then answers them. Many myths that young girls hear about sex are also demystified.

Answer Key

Key Terms
1. sexual script A stereotypical pattern of role prescriptions for how individuals should behave sexually. Females and males have been socialized to follow different sexual scripts.
2. **bisexual** A person who is attracted to people of both sexes.
3. **sexually transmitted diseases (STDs)** Diseases that are contracted primarily through sexual contact. This contact is not limited to vaginal intercourse but includes oral-genital contact and anal-genital contact as well.
4. **gonorrhea** Reported to be one of the most common STDs in the United States, this sexually transmitted disease is caused by a bacterium called *gonococcus*, which thrives in the moist mucous membrane lining the mouth, throat, vagina, cervix, urethra, and anal tract. This disease is commonly called the "drip" or the "clap."
5. **syphilis** A sexually transmitted disease caused by the bacterium *Treponema pallidu*, a spirochete.
6. **genital herpes** A sexually transmitted disease caused by a large family of viruses of different strains. These strains produce other, nonsexually transmitted diseases such as chicken pox and mononucleosis.
7. **AIDS** Acquired immune deficiency syndrome, primarily a sexually transmitted disease caused by the HIV virus, which destroys the body's immune system.

8.   **rape** Forcible nonconsensual sexual intercourse.

9.   **date, or acquaintance rape** Coercive sexual activity directed at someone with whom the perpetrate is at least casually acquainted.

10.   **quid pro quo sexual harassment** Occurs when a school employee threatens to base an educational decision (such as a grade) on a student's submission to unwelcome conduct

11.   **hostile environment sexual harassment** Occurs when students are subjected to unwelcome sexual conduct that is so severe, persistent, or pervasive that it limits the students' ability to benefit from their education.

Key People

1. B   2. D   3. F   4. E   5. G   6. A   7. C

Thinking About Adolescent Sexuality
Guided Review

1. normal
2. healthy
3. asexual
4. sexual
5. 3, 4, 5, 6, 7, 8, 9, and 10
6. ambivalent
7. sell
8. movies
9. TV shows
10. videos
11. lyrics
12. MTV
13. Internet
14. multifaceted
15. manage
16. intimacy
17. regulate
18. physical
19. social
20. cultural
21. preference
22. homosexual
23. heterosexual
24. bisexual
25. naïve
26. unassured
27. competent
28. adventurous
29. driven
30. reluctant

Thinking About Adolescent Sexuality
Section Review
Answers will vary.

Chapter	Concept
3: Biological Differences	Early pubertal maturation in girls may lead to early dating and sexual activity.
4: Cognitive Differences	Adolescent egocentrism may lead to sexual risk-taking.
5: Families	Prolonged family conflict and lack of parental monitoring can lead to problems in sexuality.
6: Peers	Peers and friends influence learning about and discussing sexual behavior.
7: Schools	Schools have a role in sex education.
8: Culture	Sexuality in the media is often presented to adolescents in an unrealistic way.
9: The Self and Identity	Sexual identity is one dimension of identity.
10: Gender	Pubertal changes may lead to boys and girls conforming to traditional masculine and feminine behaviors.

Sexual Attitudes and Behaviors
Guided Review

1. necking
2. petting
3. sexual intercourse
4. oral
5. increased
6. females
7. males
8. half
9. 18
10. sex
11. ethnicity
12. context
13. African-American males
14. inner-city
15. scripts
16. male
17. aggressive
18. female
19. limits
20. sex
21. love
22. early
23. many
24. using contraceptives
25. drinking/delinquency
26. low-income neighborhood
27. ethnicity
28. homosexuality
29. heterosexuality
30. bisexuality
31. continuum
32. genetic
33. hormonal
34. cognitive
35. environmental
36. Self-stimulation
37. contraceptives
38. low-income
39. older
40. middle income

Sexual Attitudes and Behaviors
Section Review

1.
   a. A boy or girl pressuring them.
   b. Thinking that they are reading.
   c. Wanting to be loved;
   d. To avoid being teased about being a virgin.

2.
   a. They don't usually tell their parents first.
   b. Mothers are usually told before fathers.
   c. Mothers are more likely than fathers to know about the same-sex attraction.
   d. Approximately 50-60 percent of lesbian, gay, and bisexual adolescents disclose to a sibling.

Adolescent Pregnancy
Guided Review

1. 1 million
2. eight/ten
3. unintended
4. declining
5. highest
6. health
7. mother
8. drop out of school
9. lower paying
10. low
11. well
12. personal fable
13. medically
14. psychologically
15. raising
16. close
17. sex
18. family planning
19. contraception
20. options
21. community
22. support
23. abstention

Adolescent Pregnancy
Section Review

1.
   1. The personal fable;
   2. anxiety about sex;
   3. gender-role definitions about what is masculine and feminine;
   4. sexual themes of music;
   5. sexual overtones of magazines and television;
   6. society messages that sex is fun, harmless, adult, and forbidden; f) early physical maturation;
   7. risk-taking behavior;
   8. egocentrism;
   9. inability to think futuristically; and
   10. an ambivalent contradictory culture.

2.

Program	Description
Teen Outreach Program (TOP)	Focuses on engaging adolescents in volunteer community service.
Girls, Inc.	Intended to increase adolescent girls' motivation and to avoid pregnancy until they are mature enough to make decisions about motherhood.
Growing Together	Series of workshops for mothers and adolescents.
Will Power/Won't Power	A series of sessions that focus on assertiveness training for 12–14 year old girls.
Taking Care of Business	Emphasizes career planning, as well as information about sexuality, reproduction, and contraception.
Health Bridge	Coordinates health and education services.

Sexually Transmitted Diseases
Guided Review

1. STDs
2. sexual contact
3. vaginal intercourse
4. oral-genital
5. anal-genital
6. "the clap"/ "the drip"
7. common
8. syphilis
9. most common
10. viruses
11. strains
12. cure
13. HIV
14. immune
15. low
16. adults
17. sexual contact
18. needles
19. blood transfusions

Sexually Transmitted Diseases
Section Review

1.
   a. A higher percentage of adolescent AIDS cases are acquired by heterosexual transmission.
   b. A higher percentage of adolescents are asymptomatic individuals who will become symptomatic in adulthood.
   c. A higher percentage of African American and Latino cases occur in adolescence.
   d. A special set of ethical and legal issues are involved in testing and informing partners and parents of adolescents.
   e. There is less use and availability of contraceptives in adolescence.

2.
   a. Having more than one sex partner.
   b. Sharing drug needles and syringes.
   c. Engaging in anal, vaginal, or oral sex without a condom.
   d. Performing vaginal or oral sex with someone who ingests drugs with needles.
   e. Engaging in sex with someone you don't know well or with someone who has several sex partners.
   f. Engaging in sex without a condom with an infected individual.

3.
a. Not having sex.
b. Having sex that does not involve fluid exchange.
c. Limit sex to one mutually faithful, uninfected partner.
d. Have sex with proper protection.
e. Don't use drugs, especially drugs associated with needles.

Sexual Knowledge and Sex Education: Forcible Sexual Behavior and Sexual Harassment
Guided Review

1. misinformation
2. peers
3. literature
4. mothers
5. schools
6. experience
7. 2
8. majority
9. sex
10. STDs
11. AIDS
12. school-linked
13. community health centers
14. rape
15. 95
16. Date (acquaintance)
17. Sexual harassment
18. widespread
19. quid pro quo
20. hostile environment

Sexual Knowledge and Sex Education: Forcible Sexual Behavior and Sexual Harassment
Section Review

1. The rape victim initially feels shock and numbness. She may show distress through words or tears. She may experience depression, fear, and anxiety for months or years. She may have not have normal sexual functioning for some time. She may make lifestyle changes, like moving to a new place or refusing to go out at night. One-fifth of rape victims attempt suicide.

2. Quid pro quo sexual harassment occurs when someone in a position of power threatens to give or withhold something in exchange for sexual contact. For instance, if an employer promises a woman a promotion if she will have sex with him. Hostile environment sexual harassment occurs when there is a severe, persistent, and pervasive unwanted sexual overtures or behaviors, such as constantly commenting on a woman's appearance or teasing her about having sex.

Sexual Well-Being, Social Policy, and Adolescents
Guided Review

1. timing
2. sexual
3. co-occurrence
4. health
5. contexts
6. age
7. gender
8. improved
9. before
10. abstinence
11. exploration
12. committed
13. preintercourse
14. pregnancy
15. parenthood
16. family

Sexual Well-Being, Social Policy, and Adolescents
Section Review

Developmental Issue	Specific Concerns
Timing of Sexual Behaviors	Being an early maturing girl is associated with having sexual intercourse.
Co-Occurrence of Health-Related Behaviors	Drinking, smoking, drug abuse, delinquency, and unprotected sex.
Contexts of Sexual Behavior	Poverty, neighborhood quality, school characteristics, and peer group norms.
Timing of Sexual Experiences	Cognitively and emotionally, young adolescents have difficulty handling sex and should not have sexual intercourse.
Gender and Sexuality	Males play a dominant role and girls' early experiences are often involuntary.

Explorations in Adolescent Development

1.   a.   The New Image Teen Theatre program presents contraceptive and sex education information through an improvisational theatre.

        b.   Another program utilizes a workbook containing role-playing exercises, quizzes, handouts, and homework assignments.

        c.   The Young Men's Sexuality Awareness Program is geared toward increasing male awareness of how to be affectionate without having sexual intercourse.

2.   Holland does not have mandated sex education, but adolescents can obtain contraceptive counseling at government-sponsored clinics for a small fee. The media also educates the public about sex, birth control, and abortion. Most Dutch adolescents use birth control. Swedish adolescents are sexually active early and the Swedes have a national sexual education program that begins at the age of 7 and continues to the age of 10 or 12. Teachers are instrumental in sex education.

Adventures for the Mind

1. Individual activity. No answer provided.

2. Individual activity. No answer provided.

Adolescence in Research

The hypothesis was that there was a genetic basis for homosexuality. They studied homosexuals who had twin siblings and investigated the sexual orientation of the siblings. Of the monozygotic twins (who are genetically identical), two-thirds of the siblings of homosexuals were homosexual themselves. Among dizygotic twins, who are not genetically identical, only one-third of the siblings of homosexuals were homosexuals. This finding supports a biological interpretation of homosexuality, but not entirely, for not all of the monozygotic twin siblings were homosexuals.

Comprehensive Review

1. d	5. c	9. d	13. c	17. d
2. d	6. c	10. a	14. c	18. d
3. c	7. d	11. a	15. c	19. a
4. a	8. d	12. c	16. b	20. c

◆ Chapter 12   Moral Development, Values, and Religion

Learning Objectives with Key Terms and Key People in Boldface

1.0   What is the Nature of Moral Development and Moral Thought?
-    **A.   What is Moral Development?**
        -    1.1   What is involved in moral development?
        -    1.2   What are the dimensions of moral development?
-    **B.   Moral Thought**
        -    1.3   What is the difference between Piaget's **heteronomous morality** and his **autonomous morality**?
        -    1.4   What is the concept of **immanent justice**?
        -    1.5   What does the development of formal operational thought have to do with adolescent moral reasoning?
        -    1.6   What is Hoffman's proposed **cognitive disequlibrium theory** of moral development?
        -    1.7   What is **internalization**?
        -    1.8   What is Kohlberg's theory of moral development?
        -    1.9   What are the differences between **preconventional reasoning, conventional reasoning,** and **postconventional reasoning**?
        -    1.10   What stage of moral reasoning is characterized by **heteronomous morality**?
        -    1.11   What stage of moral reasoning is characterized by **individualism, instrumental purpose and exchange**?
        -    1.12   What state of moral reasoning is characterized by mutual interpersonal expectations, relationships, and interpersonal conformity?
        -    1.13   What is the meaning of the social contract or utility and individual rights?
        -    1.14   What are universal ethical principles?
        -    1.15   What are the justice perspective and care perspective?
        -    1.16   What is social conventional reasoning?

2.0   What is Moral Behavior?
-    **A.   Basic Processes**
    -    **2.1   How is moral behavior determined by the processes of reinforcement, punishment, and imitation?**
    -    **2.2   What situational variations are involved in moral behavior?**
    -    **2.3   What did Hartshorne and May find about situational variation in moral behavior?**
-    **B.   Social Cognitive Theory**
        -    2.4   What is the nature of the social cognitive theory of moral development?
        -    2.5   What is the difference between moral competence and moral performance?
        -    2.6   What are the social cognitive theorists' criticisms of Kohlberg's theory of moral development?

3.0   What are Moral Feelings and Altruism?
-    **A.   Moral Feelings**
        -    3.1   According to Freud, what is the moral part of personality?
        -    3.2   How does the process of identification affect moral development?
        -    3.3   Why do children conform to moral standards, according to Freud?
        -    3.4   What did Freud mean by the **ego ideal** and the **conscience**?
        -    3.5   What do child-rearing techniques have to do with moral development?

3.6 How do love **withdrawal**, **power assertion**, and **induction** affect a child's moral development?

3.7 What is **empathy** and how does it contribute to moral development?

3.8 How are emotions interwoven with moral development?

B. Altruism

3.9 What is the nature of **altruism**?

3.10 How are reciprocity and exchange involved in altruism?

3.11 What is the role of **forgiveness** in altruism?

3.12 Is there a developmental sequence for the development of altruism?

4.0 What is Moral Education?

A. The Hidden Curriculum

4.1 What is meant by the **hidden curriculum**?

4.2 Who was John Dewey?

B. Character Education

4.3 What is character education?

4.4 What is the nature of moral literacy?

C. Values Clarification

4.5 What is the nature of **values clarification**?

D. Cognitive Moral Education

4.6 What is cognitive moral education?

4.7 Whose theory of moral development is the basis for many **cognitive moral education** programs?

E. Rest's Four-Component Model

4.8 What is Rest's four-component model of moral development?

4.9 What are **moral sensitivity**, **moral judgment**, **moral motivation**, and **moral character**?

5.0 What are the Nature and Characteristics of Values, Religion, and Cults?

A. Values

5.1 How are **values** defined?

5.2 How are adolescent values changing?

5.3 What is **service learning**?

B. Religion

5.4 What is the scope of religion interest in children and adolescents?

5.5 Is adolescence a special juncture in religious development?

5.6 What is Piaget's theory about the role of religion in development?

5.7 Are there links between religiousness and sexuality?

5.8 What is Fowler's life-span development view of the six stages of finding meaning in life?

C. Cults

5.9 What is the nature of cults?

5.10 Why do people join cults?

5.11 What is a cult's potential for abuse?

6.0 Explorations in Adolescent Development

6.1 What role can volunteering play in adolescent development?

7.0 Adventures for the Mind

7.1 Should a man who escaped from prison and became a model citizen be returned to serve his time? Should life support be removed from a young woman who is "brain dead"?

7.2 What are your values and where did they come from?

7.3 How have your efforts to make meaning of your life resembled or differed from Fowler's stages?

Key Terms

Write a sentence using each of these key terms by either defining the term or giving an example of it. For instance, you might write, "Altruism is..." or, "(give example) is an example of altruism." Compare your definitions with those given at the end of study guide chapter, and check your examples by referring to the text. Review the text for those terms you don't know or define incorrectly.

1. moral development

_____

_____

2. heteronomous morality

_____

_____

3. autonomous morality

_____

_____

4. immanent justice

_____

_____

5. cognitive disequlibrium theory

_____

_____

6. internalization

_____

_____

7. preconventional reasoning

_____

_____

8. heteronomous morality

_____

_____

9. individualism, instrumental purpose, and exchange

_____

_____

10. conventional reasoning

_____

_____

11.   mutual interpersonal expectations, relationships, and interpersonal conformity

_____

_____

12.   social systems morality

_____

_____

13.   postconventional reasoning

_____

_____

14.   social construct or utility and individual rights

_____

_____

15.   universal ethical principles

_____

_____

16.   justice perspective

_____

_____

17.   care perspective

_____

_____

18.   social conventional reasoning

_____

_____

19.   social cognitive theory of moral development

_____

_____

20.   ego ideal

_____

_____

21.   conscience

_____

_____

22. power assertion

_____

_____

23. induction

_____

_____

24. empathy

_____

_____

25. altruism

_____

_____

26. forgiveness

_____

_____

27. hidden curriculum

_____

_____

28. character education

_____

_____

29. values clarification

_____

_____

30. cognitive moral education

_____

_____

31. moral sensitivity

_____

_____

32. moral judgment

_____

_____

33.　moral motivation

_____

_____

34.　moral character

_____

_____

35.　values

_____

_____

36.　service learning

_____

_____

Key People
Match the person with the concept of adolescent development with which they are associated.

___	1.	Lawrence Walker	A.	Believed that adolescents develop an ideology as part of their identity.
___	2.	Jean Piaget	B.	Associated with social-cognitive perspective of moral development.
___	3.	Martin Hoffman	C.	Believes that parents play a role in moral development.
___	4.	Lawrence Kohlberg	D.	Believes that morality has social and interpersonal implications that are governed by internal cognitive and emotional processes.
___	5.	James Rest	E.	Believed that there were two types of morality, depending upon the age of the child.
___	6.	Robert Shweder	F.	Believed that moral education was the schools' hidden curriculum.
___	7.	Carol Gilligan	G.	Developed a six-stage model of religious development.
___	8.	Hugh Hartshorne and Mark May	H.	Studied value education in schools.
___	9.	Albert Bandura	I.	Thought that resolution of the Oedipus complex was associated with moral development.
___	10.	Sigmund Freud	J.	Developed the Defining Issues Test to measure morality.
___	11.	Erik Erikson	K.	Believes that there are three types of ethical orientation.
___	12.	Nancy Eisenberg	L.	Insists that girls' need for relationships is significant factor in their sense of morality.
___	13.	John Dewey	M.	Involved in large study of situational morality.
___	14.	Larry Nucci	N.	Developed a six-stage model of moral development, with three levels of moral reasoning.
___	15.	James Fowler	O.	Developed the cognitive disequilibrium theory.

The Nature of Moral Development and Moral Thought
Guided Review

　　Moral development involves (1) _____, (2) _____, and (3) _____ regarding (4) _____ of right and wrong. It has (5) _____ dimension and (6) _____ dimensions. How adolescents think about right and wrong involves their use of (7) _____. How they (8) _____, involves what they do in a situation. How they (9) _____ considers whether they feel guilt, as an example. Piaget was interested in how children (10) _____ about moral issues. He concluded that they do so in two distinct ways. (11) _____ morality is the first stage of moral development, occurring at (12) _____ to _____ years of age. In this view, (13) _____ and _____ are interchangeable and removed from the control of people. (14) _____ morality is displayed by children about (15) _____ years of age and older. The child become aware that rules and laws are created by (16) _____, and that a person's (17) _____ should be considered, as well as the consequence s of the behavior. The heteronomous thinker believes in (18) _____, meaning that if a rule is broken, (19) _____ will be handed down immediately. As adolescents become (20) _____ thinkers, they can introduce concepts of (21) _____, _____, and _____ into their definitions of religious identities. Martin Hoffman's (22) _____ theory, sees adolescents as faced with (23)_____ between moral concepts outside their family and neighborhoods, especially at school.

Lawrence Kohlberg is famous for his research involving moral (24) _____. From the answers interviewees gave, Kohlberg hypothesized three levels of moral development: (25) _____, (26) _____, and (27) _____. He believed that a key concept in understanding moral development is (28) _____. Like Piaget, Kohlberg believed that (29) _____ interaction has a large role in moral orientation. Kohlberg has been criticized for placing too much emphasis on moral (30) _____ and not enough on moral (31) _____. Others say that more attention should be paid to the way moral development is (32) _____. Some say that Kolhberg's dilemmas are (33) _____ and that his research is (34) _____ biased. Richard Shweder believes that there are (35) _____ ethical orientations or worldviews: those of (36) _____, (37) _____, and (38) _____. Carol Gilligan developed a (39) _____ perspective of morality that applies to girls, and one that she believed Kohlberg's theory does not adequately (40) _____. Gilligan believes that girls are more concerned for (41) _____ than are males, and they reflect this in their moral reasoning. Social conventional reasoning refers to (42) _____ about social (43) _____ and _____, as opposed to moral reasoning that stresses (44) _____ issues.

The Nature of Moral Development and Thought
Section Review

Complete the table by listing the main characteristics of each of Kohlberg's stages of moral development.

Stage	Characteristic
Preconventional Reasoning	
Heteronomous morality	
Individualism, instrumental purpose, and exchange	
Conventional Reasoning	
Mutual interpersonal expectations, relationships, and interpersonal conformity	
Social systems morality	
Postconventional Reasoning	
Social contract or utility and individual rights	
Universal ethical principles	

Moral Behavior
Guided Review

Behaviorists emphasize that children's moral behavior is determined by the processes of (1) _____, (2) _____, and (3) _____. The effectiveness of reinforcement and punishment depends on how (4) _____ they are administered. The effectiveness of modeling depends on the (5) _____ of the model, and the presence of (6) _____ processes enhances (7) _____ of the modeled behavior. Evidence indicates that many adults display a (8) _____ standard. What they (9) _____ about right and wrong does not always correspond with how they will (10) _____ in moral situations. Behaviorists also emphasize that moral behavior is (11) _____ dependent. The social cognitive theory of moral development emphasizes a distinction between adolescents' moral (12) _____ and moral (13)

_____. (14) _____ depend primarily on cognitive-sensory processes. Albert Bandura believes that moral development is best understood by considering a combination of (15) _____ and (16) _____ factors, especially those involving (17) _____-_____. Behaviorists believe that Kohlberg placed too little emphasis on moral (18) _____, but Kohlberg also mentioned (19) _____ factors.

Moral Feelings
Guided Review

Sigmund Freud's psychoanalytic theory describes the (1) _____ as one of the three main structures of personality, the (2) _____ and the (3) _____ being the other two. In Freud's theory, the moral branch of the personality is the (4) _____. It develops in early childhood when the child resolves the (5) _____ complex through (6) _____ with the same-sex parent. The superego consists of two main components, the (7) _____ and the (8) _____. Erik Erikson argued that there are three stages of moral development: (9) _____ moral learning in childhood, (10) _____ concerns in adolescence, and (11) _____ consolidation in adulthood. For Erikson, (12) _____ surfaces as the (13) _____ of identity in adolescence because it provides a (14) _____, assists in (15) _____ the present to the future, and contributes (16) _____ to behavior.

Piaget and Kohlberg did not think that (17) _____ provide any unique or essential inputs to children's (18) _____ development, reserving that role for (19) _____. Developmentalists identify three types of parental discipline: (20) _____ withdrawal, (21) _____ assertion, and (22) _____. Induction, in which the parent relies on (23) _____ and _____ for the consequences of the child's action, is believed the best for encouraging moral development.

Reacting to another's feelings with an emotional response similar to the other's response is known as (24) _____, which children develop at about the age of (25) ____ to _____ years. Not all adolescents, especially some (26) _____, show empathy. A recent study associated (27) _____ empathy with (28) _____ empathy. Today, many developmentalists believe that positive feelings like (29) _____, (30) _____, (31) _____, and (32) _____, as well as the negative feelings of (33) _____, (34) _____, (35) _____ and _____, contribute to moral development. However, these (36) _____ emotions are interwoven with the (37) _____ and _____ aspects of adolescent development. Having an unselfish interest in helping another person is known as (38) _____, an emotion that is often motivated by (39) _____ and (40) _____. An aspect of altruism is (41) _____, which involves being willing to release the injurer from possible (42) _____.

Moral Feelings
Section Review

1. What is the best way for parents to help children develop moral maturity, other than setting a good behavioral example?

_____

_____

2. Why is an adolescent more likely to forgive someone if his friends encourage him to do so?

_____

_____

Moral Education
Guided Review

(1)_____ called moral education in schools the (2) _____. (3) _____ are models of ethical or unethical behavior, classroom (4) _____ and (5) _____ relations transmit attitudes about (6) _____, _____, _____, and (7) _____ of others. Through its rules and regulations, the school (8) _____ gives the school its (9) _____ system. (10) _____ education involves directly teaching a basic moral (11) _____ to help prevent students from engaging in (12) _____ behavior. (13) _____ clarification means helping clarify what their lives are all about. Advocates say it is (14) _____-free, but critics say its content often offends (15) _____ standards. (16) _____ is based on the belief that students should learn to value things like (17) _____ and (18) _____. (19) _____ theory has been a basis for a number of cognitive moral education programs.

James Rest believes that moral development builds on four processes: moral (20) _____, moral (21) _____, moral (22) _____, and moral (23) _____. Rest's model is useful in comparing different approaches to (24) _____.

Moral Education
Section Review
1.   Name four character education movements and two books that promote character education.

_____

_____

2.   List and define James Rest's four basic processes of moral development.

_____

_____

3.   Complete the table by specifying how Rest's four-component model of moral development fits into the four different approaches to moral education.

Approach to Moral Education	Rest Component
Dilemma discussion approach	
Character education approach	
Sensitivity approach	
Communitarian Approach	

Values, Religion, and Cults
Guided Review
Values are (1) _____ and (2) _____ about the way people think (3) _____ be. Adolescents have recently been showing (4) _____ concern for (5) _____ and (6) _____ concern for the (7) _____. Most are more motivated to (8) _____ and are less motivated to develop a (9) _____ of life. Many adolescents show greater interest in their (10) _____ health and well-being. (11) _____ learning is a form of education that promotes social responsibility and service to the (12) _____. It takes education out into the (13) _____. Societies have invented (14) _____ schools, (15) _____ education, (16) _____ transmission of religious traditions, and (17) _____ teaching at home in order to introduce children to (18) _____ beliefs and try to insure that the children carry on (19) _____ traditions. Most adults adopt the (20) _____ teachings of their upbringing, but if a change occurs, it is likely to take place during (21) _____. One survey reported that (22) _____ percent of adolescents say that they (23) _____, and (24) _____ attended church within the past week. Adolescence is a (25) _____ juncture for religious development.

Most churches discourage (26) _____, so involvement in religious organizations enhances the probability that adolescents may have less (27) _____ attitudes toward premarital sex. However, adolescents who are involved in church and do have sex are less likely to (28) _____.

James Fowler proposed a theory of religious development that focuses on the (29) _____ to discover (30) _____ in life, either within or outside of (31) _____. He proposed (32) _____ stages of religious development that are related to the theories of (33) _____, _____, and _____.

(34) _____ foster the idea that there is only one right belief and set of practices. The purpose of cults are to (35) _____ the purposes of the leader. The purpose of religion is to (36) _____ the lives of its members and (37) _____. Most people who join cults are (38) _____ healthy. (39) _____ have depressive symptoms, and five percent have (40) _____. Many cult members are in a (41) _____ stage of their life. Many cult leaders portray themselves as inspired by or called upon by (42) _____. Cult members can be abused easily because they are usually (43) _____ and _____ isolated from the outside community.

Values, Religion, and Cults
Section Review

1.   List five ways researchers have found that service learning benefits adolescents.

_____

_____

2.   Complete the table by filling in the name of Fowler's stage of religious development, the period of development in which it occurs, and brief descriptions of the characteristics of the stage.

Name of Stage	Developmental Period	Characteristics
1		
2		
3		
4		
5		
6		

Explorations in Adolescent Development

What role can volunteering play in adolescent development? Give some examples of volunteer experiences and opportunities from the text.

_____

_____

Adventures for the Mind

1.   A man who had been sentenced to serve 10 years for selling a small amount of marijuana walked away from a prison camp six months after he was there. Twenty-five years later he was caught. He is now in his 50s and has been a model citizen. Should he be sent back to prison? Why or why not? At what Kohlberg stage is your response?

_____

_____

2. What are the five most important values to you? How did you get these values? Did they come from your parents, friends, teachers, or some event or experience?

_____

_____

3. As you progressed through the first four stages of Fowler's stages of religious development, how were your experiences different from or similar to his characterizations? Are you resolved about your choice of religious practice, or do you have some doubts?

_____

_____

Adolescence in Research

Concerning Hartshorne and May's research (1928–1930), state the hypothesis, the research methods (if known), the research conclusions, and the implications and applications for adolescent development.

_____

_____

Comprehensive Review

1. The three major aspects of moral development include
   a. stimulus, response, and consequences.
   b. thought, feeling, and behaving.
   c. individual, family, and society.
   d. id, ego, and superego.

2. Jean Piaget indicates that the heteronomous thinker
   a. believes that rules can be changed because they are merely conventions.
   b. recognizes that punishment for wrongdoing is not inevitable.
   c. judges the goodness of behavior by focusing on the consequences of the behavior.
   d. is usually a child between the ages of 10 and 12.

3. Martin Hoffman indicates that going to high school is associated with a dramatic change in moral reasoning because
   a. there is more opportunity for sexual exploitation.
   b. parental supervision is nullified.
   c. peer pressure to violate community standards is high.
   d. discussions reveal the variety of moral beliefs.

4. Lawrence Kohlberg argues that the distinctions between the three levels of moral reasoning have to do with
   a. the degree of internalization.
   b. the immediacy of the consequences for moral actions.
   c. the severity of punishments experienced.
   d. the social pressure of peers.

5. An adolescent at Kohlberg's conventional level of moral reasoning
   a. obeys rules in order to meet his defined obligations.
   b. obeys rules in order to avoid punishment.
   c. will follow rules if they are in his immediate best interest.
   d. has developed a social contract involving self-chosen ethical principles.

6. James Rest developed the Defining Issues Test because
   a. there were no available measures of moral reasoning.
   b. he found Piaget's tests too hard for adolescents.
   c. Kohlberg's stories were too difficult to score.
   d. he didn't know hat several other tests were available.

7. There is general agreement that Lawrence Kohlberg's theory
   a. is correct for adolescents, but not for adults.
   b. confused autonomy with autonomous morality.
   c. confused moral reasoning with moral behavior.
   d. underestimates the importance of culture.

8. Carol Gilligan has criticized Kohlberg's theory for
   a. overemphasizing people's connectedness and communication with other people.
   b. emphasizing moral behavior and ignoring moral reasoning.
   c. relying on a single method to assess individual's moral reasoning.
   d. understanding the importance of interpersonal relationships in moral development.

9. Adolescents' moral performance is influenced by
   a. skills.
   b. awareness of moral rules.
   c. cognitive-sensory processes.
   d. motivation.

10. Which theory distinguishes between moral competence and moral performance?
    a. psychosocial
    b. moral development
    c. cognitive social learning
    d. behavioral moral reasoning

11. Psychoanalytic theorists say that guilt develops when a child
    a. turns her hostility inward following the withdrawal of parental love.
    b. harnesses the drives of the superego and maintains the world as a safe place.
    c. becomes disillusioned with the moral and religious beliefs she acquired during childhood.
    d. participates in the feelings of an adult with whom she has identified.

12. The part of the superego that enables us to feel proud when we do the right thing, even if no one else will know, is the
    a. conscience.
    b. ego ideal.
    c. empathic aspect.
    d. altruistic channel.

13. Martin Hoffman believes that parents promote the moral development of their children and adolescents through
    a. love withdrawal.
    b. power assertion.
    c. induction.
    d. altruism.

14. The failure to develop empathy, if not altruism, is associated with
    a. excessive achievement orientation.
    b. vulnerability to cults.
    c. antisocial behaviors.
    d. chronic depression.

15. If a person can experience another's feelings and respond in a similar way, this is called
    a. pity.
    b. empathy.
    c. sympathy.
    d. understanding.

16. Which of the following is an example of altruism?
    a. sharing possessions
    b. resisting temptation
    c. saying thank you
    d. not eating with your fingers

17. Which term is used when a person "releases the injurer from possible behavioral retaliation"?
    a. altruism
    b. empathy
    c. sympathy
    d. forgiveness

18. Schools are one of the settings in which moral development occurs. The moral climate of the school is called the
    a. administrative morale.
    b. Damon Comprehensive Approach.
    c. hidden curriculum.
    d. classroom conscience.

19. According to a poll, _____ percent of the adolescents said that they prayed.
    a. 10
    b. 35
    c. 50
    d. 75

20. An adolescent refused to attend church, telling his parents that he would believe what he wants to believe, not what they tell him to believe. This adolescent demonstrates
    a. reflective faith.
    b. individuating-reflective faith.
    c. catastrophic conversion.
    d. moral fundamentalism.

Adolescence on the Screen
- *Clockwork Orange* An immoral and violent young man become the subject of an experiment to eradicate his violent tendencies.

- *Saving Private Ryan* Examines morality and the need for personal sacrifice in the context of war and military duty.

- *Stand by Me* Four 12-year-old boys trek into the wilderness to find the body of a missing boy.

Adolescence in Books
- *Meeting at the Crossroads*, by Lyn Mikel Brown and Carol Gilligan (Harvard University Press, 1992), provides a vivid portrayal of how adolescent girls are often ignored and misunderstood.

- *Postconventional Thinking*, by James Rest, Darcia Naraez, Muriel Bebeau, and Stephen Thoma. (Erlbaum, 1999), presents a neo-Kolhbergian analysis of moral development.

Answer Key

Key Terms
1. **moral development** Thoughts, feelings, and behaviors regarding standards of right and wrong.
2. **heteronomous morality** The first stage of moral development in Piaget's theory, occurring at 4 to 7 years of age. Justice and rules are conceived of as unchangeable properties of the world, removed from the control of people.
3. **autonomous morality** The second stage of moral development in Piaget's theory, displayed by older children (about 10 years of age and older). The child becomes aware that rules and laws are created by people and that, in judging an action, one should consider the actor's intentions as well as the consequences.
4. **immanent justice** Piaget's concept that if a rule is broken, punishment will be meted out immediately.
5. **cognitive disequilibrium theory** Hoffman's theory that adolescence is an important period in moral development, in which, because of broader experiences associated with the move to high school or college, individuals recognize that their set of beliefs is but one of many and that there is considerable debate about what is right and wrong.
6. **internalization** The developmental change from behavior that is externally controlled to behavior that is controlled by internal standards and principles.
7. **preconventional reasoning** The lowest level in Kohlberg's theory of moral development. The individual shows no internalization of moral values—moral reasoning is controlled by external rewards and punishment.
8. **heteronomous morality** Is the first stage in Kohlberg's theory. At this stage, moral thinking is often tied to punishment.
9. **individualism, instrumental purpose, and exchange** The second Kolhberg stage of moral development. At this stage, individuals pursue their own interests but also let others do the same.
10. **conventional reasoning** The second, or intermediate, level in Kohlberg's theory of moral development. Internalization is intermediate. Individuals abide by certain standards (internal), but they are the standards of others (external), such as parents or the laws of society
11. **mutual interpersonal expectations, relationships, and interpersonal conformity** Is Kolhberg's third stage of moral development. At this stage, individuals value trust, caring, and loyalty to others as a basis of moral judgments.
12. **social systems morality** The fourth stage in Kohlberg's theory of moral development. Moral judgments are based on understanding the social order, law, justice, and duty.

13. **postconventional reasoning** The highest level in Kohlberg's theory of moral development. Morality is completely internalized.

14. **social contract or utility and individual rights** The fifth Kohlberg stage. At this stage, individuals reason that values, rights, and principles undergird or transcend the law.

15. **universal ethical principles** The sixth and highest stage in Kohlberg's theory of moral development. Individuals develop a moral standard based on universal human rights.

16. **justice perspective** A moral perspective that focuses on the rights of the individual; individuals independently make moral decisions.

17. **care perspective** The moral perspective of Carol Gilligan, that views people in terms of their connectedness with others and emphasizes interpersonal communication, relationships with others, and concern for others.

18. **social conventional reasoning** Thoughts about social consensus and convention, as opposed to moral reasoning that stresses ethical issues.

19. **social cognitive theory of moral development** The theory that distinguishes between moral competence—the ability to produce moral behaviors—and moral performance—those behaviors in specific situations.

20. **ego ideal** The component of the superego that involves ideal standards approved by parents.

21. **conscience** The component of the superego that involves behaviors disapproved of by parents.

22. **power assertion** A discipline technique in which a parent attempts to gain control over a child or a child's resources.

23. **induction** A discipline technique in which a parent uses reason and explanation of the consequences for others of a child's actions.

24. **empathy** Reacting to another's feelings with an emotional response that is similar to the other's response.

25. **altruism** Unselfish interest in helping another person.

26. **forgiveness** This is an aspect of altruism that occurs when an injured person releases the injured from possible behavioral retaliation.

27. **hidden curriculum** The pervasive moral atmosphere that characterizes schools.

28. **character education** A direct moral education approach that involves teaching students a basic moral literacy to prevent them from engaging in immoral behavior or doing harm to themselves or others.

29. **values clarification** Helping people to clarify what their lives are for and what is worth working for. Students are encouraged to define their own values and understand others' values.

30. **cognitive moral education** Is based on the belief that students should learn to value things like democracy and justice as their moral reasoning develops; Kohlberg's theory has been the basis for many of the cognitive moral education approaches.

31. **moral sensitivity** Interpreting situations and being aware of how our actions affect other people.

32. **moral judgment** Making decisions about which actions are right and which are wrong.

33. **moral motivation** Prioritizing moral values over other personal values.

34. **moral character** Having the strength of your convictions, persisting, and overcoming distractions and obstacles.

35. **values** Beliefs and attitudes about the way people think things should be.

36. **service learning** A form of education that promotes social responsibility and service to the community.

Key People

1. D	**4.** N	**7.** L	**10.** I	**13.** F
2. E	**5.** J	**8.** M	**11.** A	**14.** H
3. O	**6.** K	**9.** B	**12.** C	**15.** G

The Nature of Moral Development and Moral Thought
Guided Review

1. thoughts
2. feelings
3. behaviors
4. standards
5. interpersonal
7. reassuring
8. behave
9. feel
10. think
11. heteronomous
12. 4/7
13. justice/rules
14. Autonomous
15. 10
16. people

17. intentions
18. immanent justice
19. justice
20. formal operational
21. belief/intelligence/faith
22. cognitive disequilibrium theory
23. contradictions
24. dilemmas
25. preconventional
26. conventional
27. postconventional
28. internalization
29. peer
30. reasoning

31. behavior
32. assessed
33. unrealistic
34. biased
35. three
36. autonomy
37. community
38. divinity
39. care
40. address
41. relationships
42. thoughts
43. consensus/convention
44. ethical

The Nature of Moral Development and Thought
Section Review

Stage	Characteristic
Preconventional Reasoning	Individual shows no internalization of moral values; moral reasoning is controlled by external rewards and punishment.
Heteronomous morality	Moral thinking is tied to punishment.
Individualism, instrumental purpose, and exchange	Individuals pursue their own interests but let others do the same.
Conventional Reasoning	Internalization is intermediate. Individuals abide by certain internal standards, but they are the standards of others, such as parents or the laws of society.
Mutual interpersonal expectations, relationships, and interpersonal conformity	Individuals value trust, caring, and loyalty to others as a basis of moral judgment.
Social systems morality	Moral judgments are based on understanding the social order, law, justice, and duty.
Postconventional Reasoning	Morality is completely internalized and is not based on others' standards. The individual recognizes alternative moral courses, explores the options, and then decides on a personal moral code.
Social contract or utility and individual rights	Individuals reason that values, rights, and principles undergird or transcend the law.
Universal ethical principles	The person has developed a moral standard based on universal human rights.

Moral Behavior
Guided Review

1. reinforcement
2. punishment
3. imitation
4. consistently
5. characteristics
6. cognitive
7. retention
8. double
9. think
10. act
11. situationally
12. competence
13. performance
14. competence
15. social
16. cognitive
17. self-control
18. behavior
19. extramoral

Moral Feelings
Guided Review

1. superego
2. id
3. ego
4. superego
5. Oedipus
6. identifying
7. ego ideal
8. conscience
9. specific
10. ideological
11. ethical
12. ideology
13. guardian
14. sense of purpose
15. tying
16. meaning
17. parents
18. moral
19. peers
20. love withdrawal
21. power assertion
22. induction
23. reason/explanation
24. empathy
25. 10/12
26. delinquent
27. parental
28. adolescent
29. empathy
30. sympathy
31. admiration
32. self-esteem
33. anger
34. outrage
35. shame/guilt
36. moral
37. cognitive/social
38. altruism
39. reciprocity
40. exchange
41. forgiveness
42. behavioral retaliation

Moral Feelings
Section Review

1. Trying to probe and elicit their child's opinions, in a general Socratic style, instead of giving too much information that may come across as preaching or lecturing.

2. It is often difficult for the victim of harm to try to take steps towards forgiveness. His friends can encourage him to consider why that might be the better response.

Moral Education
Guided Review

1. John Dewey
2. hidden curriculum
3. Teachers
4. rules
5. peers
6. cheating/lying/stealing
7. consideration
8. Administration
9. moral
10. character
11. literacy
12. immoral
13. values
14. value
15. community
16. Cognitive moral education
17. democracy
18. justice
19. Kohlberg's
20. sensitivity
21. judgment
22. motivation
23. character
24. moral education

Moral Education
Section Review

1. Character Education Partnership, Character Education Network, Aspen Declaration on Character Education, and Character Counts. Books include William Bennett's *Book of Virtues* (1993) and William Damon's *Greater Expectations* (1995).

2.
   a. Moral sensitivity involves interpreting situations and being aware of how our actions affect other people.
   b. Moral judgment involves making decisions about which actions are right and wrong.
   c. Moral motivation involves prioritizing moral values over other personal values.
   d. Moral character involves having the strength of your convictions and overcoming distractions and obstacles.

3.

Approach to Moral Education	Rest Component
Dilemma discussion approach	Moral judgment
Character education approach	Moral character
Sensitivity approach	Moral sensitivity
Communitarian Approach	Moral motivation

Values, Religion, and Cults
Guided Review

1. beliefs
2. attitudes
3. things should
4. increased
5. personal well-being
6. decreased
7. well-being of others
8. be well off financially
9. meaningful philosophy
10. physical
11. service
12. community
13. community
14. Sunday
15. parochial
16. tribal
17. religious
18. religious
19. religious
20. religious
21. adolescence
22. three-fourths
23. pray
24. one-half
25. critical
26. premarital
27. permissive
28. contraception
29. motivation
30. meaning
31. religion
32. six
33. Erikson/Piaget/Kolhberg
34. Cults
35. serve
36. better
37. nonmembers
38. psychologically
39. One-third
40. major psychological problems
41. transitional
42. God
43. physically/socially

Values, Religion, and Cults
Section Review

1.
   a. Their grades improve.
   b. They become more motivated.
   c. They set goals.
   d. Their self-esteem improves.
   e. They become less alienated.
   f. They reflect on society's political organization and moral order.

2.   Complete the table by filling in the name of Fowler's stage of religious development, the period of
       development in which it occurs, and brief descriptions of the characteristics of the stage.

Name of Stage	Developmental Period	Characteristics
1. Intuitive-Projective Faith	Early Childhood	Intuitive images of good and evil; fantasy and reality are the same.
2. Mythical-Literal Faith	Middle/Late Childhood	More logical, concrete thought; literal interpretation of religious stories.
3. Synthetic-Conventional Faith	Early Adolescence	More abstract thought; conformity to religious beliefs of others.
4. Individuative-Reflective Faith	Late Adolescence, Early Adulthood	Capable of taking full responsibility for religious beliefs; In-depth exploration of one's own values and beliefs.
5. Conjunctive Faith	Middle Adulthood	More open to opposing viewpoints; awareness of one's finiteness and limitations.
6. Universalizing Faith	Middle and Late Adulthood	Transcending belief systems to achieve a sense of oneness with all.

Explorations in Adolescent Development

Adolescents can express their views at public forums, churches, and town members. Some community boards, offices, and agencies have youth advisory councils. Many cities have volunteer programs where adolescents may receive special training and even a stipend or money toward college. The National Association of Service and Conservation Corps is a clearing house for youth corps programs. Youth Service American is a source of information about service learning programs. Even poorer communities have commitments to community service.

Adventures for the Mind

1.   Individual activity. No answers provided.

2.   Individual activity. No answers provided.

3.   Individual activity. No answers provided.

Adolescence in Research

The hypothesis was that moral behavior is situationally dependent. The researchers observed the moral responses of 11,000 children and adolescents who were given the opportunity to lie, cheat, and steal in a variety of circumstances—at home, school, social events, and in athletics. Situation-specific moral behavior was the rule. Adolescents were more likely to cheat when their friends pressured them to do so and when the chances of getting caught were slim

Comprehensive Review

1. b	3. d	5. a	7. d	9. d	11. a	13. c	15. b	17. d	19. d
2. c	4. a	6. c	8. d	10. c	12. b	14. c	16. a	18. c	20. b

Chapter 13   Achievement, Careers, and Work

Learning Objectives with Key Terms and Key People in Boldface

1.0   **What is the Importance of Adolescence in Achievement and Extrinsic and Intrinsic Motivation?**
    A.   **The Importance of Adolescence in Achievement**
        1.1   What is the importance of adolescence in achievement?
        1.2   What impact do social and academic pressures have on adolescents?
        1.3   What determines how well adolescents adapt to social and academic pressures?
    B.   **Extrinsic and Intrinsic Motivation**
        1.4   What is extrinsic motivation?
        1.5   What is intrinsic motivation?
        1.6   What are the self-determining characteristics of intrinsic motivation?
        1.7   What can be done to increase students' internal motivation?
        1.8   What is flow?
        1.9   When is flow most likely to occur?
        1.10   How do rewards affect performance?
        1.11   For what purpose should rewards be used?

2.0   **What are Attribution, Mastery, Motivation, Self-Efficacy, Goal-Setting, Planning, Self-Monitoring, and Anxiety?**
    A.   **Attribution**
        2.1   What is attribution theory?
        2.2   What, according to Weidner, are the three dimensions of causal attributions?
        2.3   What are locus, stability, and controllability?
        2.4   How do these dimensions produce different explanations of failures?
    B.   **Mastery Motivation**
        2.5   What is mastery motivation?
        2.6   What is meant by helpless orientation?
        2.7   What is performance orientation?
    C.   **Self-Efficacy**
        2.8   What is **self-efficacy**?
        2.9   What is Bandura's view of self-efficacy?
        2.10   What is Schunk's view of self-efficacy?
        2.11   What are some educational applications for self-efficacy?
    D.   **Goal-Setting, Planning, and Self-Monitoring**
        2.12   How does goal-setting benefit students' self-efficacy and achievement?
        2.13   How do Dweck and Nicholls define goals?
        2.14   What are the characteristics of a good planner?
        2.15   What is self-monitoring?
    E.   **Anxiety**
        2.16   What is the nature of **anxiety**?
        2.17   Where does high anxiety come from?
        2.18   What can be done to help students cope with anxiety?

3.0 **What Roles Do Ethnicity and Culture Play in Achievement? How Can Hard-To-Reach and Low-Achieving Students Be Motivated?**

    A. **Ethnicity and Culture**

        3.1   What are the respective roles of ethnicity and culture in achievement?

        3.2   Why is it important to consider diversity of achievement within an ethnic group?

        3.3   How do American adolescents size up against their Asian counterparts in terms of achievement?

    B. **Motivating Hard-To-Reach, Low-Achieving Students**

        3.4   What are the characteristics of the discouraged student?

        3.5   What does it take to reach a discouraged student?

        3.6   What is **failure syndrome** and where does it come from?

        3.7   What strategies benefit adolescents who are motivated to protect self-worth and avoid failure?

        3.8   What is **self-handicapping**?

4.0 **What are the Components of Career Development?**

    A. **Theories of Career Development**

        4.1   What are the three theories of career development?

        4.2   What are the characteristics of Ginzberg's **developmental career choice theory**?

        4.3   What are the characteristics of Super's vocational **career self-concept theory**?

        4.4   What is the nature of Holland's **personality type theory** of career development?

    B. **Cognitive Factors**

        4.5   What are the cognitive dimensions of career development?

        4.6   What are the roles of exploration, decision making, and planning in adolescent career development?

    C. **Social Contexts**

        4.7   What are the most important social contexts that influence career development?

        4.8   What roles do socioeconomic status, parents and peers, schools, gender, and ethnicity play in career development?

5.0 **What Is The Nature of Work?**

    A. **Sociohistorical Contexts**

        5.1   How likely are adolescents to hold full-time jobs today?

        5.2   How many adolescents work part-time?

    B. **Advantages and Disadvantages of Part-Time Work**

        5.3   What are the advantages of part-time work for adolescents?

        5.4   What are the disadvantages of part-time work for adolescents?

    C. **The Transition from School to Work**

        5.5   What are the rates of adolescent unemployment?

        5.6   What can be done to bridge the gap between school and work?

    D. **Work/Career-Based Learning**

        5.7   What is career-based learning?

        5.8   What new types of high schools exemplify a college-and-career approach?

        5.9   What are single-theme schools?

        5.10   What are schools-within-schools?

        5.11   What are majors, clusters, or pathways in the school curriculum?

6.0 **Explorations in Adolescence**

        6.1   What was the nature of Jaime Escalante's experience teaching math in an East Los Angeles high school in the 1970s?

7.0   Adventures for the Mind

7.1   How did you handle achievement challenges in middle school and high school? What do you wish you had done differently?

7.2   What are your career dreams and how do they related to your long- and short-term career goals?

Key Terms

Write a sentence using each of these key terms by either defining the term or giving an example of it. For instance, you might write, "Extrinsic motivation is..." or, "(give example) is an example of extrinsic motivation." Compare your definitions with those given at the end of study guide chapter, and check your examples by referring to the text. Review the text for those terms you don't know or define incorrectly.

1.   extrinsic motivation

_____

_____

2.   intrinsic motivation

_____

_____

3.   flow

_____

_____

4.   attribution theory

_____

_____

5.   mastery orientation

_____

_____

6.   helpless orientation

_____

_____

7.   performance orientation

_____

_____

8.   self-efficacy

_____

_____

9. anxiety

_____

_____

10. failure syndrome

_____

_____

11. self-handicapping strategies

_____

_____

12. developmental career choice theory

_____

_____

13. career self-concept theory

_____

_____

14. personality type theory

_____

_____

Key People
Match the person with the concept of adolescent development with which they are associated.

___	1.	Jere Brophy	A. Examined the work experience of California students
___	2.	Mihalyi Csikszentmihalyi	B. Believes that today's parents are pressuring adolescents to achieve too much
___	3.	Bernard Weiner	C. Proponent of the career self-concept theory
___	4.	Carol Dweck	D. Believes that parent child relations play an important role in occupation selection
___	5.	Albert Bandura	E. Credited with the development of the personality type theory of career development
___	6.	Dale Schunk	F. Conceptualized the developmental career choice theory
___	7.	Sandra Graham	G. Studies cross-cultural comparisons of school performance
___	8.	Harold Stevenson	H. Believes that self-efficacy influences a student's choice of tasks
___	9.	Martin Covington	I. Believes that self-efficacy is a critical factor in student development
___	10.	Eli Ginzberg	J. Studies ethnic differences in achievement
___	11.	Donald Super	K. Proposed strategies that teachers can use to help adolescents protect self-worth and avoid failure
___	12.	John Holland	L. Believes that adolescents have either mastery orientation or helpless orientation
___	13.	David Elkind	M. Developed strategies for improving motivation of hard-to-teach and low-achieving adolescents
___	14.	Anna Roe	N. Theorized about the three dimensions of causal attribution
___	15.	Ellen Greenberger and Laurence Steinberg	O. Uses the term "flow" to refer to optimal experiences in life

The Importance of Adolescence in Achievement
Guided Review

Adolescence is a (1) _____ in achievement. New (2) _____ and _____ pressures force adolescents towards different (3) _____ that often involve more (4) _____. Whether or not adolescents effectively adapt to these new pressures is determined, in part, by (5) _____, _____, and _____ factors. Adolescent's achievement is due to much more than their (6) _____ ability. The behavioral perspective of achievement emphasizes the importance of (7) _____ motivation achievement. The (8) _____ and _____ approaches stress the importance of intrinsic motivation in achievement. Extrinsic motivation involves (9) _____ incentives such as (10) _____ and _____. Intrinsic motivation is based on (11) _____ factors such as (12) _____, (13) _____, (14) _____, and (15) _____. Mihalyi Csikszentmihalyi uses the term (16) _____ to describe optimal experiences in life. It occurs most often when people develop a sense of (17) _____ and are absorbed in a state of (18) _____ while they engage in an activity. Flow is most likely to occur in areas in which adolescents are (19) _____ and perceive themselves as having a (20) _____. (21) _____ can actually undermine learning, but they can have two good uses: to (22) _____ behavior and as (23) _____ about mastery. (24) _____ feedback can carry information that students are (25) _____ and this can undermine (26) _____ motivation.

The Importance of Adolescence in Achievement
Section Review

1. Complete the table by filling in the outcomes for each of the combinations of students' perceived level of skill and challenge.

Students' Perceived Level of Skill

Perceived Level of Challenge	Low	High
Low		
High		

2. Complete the table by listing students' reasons for failure that correspond with the given combination of Weiner's three main categories of attributions: locus (internal-external), stability (stable-unstable), and controllability (controllable-uncontrollable).

Combination of Causal Attributes	Reason Students Give for Failure
Internal-Stable-Uncontrollable	
Internal-Stable-Controllable	
Internal-Unstable-Uncontrollable	
Internal-Unstable-Controllable	
External-Stable-Uncontrollable	
External-Stable-Controllable	
External-Unstable-Uncontrollable	
External-Unstable-Controllable	

3. Compare and contrast the concerns of adolescents with (1) ego-involved goals, (2) task-involved goals, and (3) work-avoidant goals.

_____

_____

Attribution, Mastery Motivation, Self-Efficacy, Goal-Setting, Planning, Self-Monitoring and Anxiety Guided Review

(1)_____ theory states that individuals are motivated to understand the (2) _____ causes of their own behavior or performance. Attributions are (3) _____ of outcomes. Bernard Weiner identified there dimensions of causal attributions: (4) _____, which refers to whether the cause is (5) _____ or _____ to the actor; (6) _____, which focuses on the extent to which the cause (7) _____ or _____, and (8) _____, concerning the extent to which the individual can control the cause. (9) _____ motivation is closely related to intrinsic motivation and attribution. Mastery is one of the three types of achievement orientation. The other two are (10) _____ and (11) _____. Adolescents with mastery orientation focus on the (12) _____ rather than on their (13) _____. Adolescents with a helpless orientation focus on their (14) _____ inadequacies. Performance orientation involves being concerned with (15) _____ rather than _____. (16) _____ is the belief that one can master a situation and produce favorable outcomes. A teacher's (17) _____ will have a major impact on the quality of students' learning experience. Self-efficacy and achievement improve when adolescents (18) _____. Adolescents needs both (19) _____- and _____-term goals. They also need to set (20) _____ goals, which are commitments to (21) _____. In addition to setting goals, adolescents need to (22) _____ how to (23) _____ their goals and (24) _____ how well they are (25) _____ to their plan.

(26) _____ is a vague, highly unpleasant feeling of fear and (27) _____. High levels of anxiety can (28) _____ the ability to achieve. Programs that are created to reduce an adolescent's high anxiety level emphasize (29) _____ techniques and replacing (30) _____ and _____ thoughts with (31) _____, _____-focused thoughts.

Attribution, Mastery Motivation, Self-Efficacy, Goal-Setting, Planning, Self-Monitoring and Anxiety Guided Review

1. Complete the table by listing behaviors associated with each type of failure-avoiding strategy.

Strategy	Behaviors
Nonperformance	
Sham Effort	
Procrastination	
Setting Unreachable Goals	
The Academic Wooden Leg	

2. Complete the table by listing the emphasis and main goals of each cognitive retraining method used to increase the motivation of students who display a failure syndrome.

Training Method	Primary Emphasis	Main Goals
Efficacy Training		
Attribution and Achievement Orientation Training		
Strategy Training		

3. List six strategies proposed by Martin Covington and his colleagues that teachers can use to help adolescents reduce their preoccupation with protecting their self-worth and avoiding failure.

_____

_____

Ethnicity and Culture
Guided Review

There is (1) _____ in achievement of ethnic minority adolescents. Too often the achievement of ethnic minority students have been interpreted as (2) _____ when they are simply (3) _____ different and (4) _____. Sandra Graham has found ethnic differences in the general (5) _____ theory, especially the (6) _____ theory. Ethnic minority students must deal with (7) _____, conflict between their (8) _____ and those of the majority group, and lack of (9) _____. Ethnic students may be in schools that are less likely to have high quality (10) _____ services, (11) _____ courses, and courses that (12) _____ students.

In cross-cultural comparisons, (13) _____ students consistently outperform (14) _____ students. Asian teachers spent more time teaching (15) _____ and Asian students were in school an average of (16a) _____ days a year compared to (16b) _____ days in the United States. (17) _____ parents have lower expectations for their children than do (18) _____ parents.

Hard-to- reach and low-achieving adolescents include (19) _____ achievers with low (20) _____; students with (21) _____ syndrome, and (3) adolescents obsessed with (22) _____ failures. Failure syndrome refers to having (23) _____ for success and (24) _____ at the first sign of difficulty. These adolescents often have low (25) _____ or (26) _____ problems. Adolescents motivated to protect their self worth by avoiding failure use strategies such as (27) _____, putting forth a (28) _____ effort, (29) _____, setting (30) _____ goals, and suggesting that they have an (31) _____ leg. These efforts to avoid failure are collective referred to as (32) _____ strategies that precede (33) _____ or _____. Teachers can use a number of strategies to help adolescents reduce their (34) _____ with (35) _____ their self worth and (36) _____ failure.

Career Development
Guided Review

Eli Ginzberg's (1) _____ theory says that children and adolescents go through (2) _____ career-choice stages: (3) _____, (4) _____, and (5) _____. Donald Super believes that individual's (6) _____ plays a central role in their career choice, and that during adolescence individuals first construct a (7) _____ that consists of five stages: (8) _____, (9) _____, (10) _____, (11) _____, and (12) _____. John Holland's theory is known as the (13) _____ theory. He believes that an individual's career choice should match his or her (14)_____, of which there are six types: (15) _____, (16) _____, (17) _____, (18) _____, (19) _____, and (20) _____. Criticisms of career choice theories focus on the fact that they may be too (21) _____, are not supported by sufficient (22) _____, and don't account for individual (23) _____ as people get older.

Cognitive factors involved in career chose include (24) _____, (25) _____ making, and (26) _____. Adolescents often approach career exploration and decision making with considerable (27) _____, _____, and _____. One of the most important aspects of career planning is awareness of (28) _____ requirements for a particular career. Career development is related to (29) _____ development. Social contexts that influence career development are (30) _____ status, (31) _____ and _____, (32) _____, and (33) _____. Special concerns exist about the lack of (34) _____ equipment in low-income areas, as well as the need to improve the interest of (35) _____ girls in pursuing careers in sciences and computer technology. Career development and math and science awareness interventions are also needed for the four distinct subgroups of American culture, (36) _____ Americans, (37) _____ Americans, (38)_____, and Native (39) _____.

Career Development
Section Review
Complete the table by listing the career areas that match each of Holland's personality type.

Personality Type	Career
Realistic	
Intellectual	
Social	
Conventional	
Enterprising	
Artistic	

Work
Guided Review

In the late 1800s, fewer than (1) _____ of _____ high school age adolescents were in school. Today more than (2) _____ out of _____ receive high school diplomas. In 1940, only (3) _____ of _____ tenth-grade males worked while attending school. Today, (4) _____ of _____ combine school and part-time jobs. The typical part-time job today involves (5) ___ to ____ hours of work per week. Most work in (6) _____, (7) _____ stores, (8) _____, and as (9) _____ laborers. Advantage of work including learning how the (10) _____, how to (11) _____ and _____ a job, how to (12) _____ money, how to (13) _____ time, how to (14) _____ in accomplishments and _____ goals. Disadvantages include giving up (15) _____ activities at school, (16) _____ with peers, and (17) _____, as well as balancing the demands of (18) _____, (19) _____, (20) _____, and (21) _____. (22) _____ participation and (23) _____ might decline if students work long hours. (24) _____ adolescents may face (25) _____ problems. To bridge the gap between school and work, there should be better (26) _____ of adolescent's work experiences and better (27) _____ counseling. Interest in (28) _____ learning in high is increasing. Schools that have career-based learning include (29) _____-theme schools, (30) _____ within _____, and schools that have (31) _____, _____, and _____.

Work
Section Review
List the William T. Grant Foundation Commission's (1988) recommendations for bridging the gap from school to work.

_____

_____

Explorations in Adolescent Development
What, in addition to math skills, did Jaime Escalante pass on to his students?

_____

_____

Adventures for the Mind

1.   What are your career dreams? With your dreams in mind, write down your specific work, job and career goals for the next 20 years, 10 years, and 5 years. Begin with the long-term goals first so that you can envision how to plan now to reach that "dream" career goal.

_____

_____

2.   What achievement-related challenges did you encounter in middle school and high school? How did you resolve them? Looking back, how might you have coped with these challenges in a more effective way?

_____

_____

Adolescence in Research

Concerning the research of Ellen Greenberger and Laurence Steinberg (1981, 1986), state the hypothesis, the research methods (if known), the research conclusions, and the implications and applications for adolescent development.

_____

_____

Comprehensive Review

1.   The motive with the greatest impact on the quality of adult life is
        a.   sexuality.
        b.   fear.
        c.   affiliation.
        d.   achievement.

2.   Aaron studies very hard. He concentrates on the sciences because he wants to become an environmental biologist. Aaron could be described as
        a.   motivated.
        b.   intelligent.
        c.   unrealistic.
        d.   a hurried adolescent.

3.   Attribution theory indicates that individuals attribute people's behavior to two causes:
        a.   direct and indirect.
        b.   inferred and observed.
        c.   internal and external.
        d.   scientific and psychological.

4.   A parent of an adolescent decides to join the community band. His daughter asks why he joined, since he won't make any money and few people attend the concerts. He responds, "I just like playing with the band." He is _____ motivated.
        a.   achievement
        b.   intrinsically
        c.   extrinsically
        d.   mastery

5. One key feature of the helpless orientation is
   a. attributing failure to internal causes.
   b. overestimating the role of effort.
   c. underestimating the importance of external incentives.
   d. fear of failure.

6. It is very difficult and dangerous to make sweeping generalizations about achievement motivation in ethnic minority adolescents because
   a. it has never been studied systematically.
   b. there is more variability within groups than among groups.
   c. all American groups score lower than Asian groups.
   d. social class is a more powerful predictor.

7. Japanese children often outperform American children in math and science areas, perhaps because all of the following are true except that
   a. Japanese parents have higher expectations.
   b. Japanese children spend more time in school each week.
   c. Japanese teachers are better trained in math and science.
   d. the Japanese school year is longer.

8. According to your text, the major reason for the "super achiever" image of Asian American adolescents (whose parents immigrated to the United States in the late 1960s to mid-1970s) is that
   a. their families have had more time to adjust to the culture.
   b. they are more intelligent.
   c. the males are encouraged to excel more than the females.
   d. they come from better-educated families.

9. According to Eli Ginzberg, youngsters between the ages of 11 and 17 years progressively evaluate three aspects of career choice. The order of occurrence is:
   a. values, capacities, and interests.
   b. interests, capacities, and values.
   c. interests, values, and capacities.
   d. capacities, values, and interests.

10. When individuals complete their education or training and enter the work force, Donald Super refers to this as the _____ stage.
   a. crystallization
   b. implementation
   c. stabilization
   d. specification

11. Your son always had a way with words and got along well with peers and adults. According to John Holland, he would prefer the job of
   a. social worker.
   b. bank teller.
   c. construction worker.
   d. sales manager.

12. The most important contribution made by John Holland's personality type theory to the career field was its
    a. consideration of the role of motivation on job performance.
    b. introduction of the conventional personality type.
    c. focus on psychological testing as a way of insuring job suitability.
    d. emphasis on linking individuals' personalities to the characteristics of given jobs.

13. In order to benefit from career guidance courses and to show more systematic career planning, students need
    a. accurate knowledge concerning the educational requirements of careers.
    b. self-directed opportunities to engage in career exploration.
    c. courses that are taught by trained guidance counselors.
    d. to be in the implementation stage of vocational choice.

14. When both parents work and seem to enjoy it,
    a. the parents try to live vicariously through their children's occupational choices.
    b. boys and girls learn work values from both parents.
    c. boys and girls aspire to higher status occupations.
    d. schools don't need to motivate students to get a good education.

15. Which kind of job employs the most adolescents in part-time work?
    a. unskilled laborers
    b. clerical assistants
    c. restaurant work
    d. retail

16. An adolescent female (16 years of age) who takes a part-time job can expect to
    a. make more money than males.
    b. work shorter hours than males.
    c. easily find a job as a newspaper carrier.
    d. easily find a job as a gardener.

17. Which of the following represents an advantage of working during adolescence?
    a. extensive on-the-job training
    b. improved ability to manage money
    c. improved school grades
    d. greater enjoyment of school

18. A number of adolescent problem behaviors are associated with part-time work, such as insufficient sleep and exercise. At what level of work does this begin to be apparent?
    a. 1 to 5 hours per week
    b. 6 to 10 hours per week
    c. 15 to 20 hours per week
    d. more than 20 hours per week

19. Which foundation in the United States has been very active in developing programs for unemployed youth?
    a. John S. Sage
    b. William T. Grant
    c. Richard B. Williams
    d. John F. Kennedy Education

20. Jaime Ecsalante was a _____ teacher at Garfield High School, in East Los Angeles, California. lack of family support.
   a. English
   b. geography
   c. math
   d. physical education

Adolescence in Movies
- *Cider House Rules* depicts an orphan who rejects the medical profession his foster father planned for him—until he chooses it for himself.

- *October Sky* is the true story of Homer Hickman, a West Virginia coal miner's son, who went from setting off rockets in his back yard to joining the NASA space program.

- *Stand and Deliver* is the story of Jaime Escalante's math classrooms in a largely Latino California high school.

Adolescence in Books
- *All Grown Up & No Place to Go: Teenagers in Crisis*, by David Elkind (Addison-Wesley, 1984), argues that teenagers are expected to confront adult challenges too early in their development.

- *Mentors*, by Thomas Evans (Peterson's Guides, 1992), describes the experiences of motivated individuals, from corporate executives to parents.

- *What Color Is Your Parachute?* by Richard Bolles (Ten Speed Press, 2000), is a popular book on career choice that is updated annually.

Answer Key
Key Terms

1. **extrinsic motivation** Response to external incentives such as rewards and punishments.
2. **intrinsic motivation** Internal motivational factors such as self-determination, curiosity, challenge, and effort.
3. **flow** Csikszentmihalyi's concept that describes optimal life experiences, which he believes occur most often when people develop a sense of mastery and are absorbed in a state of concentration when they are engaged in a activity.
4. **attribution theory** The concept that individuals are motivated to discover the underlying causes of their own behavior or performance in their effort to make sense of it.
5. **mastery orientation** An outlook in which individuals focus on the task rather than on their ability, have positive affect, and generate solution-oriented strategies that improve performance.
6. **helpless orientation** An outlook in which individuals focus on their personal inadequacies often attribute their difficulty to a lack of ability, and display negative affect (including boredom and anxiety). This orientation undermines performance.
7. **performance orientation** An outlook in which individuals are concerned with performance outcome rather than performance process. For performance-oriented students, winning is what matters.
8. **self-efficacy** The belief that one can master a situation and produce positive outcomes.
9. **anxiety** A vague, highly unpleasant feeling of fear and apprehension.
10. **failure syndrome** Having low expectations for success and giving up at the first sign of difficulty

11. **self-handicapping strategies** Some adolescents deliberately do not try in school, put off studying until the last minute, and use other self-handicapping strategies so that if their subsequent performance is at a low level, these circumstances, rather than lack of ability, will be seen as the cause.

12. **developmental career choice theory** Ginzberg's theory that children and adolescents go through three career-choice stages: fantasy, tentative, and realistic.

13. **career self-concept theory** Super's theory that individuals' self-concepts play a central role in their career choices and that in adolescence individuals first construct their career self-concept.

14. **personality type theory** Holland's belief that an effort should be made to match an individual's career choice with his or her personality.

Key People

1. M	4. L	7. J	10. F	13. B
2. O	5. I	8. G	11. C	14. D
3. N	6. H	9. K	12. E	15. A

The Importance of Adolescence in Achievement
Guided Review

1. critical juncture
2. social/academic
3. different roles
4. responsibility
5. psychological/ motivational/contextual
6. intellectual
7. extrinsic
8. humanistic/cognitive
9. external
10. rewards/punishments
11. internal
12. self-determination
13. curiosity
14. challenge
15. effort
16. flow
17. mastery
18. concentration
19. challenged
20. high degree of skill
21. Rewards
22. control behavior
23. information
24. negative
25. incompetent
26. intrinsic

The Importance of Adolescence in Achievement
Section Review

1.
Student's Perceived Level of Skill

Perceived Level of Challenge	Low	High
Low	Apathy	Boredom
High	Anxiety	Flow

2.

Combination of Causal Attributes	Reason Students Give for Failure
Internal-Stable-Uncontrollable	Low aptitude
Internal-Stable-Controllable	Never study
Internal-Unstable-Uncontrollable	Sick the day of the test
Internal-Unstable-Controllable	Did not study for this particular test
External-Stable-Uncontrollable	School has tough requirements
External-Stable-Controllable	The instructor is biased
External-Unstable-Uncontrollable	Bad luck
External-Unstable-Controllable	Friends failed to help

3. a. Ego-involved goals—They strive to maximize favorable evaluations. They are concerned with how smart they will look and how effectively they can outperform others
   b. Task-involved goals—They focus on mastering the task. They are concerned with how they can do the task and what they will learn.
   c. Work-avoidant goals—They want to avoid work. They are concerned with how to exert as little effort as possible when faced with a task.

Attribution, Mastery Motivation, Self-Efficacy, Goal-Setting, Planning, Self-Monitoring and Anxiety Guided Review

1. Attribution
2. underlying
3. perceived causes
4. locus
5. internal/external
6. stability
7. remains the same/changes
8. controllability
9. mastery
10. helpless
11. performance
12. task
13. ability
14. personal
15. outcome/process
16. self-efficacy
17. self-efficacy
18. set goals
19. short/long
20. challenging
21. commitments
22. plans to
23. reach
24. monitor
25. sticking
26. Anxiety
27. apprehension
28. impair
29. relaxation
30. negative/self-damaging
31. positive/task

Attribution, Mastery Motivation, Self-Efficacy, Goal-Setting, Planning, Self-Monitoring and Anxiety Guided Review

1.

Strategy	Behaviors
Nonperformance	Appear eager to answer but hope teacher will call on someone else; scrunch down in seat to avoid being seen by teacher; avoid eye contact; dropping out of school; excessive absences.
Sham Effort	Asking a question even if they know the answer; adopting a pensive, quizzical expression; feigning focused attention during class discussion.
Procrastination	Postpone studying for a test until the last time minute; take on so many activities and responsibilities that they have an excuse for not doing any of them competently.
Setting Unreachable Goals	Setting goals that are impossible to attain so that anyone would fail.
The Academic Wooden Leg	Admit to minor weakness; blame a bad test score on text anxiety.

2.

Training Method	Primary Emphasis	Main Goals
Efficacy Training	Improve students' self-efficacy perceptions	Teach students to set challenging goals; monitor students' progress; use adult and peer modeling; individualize instruction to student's knowledge and skills; keep social comparison to a minimum; be an efficacious teacher; view students with failure syndrome as a challenge, rather than a failure.
Attribution and Achievement Orientation Training	Change students' attributions and achievement orientation	Teach students to attribute failures to factors that can be changed; work with students to develop a mastery orientation; help them focus on achievement rather than winning or losing.
Strategy Training	Improve students' domain- and task-specific skills and strategies	Help students acquire and self-regulate their use of effective learning and problem-solving strategies; teach students what to do, how tot do it, and when and why to do it.

3. a. Give interesting assignments that stimulate curiosity.
    b. Establish a reward system so that all can attain rewards if they put forth the effort.
    c. Help adolescents set challenging but realistic goals and provide them with academic and emotional support to reach those goals.
    d. Strengthen adolescent's association between effort and self-worth. Minimize social comparison.
    e. Encourage adolescents to have positive beliefs about their abilities.
    f. Improve teacher-adolescent relationships by emphasizing teacher's role as a resource person who will guide and support learning, rather than an authority figure who controls student behavior.

Ethnicity and Culture
Guided Review

1. diversity
2. deficits
3. culturally
4. distinct
5. motivational
6. attribution
7. racial prejudice
8. values
9. positive role models
10. academic
11. advanced
12. challenge
13. Asian
14. American
15. math
16. 240/178
17. American
18. Asian
19. low
20. ability
21. failure
22. avoiding
23. low expectations
24. giving up
25. self-esteem
26. attribution
27. nonperformance
28. sham
29. procrastination
30. unreachable
31. academic wooden
32. self-handicapping
33. success/failure
34. preoccupation
35. protecting
36. avoiding

Career Development
Guided Review

1. developmental career choice
2. three
3. fantasy
4. tentative
5. realistic
6. self-concept
7. career self-concept
8. crystallization
9. specification
10. implementation
11. stabilization
12. consolidation
13. personality type
14. personality
15. realistic
16. intellectual
17. social
18. conventional
19. enterprising
20. artistic
21. simple
22. data
23. change
24. exploration
25. decisions
26. planning
27. ambiguity/uncertainty/stress
28. educational
29. identity
30. socioeconomic
31. parents/peers
32. schools
33. gender
34. modern technology
35. ethnic minority
36. African
37. Asian
38. Latinos
39. Native

Career Development
Section Review

Personality Type	Career
Realistic	labor, farming, truck driving, construction
Intellectual	math and science careers
Social	teaching, social work, counseling
Conventional	bank tellers, secretaries, file clerks
Enterprising	sales, politics, management
Artistic	art and writing

Work
Guided Review
1. 1/20
2. 9/10
3. 1/25
4. 3/4
5. 16/20
6. restaurants
7. retail
8. offices
9. unskilled
10. business world works
11. get/keep
12. marriage
13. budget
14. take pride/evaluate
15. extracurricular
16. social affairs
17. sleep
18. school
19. family
20. peers
21. work
22. school
23. grades
24. Ethnic minority
25. unemployment
26. monitoring
27. career
28. work-based
29. single
30. schools/schools
31. majors/clusters/ pathways

Work
Section Review
1. Implement monitored work experiences, like cooperative education, internships, apprenticeships, preemployment training, and youth-operated enterprises.
2. Expand community and neighborhood services so adolescents can volunteer as citizens.
3. Redirect vocational education to prepare youth for specific jobs.
4. Introduce incentives, like guaranteed postsecondary education, employment, and work-related training, so that students will work harder and be more successful in school.
5. Improve career information and counseling.
6. Use adults as friends to help students master stress and as mentors to open up for career opportunities.

Explorations in Adolescence
His commitment and motivation were transferred to his students.

Adventures for the Mind

1. Individual activity. No answers provided.

2. Individual activity. No answers provided.

Adolescence in Research
Greenberger and Steinberg examined the work experiences of students in four California high schools. Their hypothesis was not stated in the text, but they are said to have disproved some common myths about adolescents and work. They found that students got little on-the-job-training, and did not feel close to the adults with whom they worked. The found that work helped adolescents to learn how the business world works, how to get and keep a job, how to manage money, how to budget time, take pride in accomplishments, and evaluate goals. They found also that working adolescents had lower GPAs, which were lower the more hours they worked. They also felt less involved in school and were absent more. The significance for adolescent development is that students should be encouraged to work less hours and more states ought to adopt laws putting limit on the number of hours a week that students can work while school is in session.

Comprehensive Review
1. d
2. a
3. c
4. b
5. a
6. d
7. c
8. d
9. b
10. b
11. a
12. d
13. a
14. b
15. d
16. b
17. b
18. a
19. b
20. c

Section V
Adolescent Problems, Stress, Health and Coping

◆ **Chapter 14   Adolescent Problems**

Learning Objectives with Key Terms and Key People in Boldface

1.0   What Is Abnormality?
    A.   What Is Abnormal Behavior?
        1.1   What is the nature of abnormal behavior?
    B.   What Causes Abnormal Behavior?
        1.2   What are the biological, psychological, and sociocultural factors that cause abnormal behavior?
        1.3   What is the biopsychosocial model of abnormal behavior?
        1.4   What is the **developmental psychopathology** approach to abnormal behavior?
    C.   Characteristics of Adolescent Disorders
        1.5   What is the spectrum of disorders associated with adolescence?
        1.6   What are internalizing problems?
        1.7   What are externalizing problems?
        1.8   Are there gender differences in adolescent disorders?
        1.9   What developmental assets protect adolescents against disorders?

2.0   How Are Drugs and Alcohol Related to Adolescent Problems?
    A.   Why Do Adolescents Take Drugs?
        2.1   Why do people use drugs?
        2.2   What is **tolerance**?
        2.3   What is **physical dependence**?
        2.4   What is the nature of addiction?
        2.5   What are the characteristics of **psychological dependence**?
    B.   Trends in Overall Drug Use
        2.6   What was the nature of drug use in the 1960s and 1970s?
        2.7   What has been the trend of drug use in the 1980s and 1990s?
        2.8   How does adolescent drug use in the United States compare to that in other industrialized countries?
    C.   Alcohol
        2.9   What type of drug is alcohol?
        2.10   How much is alcohol used by American adolescents?
        2.11   What are the risk factors for adolescent alcohol use?
    D.   Other Drugs
        2.12   What drugs other than alcohol are harmful to adolescents?
        2.13   What are the nature and characteristics of **hallucinogens**, **LSD**, **marijuana**, **stimulants**, **cocaine**, **amphetamines**, **depressants**, **barbiturates**, **tranquilizers**, and **opiates**?
        2.14   What are the risks of using **anabolic steroids**?

6.0 Explorations in Adolescent Development

    6.1   Why do young people kill?

7.0 Adventures for the Mind

    7.1   If you were named as the Chair of the President's Commission on Adolescent Drug Abuse, what type of program would you first initiate and what would be the locus of the intervention?

    7.2   Why is risk-taking behavior likely to have more serious consequences today than in the past?

Key Terms

Write a sentence using each of these key terms by either defining the term or giving an example of it. For instance, you might write, "Abnormal behavior is..." or, "(give example) is an example of abnormal behavior." Compare your definitions with those given at the end of study guide chapter, and check your examples by referring to the text. Review the text for those terms you don't know or define incorrectly.

1.   abnormal behavior

_____

_____

2.   developmental psychopathology

_____

_____

3.   tolerance

_____

_____

4.   physical dependence

_____

_____

5.   psychological dependence

_____

_____

6.   hallucinogens

_____

_____

7.   LSD

_____

_____

8.   marijuana

_____

_____

9.   stimulants

_____

_____

10.   cocaine

_____

_____

11.   amphetamines

_____

_____

12.   depressants

_____

_____

13.   barbiturates

_____

_____

14.   tranquilizers

_____

_____

15.   opiates

_____

_____

16.   anabolic steroids

_____

_____

17.   juvenile delinquency

_____

_____

18.   index offenses

_____

_____

19.   status offenses

_____

_____

20.   conduct disorder

_____

_____

21.   cadre approach

_____

_____

22.   total student body approach

_____

_____

23.   major depressive disorder

_____

_____

24.   anorexia nervosa

_____

_____

25.   bulimia

_____

_____

26.   stress

_____

_____

27.   problem-focused coping

_____

_____

28.   emotion-focused coping

_____

_____

Key People

Match the person with the concept of adolescent development with which they are associated.

___ 1. Alan Sroufe

    A. Uses the term "developmental pathways" to discuss developmental psychopathology.

___ 2. Byron Egeland

    B. Found that anxiety problems in adolescence are linked with anxious/resistant attachment in infancy.

___ 3. Thomas Achenbach and Craig Edelbrock

    C. Analyzed research literature on resilience.

___ 4. Lloyd Johnston, Patrick O'Malley, and Gerald Bachman

    D. Found that adolescents from lower-SES background were more likely to have problems than those from a middle-SES background.

___ 5. Cheryl Perry

    E. Monitor the drug use of America's high school students through a project at the University of Michigan.

___ 6. Judith Brook

    F. Believes that resilient children triumph over life's adversities.

___ 7. Joy Dryfoos

    G. Believes that there are two basic coping styles.

___ 8. Gerald Patterson

    H. Interested in the interrelationship between adolescent problem behaviors.

___ 9. David and Roger Johnson

    I. Conducts research in the parental factors associated with antisocial conduct in boys.

___ 10. James Garbarino

    J. Proposed a developmental model of adolescent drug abuse.

___ 11. Anne Petersen

    K. Developed a comprehensive approach to curb adolescent cigarette smoking.

___ 12. Ann Masten

    L. Believe in teaching conflict resolution skills in schools.

___ 13. Norman Garmezy

    M. Believes that depression is a major problem in adolescence.

___ 14. Richard Lazarus

    N. Interviewed young men who were murderers.

Abnormality
Guided Review

Today, scientists who adopt a biological approach to mental disorders often focus on (1) _____ processes, such as (2) _____ and (3) _____ factors as the causes of abnormal behavior. In this approach, (4) _____ therapy is a frequent treatment. The medical model describes mental disorders as (5) _____ diseases with a (6) _____ origin. From this perspective, abnormalities are called (7) _____ illnesses, the individuals afflicted are (8) _____, and they are treated by (9) _____. Psychological factors that contribute to abnormal behavior are (10) _____ thoughts, (11) _____ turmoil, inappropriate (12) _____, and troubled (1) _____. Among the sociocultural factors that influence mental disorders are (14) _____ and _____ quality. Socioeconomic status plays a much stronger role in mental disorders than does (15) _____. The interactionist approach to abnormal behaviors, the belief that abnormal behavior can be influenced by (16) _____, _____ and _____ factors, is called the (17) _____ approach.

The field of developmental (18) _____ focuses on describing and exploring the developmental (19) _____ of problems and disorders. Links have been established between (20) _____ and (21) _____ behaviors in childhood and (22) _____ diagnosis in adulthood. Internalizing patterns consist of turning problems (23) _____, such as (24) _____ and _____, while externalizing problems consist of turning problems (25) _____, such as (26) _____ out and engaging in (27) _____ behaviors. The spectrum of adolescent disorders varies in severity in terms of the adolescent's (28) _____ level, (29) _____, and (30) _____ status. Some disorders are more likely to appear at one (31) _____ level than another. For instance, (32) _____ are more common in early childhood, while (33) _____ problems are more common in adolescence. The behavioral problems most likely to cause adolescents to be referred to a clinic for mental heath treatment were feelings of (34) _____, _____, or _____ and poor (35) _____. (36) _____ Institute has prescribed (37) _____ developmental assets that they believe adolescents need to achieve positive outcomes in their lives; (38) ___ of them are (39) _____ and (40)

_____ are internal. Adolescents with more assets engage in (41) _____ risk-taking behaviors, such as (42) _____ and _____ use, (43) _____, and (44) _____.

Abnormality
Section Review

Give an example of each of these internal and external assets identified by The Search Institute.

External Assets	Example
Support	
Empowerment	
Boundaries and Expectations	
Constructive Use of Time	
Internal Assets	**Example**
Commitment to Learning	
Positive Values	
Social Competencies	
Positive Identity	

Drugs and Alcohol
Guided Review

Individuals use drugs for (1) _____ reasons, most commonly for personal (2) _____ and temporary (3) _____. The price tag for drug use includes drug (4) _____, (5) _____ and _____ disorganization, and a predisposition to (6) _____ and _____ diseases. Adolescent drug use can lead to (7) _____, meaning a greater amount of drug is needed to produce (8) _____. Physical dependence is the (9) _____ need for a drug that is accompanied by (10) _____ symptoms when the drug is (11) _____. Psychological dependence is the strong desire and (12) _____ to repeat the use of a drug because of various (13) _____ reasons, such as a feeling of (14) _____ and a (15) _____ of stress. Since 1975, the (16) _____ Study has monitored drug use of American students. Though drug use is (17) _____, the United States still has the (18) _____ rate of adolescent drug use of any (18) _____.

Alcohol is a (19) _____ drug that acts on the body as a (20) _____. Alcohol is the most (21)_____ use drug by adolescents in the United States. Binge drinking is defined as having (22) _____ or more drinks in a row in the last _____. More (23) _____ than _____ report binge drinking. Risk factors for adolescent alcohol abuse include (24) _____, (25) _____ influences, (26) _____ relations and (27) _____ characteristics. Personality traits associated with alcoholism are being (28) _____ bored and needing (29) _____ and _____; being (30) _____ to avoid (31) _____ of actions and craving (32) _____, _____ reward for effort.

(33) _____ are drugs that modify an individual's perceptual experiences and produce hallucinations. They are also called (34) _____ or _____ drugs. LSD, or (35) _____, produces striking (36) _____ changes. Marijuana is a milder (37) _____ than LSD, and it comes from the (38) _____ plant. Its effects may be felt for several days because it is (39) _____ slowly. Stimulants increase the activity of the (40)_____. They include (41) _____, _____, _____ and _____. They can be (42) _____ addictive. Cigarette smoking is one of the most (43) _____ yet _____ health problems. Adolescent cigarette us is (44) _____. The most popular first-time brand of cigarettes is (45) _____. Peer disapproval of cigarette smoking has (46) _____ and the percentage of adolescents who see smoking as dangerous is (47) _____. Recent research suggests that smoking in adolescent years causes permanent (48) _____ changes in the lungs and increase the risk of (49) _____, even if the smoker quits.

Cocaine is a (50) _____ that comes from the (51) _____ plant. It is either (52) _____ or _____ in the form of (53) _____ or _____. Its damaging effects include (54)

_____, _____, or brain _____. About one in every (55) _____ high school seniors has tried cocaine at least once. Amphetamines are (56) _____ that are also called (57) _____ or _____. Though amphetamine use is declining, many students use over-the counter pills that contain (58) _____. Depressants are drugs that (59) _____ the central nervous system. The most widely used depressants are (60) _____, _____, and _____. (61) _____ are also dangerous depressants. Barbiturates, such as (62) _____ and _____, are depressants that reduce (63) _____ and induce (64) _____. Opiates are more commonly known as (65)_____, the most common forms being (66) _____ and _____. (67) _____ are drugs derived from the male sex hormone, (68) _____. Men and women who use them usually experience changes in (69) _____. There are both negative (70) _____ and _____ effects. Anabolic steroid use among adolescents is (71) _____.

(72) _____ relationships with parents is important in reducing adolescent drug use. Adolescents are most likely to use drugs when (73) _____ and _____ took drugs. A number of different programs have to be in place for effective (74) _____. The Midwestern Prevention Program used local (75) _____, (76) _____ education, (77) _____ programs and (78) _____ curriculum in the schools.

Drugs and Alcohol
Section Review
1. Identify the class of drugs by placing a "D" for depressants, "S" for stimulants, and "H" for hallucinogens.

_____1. marijuana

_____2. alcohol

_____3. barbiturates

_____4. amphetamines

_____5. tranquilizers

_____6. cocaine

_____7. narcotics

_____8. LSD

2. What seven criteria have been generally accepted as necessary for effective school-based drug abuse prevention programs?

_____

_____

_____

_____

_____

_____

_____

Juvenile Delinquency
Guided Review
Juvenile delinquency refers to (1) _____ unacceptable behaviors, (2) _____ offenses, and (3) _____ acts. Index offenses are (4) _____ acts, whether they are committed by(5) _____ or _____. Status offenses are less serious acts performed by (6) _____ under a certain age. Most states set the age of (7) _____ as the maximum for defining who is a juvenile.

Trying adolescents as adults is (8) _____ the crime rate. A recent proposal suggested that juveniles under the age of (9) _____ should not be evaluated as adults, but those (10) _____ and over should be. Individuals (11) ____ to _____ years of age should receive (12) _____-assessment to determine whether they should be tried as juveniles or adults.

(13) _____ is a psychiatric diagnostic category for behaviors such as (14) _____, (15) _____, (16) _____, cruelty to (17) _____, (18) _____ and _____, and excessive (19) _____. About (20) _____ percent of adolescents 10-18 years of age are (21)_____ each year.

Predictors of juvenile delinquency include (22) _____ identity, (23) _____ self-control, (24) _____ initiation, low commitment to (25) _____, and (26) _____ influence. (27) _____ status, lack of parental (28) _____, (29) _____ discipline and (30) _____ quality also are factors.

In a recent school year, (31) _____ percent of elementary and secondary school principles reported that one or more (32) _____ had occurred. (33) ___ percent of all public schools report one or more serious violent crimes, such as (34) _____, _____, _____ attack, or _____. Two types of conflict resolution programs operating in schools that contribute to violence prevention are the (35) _____ approach, in which as small number of students are trained to serve as (36) _____, and the (37) _____ approach, in which every student learns how to manage conflicts constructively by (38) _____ agreements and (39) _____ schoolmates' conflict.

Juvenile Delinquency
Section Review

1. Complete the table for listing the association with delinquency that matches each antecedent of delinquency.

Antecedent	Association with Delinquency
Identity	
Self-control	
Age	
Sex	
Expectations for education and school grades	
Parental influences	
Peer influences	
Socioeconomic status	
Neighborhood quality	

2. What are the four factors often present in at-risk youth that seem to propel them toward acts of violence?

_____

_____

_____

_____

3. What four recommendations for reducing youth violence were suggested by The Oregon Social Learning Center?

_____

_____

_____

_____

4.   a.   What are the 6 steps to negotiation taught in the Teaching Students to Be Peacemakers Program?

_____

_____

_____

_____

_____

_____

b.   What are the four steps to medication taught in the Teaching Students to Be Peacemakers Program?

_____

_____

_____

_____

Depression and Suicide
Guided Review

Adolescents are often referred for psychological treatment for (1) _____ or (2) _____. If an individual experiences characteristics such as (3) _____ and _____ for at least (4) _____ or longer and (5) _____ is impaired, the person may be said to have a (6) _____ disorder. Adolescents may manifest the symptoms in such ways as wearing (7) _____, writing (8) _____ with _____ themes, or being preoccupied with (9) _____ that has _____ themes. Adolescent depression may occur in conjunction with (10) _____ problems, (11) _____ disorder, (12) _____ abuse, or an (13) _____ disorder. Adolescent (14) _____ have a higher rate of depression than adolescent (15) _____. Depressed adolescents may experience (16) _____ in adulthood. Having a depressed (17) _____ is a risk for depression, as is having parents who are emotionally (18) _____, immersed in (19) _____, and who have (20) _____ problems. Depression is usually treated through (21) _____ therapy, such as (22) _____ and (23) _____ techniques, such as (24) _____ therapy.

(25) _____ is the third leading cause of death in 15-24 year-olds. It is helpful to think of suicide in terms of (26) _____, or _____ factors, and (27) _____, or _____- experience, factors. Proximal factors include the loss of a (28) _____ or _____, (29) _____ at school, or an unwanted (30) _____. Distal factors include a history of (31) _____ instability and lack of supportive (32) _____. (33) _____ is the most frequently cited factor associated with a adolescent suicide. A sense of (34) _____, low (35) _____, and high (36) _____ are also factors.

Depression and Suicide
Section Review

1.   For each appropriate behavior associated with suspecting that someone is suicidal, write "Y" for yes. For each inappropriate behavior associated with suspecting that someone is suicidal, write "n" for no.

___1.   Ignore the warning signs.

___2.   Ask, "Are you thinking about hurting yourself?"

___3.   Don't talk about it if the person brings it up.

___4.   Try to persuade the person to seek professional help.

___5.   React with horror, disapproval, or repulsion.

___6.   Tell them, "Everything is going to be all right."

___7.   Don't give false reassurances.

___8.   Try to assess the serious of their intent by asking questions about feelings, relationships, and how much thought they have given to suicide.

___9.   Once the person has sought professional help, back off and stay out of their life.

Eating Disorders, The Interrelationship of Problems, and Prevention/Intervention
Guided Review

Adolescent girls who feel (1) _____ about their bodies in early adolescence are more likely to develop eating disorders (2) _____ later, as are girls who were (3) _____ involved with their boyfriends and in (4) _____ transition. The three most common eating disorders in adolescence are (5) _____, (6) _____, and (7) _____. (8) _____ percent of today's adolescence are obese. Both (9) _____ and _____ factors are involved in obesity. (10) _____ percent of obese children have (11) _____ obese parents. The dramatic increase in obesity in the United States is due to the greater availability of food (12) _____ in fat, (13) _____ devices, and declining (14) _____. The pursuit of thinness through starvation is known as (15) _____. The societal factor most often held responsible is the current fashion image of (16) _____. Psychological factors include desire for (17) _____, denial of (18) _____, and a way of coping with (19) _____ parents. Physiological causes involve abnormal functioning of the (20) _____. A pattern of (21) _____ eating is known as bulimia. True bulimics make up less than (22) _____ of the college female population. Anorexics can (23) _____ their eating, while (24) _____ cannot. (25) _____ is a common characteristic of bulimics. Bulimia can produce (26) _____ and _____ imbalances in the body.

Researchers are finding that adolescent problem behaviors are (27) _____. Most at-risk adolescents have (28) _____ problem. Many at-risk adolescents engage in (29) ____ to _____ problem behaviors. The common components of successful interventions for at-risk adolescents are (30) _____, _____ attention, community-wide multiagency (31) _____ approaches, and early (32) _____ and _____.

Eating Disorders, The Interrelationship of Problems, and Prevention/Intervention
Section Review

Give several examples of adolescent problem behaviors that are interrelated.

_____

_____

_____

Stress and Coping
Guided Review

The response of individuals to (1) _____ and _____ that (2) _____ them and (3) _____ their coping abilities, is known as (4) _____. Stress is determined by (5) _____ factors: (6) _____, (7) _____, (8) _____ and _____ factors, and (9) _____ factors. Characteristics that help buffer children and adolescents from adverse conditions include good (10) _____ functioning, close (11) _____ to a _____ figure, and (12) _____ bonds. Children who can overcome adverse conditions are known as (13) _____. The adolescent's ability to (14) _____ with stress is important. Richard Lazarus believes that coping takes two forms: (15) _____ focused coping is used by people who (16) _____ their troubles and try to (17) _____ them. Emotion-focused coping means responding to stress in an (18) _____ way, especially using (19) _____ appraisal. Adolescents using this style might (20) _____ something, (21) _____ what is happening, (22) _____ that it is occurring, or (23) _____ at it. (24) _____, _____ attachments to others are important stress buffers. (25)_____, _____, and _____ can be important supports. Adolescents can often use (26) _____ coping strategy to help them deal with stress.

Stress and Coping
Section Review
Complete the table by filling in the characteristics associated with the nature of the source of resilience.

Source	Characteristics
Individual	
Family	
Extrafamilial context	

Explorations In Adolescence
What are some factors shared by recent young men involved in shootings and murders?

_____

_____

Adventures for the Mind

1. Imagine that you have just been appointed the head of the President's Commission on Adolescent Drug Abuse. What would be the first program you would try to put into place? What would be its main components? Would it be school-focused? What role, if any, would the media play in promoting the program?

_____

_____

2. Why are the consequences of risky behavior more serious today than they have ever been?

_____

_____

Adolescence in Research

Concerning Ann Masten's research concerning resilience, state the hypothesis, the research methods (if known), the research conclusions, and the implications and applications for adolescent development.

_____

_____

Comprehensive Review

1. _____ behavior is maladaptive and harmful to oneself or to others.
   a. Atypical
   b. Delinquent
   c. Idiosyncratic
   d. Abnormal

2. The medical model of abnormal behavior
   a. represents the biological viewpoint.
   b. is well documented; abnormal behavior is caused by diseases.
   c. has been discarded as too inflexible.
   d. does not seem to apply to adolescents.

3. Most developmentalists accept an interactionist approach to the study of abnormal behavior because
   a. the evidence shows that all disorders have both psychological and sociocultural causes.
   b. neither the biological nor psychological and sociocultural viewpoints can account for the complexity of problems.
   c. it's the only way to keep peace in the profession.
   d. adolescents tell us that the interactionist approach is best.

4. Which two behavioral problems are the most common causes for referring adolescents to mental health clinics?
   a. conflict with parents and substance abuse
   b. poor school work and depression
   c. suicide attempt and depression
   d. substance abuse and poor school work

5. Your textbook indicates that adolescents use drugs
   a. because Sigmund Freud used cocaine.
   b. as adaptations to changing environments.
   c. as aids to sexual gratification.
   d. because their parents use drugs at home.

6. An adolescent has been drinking white wine for about three years. He has noticed that over this period, it takes more and more wine to get "looped." This indicates
   a. the wine producers have decreased the alcoholic content.
   b. tolerance.
   c. the disorganized thinking associated with ingesting alcohol at a young age.
   d. his psychological dependence.

7.   The most widely used illicit drug is
     a.   marijuana.
     b.   cocaine.
     c.   barbiturates.
     d.   alcohol.

8.   Which of the following is not a risk factor for alcohol abuse?
     a.   secure attachment to parents
     b.   having friends who abuse alcohol
     c.   coming from an unhappy home
     d.   susceptibility to peer pressure

9.   The parents of an 11-year-old boy have been advised by a psychologist to provide more structure in the home, more caring support, and a more stimulating environment. According to Robert Cloninger, what are they trying to prevent in their youngsters?
     a.   eventually acquiring a sexually transmitted disease
     b.   attempting suicide
     c.   alcoholism as an adult
     d.   the youngster from eventually abusing his parents

10. Nembutal and Seconal are
     a.   stimulants.
     b.   hallucinogens.
     c.   opiates.
     d.   depressants.

11. Which of the new school-based drug prevention programs appears to be the most promising?
     a.   counselor-led programs
     b.   the use of testimonials from ex-drug users
     c.   social skills training
     d.   attendance at juvenile court when drug cases are heard

12. In the United States, theft, rape, and assault are _____ offenses.
     a.   status
     b.   index
     c.   matrix
     d.   conduct

13. Between February and September, Harry, a 14-year-old, ran away from home and got involved in a series of break-and-enter offenses. The parents say he is "out of control." According to your text, the court psychiatrist will likely diagnose him as
     a.   being a delinquent.
     b.   having a conduct disorder.
     c.   a problem child.
     d.   having poor parents.

14. Which of the following individuals would say that delinquency is a manifestation of the search for "Who am I?"
    a. Gilbert Botvin
    b. Peter Blos
    c. John Bowlby
    d. Erik Erikson

15. Which of the following is not associated with juvenile delinquency?
    a. negative identity
    b. learned helplessness
    c. failed self-control
    d. lower-class culture

16. A recent review of all the approaches to prevention of delinquency has revealed that _____ seems to be effective.
    a. a multiple components approach
    b. work experience
    c. preventative casework
    d. security guards in school

17. Which is not a recommendation for dealing with a suicidal adolescent?
    a. Find out if the person has a plan for killing himself.
    b. Pay attention to warning signs and take them seriously.
    c. Assure the person that everything is under control.
    d. Help the person find appropriate counseling.

18. _____ percent of all adolescents are "very high risk" or "high risk" in developing major problem behaviors.
    a. 5
    b. 25
    c. 10
    d. 1

19. All but one of the following is a characteristic of successful programs for reducing adolescent problems. Which one is the exception?
    a. Remove adolescents from the situation that seems to be causing their problems.
    b. Make sure that each adolescent gets personal attention from a responsible adult.
    c. Coordinate the activities of different agencies and institutions.
    d. Begin intervention programs early in adolescent's lives.

20. _____ helps provide a buffer to stress for children and adolescents.
    a. Resilience
    b. Acculturation
    c. Cheerful optimism
    d. Self-efficacy

Adolescence in Movies

- *Ordinary People* A young man struggles with depression and thoughts of suicide as a result of surviving an accident that took his younger brother's life.

■ *Trainspotting* Portrays the grim reality of lives ruined by heroin addiction.

Adolescence in Books
■ *Developmental Psychopathology*, edited by Suniya Luthar, Jacob Burack, Dante Cicchetti, and John Weisz (Cambridge University Press, 1999), explores the many aspects of developmental psychopathology.

■ *Lost Boys*, by James Garbarino (The Free Press, 1999), examines why young men grow up to be murderers.

Answer Key

Key Terms
1. **abnormal behavior** Behavior that is deviant, maladaptive, and personally distressful.
2. **developmental psychopathology** Focuses on describing and exploring the developmental pathways of problems and disorders.
3. **tolerance** A greater amount of a drug is needed to produce the same effect.
4. **physical dependence** The physical need for a drug that is accompanied by unpleasant withdrawal symptoms when the drug is discontinued.
5. **psychological dependence** The strong desire and craving to repeat the use of a drug for various emotional reasons, such as a feeling of well-being and reduction of distress.
6. **hallucinogens** Drugs that alter an individual's perceptual experiences and produce hallucinations—also called psychedelic or mind-altering drugs.
7. **LSD** Lysergic acid diethyl amide, a hallucinogen that, even in low doses, produces striking perceptual changes.
8. **marijuana** Originally from central Asia but now grown in most parts of the world, this mild hallucinogen comes from the hemp plant Cannabis sativa.
9. **stimulants** Drugs that increase the activity of the central nervous system.
10. **cocaine** A stimulant that comes from the coca plant, which is native to Bolivia and Peru.
11. **amphetamines** Called pep pills or uppers, these are widely prescribes stimulants, sometimes in the form of diet pills.
12. **depressants** Drugs that slow the central nervous system, bodily functions, and behavior.
13. **barbiturates** Depressant drugs that induce sleep or reduce anxiety; examples are Nembutal and Seconal.
14. **tranquilizers** Depressant drugs that reduce anxiety and induce relaxation; examples are Valium and Xanax.
15. **opiates** Opium and its derivatives, drugs that depress the activity of the central nervous system; commonly known as narcotics.
16. **anabolic steroids** Drugs derived from the male sex hormone, testosterone. They promote muscle growth and lean body mass.
17. **juvenile delinquency** A broad range of child and adolescent behaviors, including socially unacceptable behavior, status offenses, and criminal acts.
18. **index offenses** Whether they are committed by juveniles or adults, these are criminal acts, such as robbery, rape, and homicide.
19. **status offenses** Performed by youths under a specified age, these are juvenile offenses that are not as serious as index offenses. These offenses may include such acts as drinking under age, truancy,. and sexual promiscuity.
20. **conduct disorder** The psychiatric diagnostic category for the occurrence of multiple delinquent activities over a 6-month period. These behaviors include truancy, running away, fire setting, and cruelty to animals, breaking and entering, and excessive fighting.
21. **cadre approach** A conflict resolution strategy in which a small number of students are trained to serve as peer mediators for the entire school.

22. **total student body approach** A conflict resolution strategy in which every student learns how to manage conflicts constructively by negotiating agreements and mediating schoolmates' conflicts.

23. **major depressive disorder** The diagnosis when an individual experiences a major depressive episode and depressed characteristics, such as lethargy and depression, for two weeks or longer and daily functioning becomes impaired.

24. **anorexia nervosa** An eating disorder that involves the relentless pursuit of thinness through starvation.

25. **bulimia** In this eating disorder, the individual consistently follows a bang-and-purge eating pattern.

26. **stress** The response of individuals to the circumstances and events, called stressors, that threaten and tax their coping abilities.

27. **problem-focused coping** Lazarus' term for the cognitive coping strategy used by individuals who face their troubles and try to solve them.

28. **emotion-focused coping** Lazarus' term for the coping strategy in which individuals respond to stress in an emotional manner, especially using defensive appraisal.

Key People

1. B
2. A
3. D
4. E
5. K
6. J
7. H
8. I
9. L
10. N
11. M
12. C
13. F
14. G

Abnormality
Guided Review

1. biological
2. neurotransmitters
3. genetic
4. drug
5. mental
6. biological
7. mental
8. patients
9. doctors
10. abnormal
11. emotional
12. learning
13. relationships
14. socioeconomic status/neighborhood
15. ethnicity
16. biological/ psychological/sociocultural
17. interactionist
18. psychopathology
19. pathways
20. internalizing
21. externalizing
22. psychiatric
23. inward
24. anxiety/depression
25. outward
26. acting
27. antisocial
28. developmental
29. sex
30. socioeconomic
31. developmental level
32. fears
33. drug-related
34. unhappiness/ sadness/depression
35. school performance
36. The Search
37. 40
38. 20
39. external
40. 20
41. less
42. alcohol/tobacco
43. sexual intercourse
44. violence

Abnormality
Section Review

External Assets	Example
Support	Family and neighborhood
Empowerment	Adults in the community valuing youth; youth being given useful community roles.
Boundaries and Expectations	Family setting clear rules and consequences; family monitoring adolescent's whereabouts; positive peer influences.
Constructive Use of Time	Engaging in creative activities 3 or more times a week; participating in 3 or more hours a week in organized youth programs.
Internal Assets	**Example**
Commitment to Learning	Motivation to achieve in school; doing at least one hour of homework on school days.
Social Competencies	Knowing how to plan and make decisions; having interpersonal competencies like empathy and friendship skills.
Positive Identity	Having a sense of control and high self-esteem.

Drugs and Alcohol
Guided Review

1. many
2. gratification
3. adaptation
4. dependence
5. personal/social
6. serious/fatal
7. tolerance
8. the same effect
9. physical
10. withdrawal
11. discontinued
12. craving
13. emotional
14. well-being
15. reduction
16. declining
17. highest
18. industrialized country
19. potent
20. depressant
21. widely
22. five/two
23. males/females
24. hereditary
25. family
26. peer
27. personality

28. easily
29. activity/challenge
30. driven
31. negative
32. immediate/external
33. Hallucinogens
34. psychedelic/mind altering
35. lysergic acid diethylamide
36. perceptual
37. hallucinogens
38. hemp
39. metabolize
40. central nervous system
41. heart rate/breathing/temperature
42. physically
43. serious/preventable
44. increasing
45. Marlboro
46. dropped
47. declining
48. genetic
49. lung cancer
50. stimulant
51. coca
52. snorted/injected
53. crystals/powder

54. heart attacks/strokes/seizures
55. 13
56. stimulants
57. "pep pills"/"uppers"
58. caffeine
59. slow down
60. alcohol/barbiturates/ tranquilizers
61. opiates
62. Nembutal and Seconal
63. anxiety
64. relaxation
65. narcotics
66. heroin/morphine
67. Anabolic steroids
68. testosterone
69. sexual characteristics
70. physical/psychological
71. increasing
72. positive
73. parents/peers
74. prevention
75. media
76. community
77. parent
78. substance abuse

Drugs and Alcohol
Section Review

1.
   1. H
   2. D
   3. D
   4. S
   5. D
   6. S
   7. D
   8. H

2.
   1. Early intervention is more effective than late intervention.
   2. A kindergarten—12th grade approach is necessary, with age-appropriate components.
   3. Teacher training is an important element in school-based programs.
   4. Social skills training focused on coping skills and resistance to peer pressure is the most promising of the new wave of school–based curriculum.
   e. Peer-led programs are often more effective than teacher-led or counselor programs.
   f. More programs aimed at the high-risk group of students are needed.
   g. The most effective school-based programs are often part of community-wide prevention efforts.

Juvenile Delinquency
Guided Review

1. socially
2. status
3. criminal
4. criminal
5. juveniles/adults
6. youth
7. 18
8. increasing
9. 12
10. 17
11. 13 - 16
12. individual
13. Conduct disorder
14. truancy
15. running away
16. fire setting
17. animals
18. breaking/entering
19. fighting
20. 10
21. arrested
22. negative
23. low
24. early
25. education
26. peer
27. Socioeconomic
28. monitoring
29. ineffective
30. neighborhood
31. 57
32. incidents/crime/ violence
33. 10
34. murder/rape/ physical/robbery
35. cadre
36. peer mediators
37. total student body approach
38. negotiating
39. mediating

Juvenile Delinquency
Section Review

1.

Antecedent	Association with Delinquency
Identity	Negative identity
Self-control	Low degree
Age	Early initiation
Sex	Males
Expectations for education and school grades	Low expectations and low grades
Parental influences	Low monitoring, low support, ineffective discipline
Peer influences	Heavy influence, low resistance
Socioeconomic status	Low
Neighborhood quality	Urban, high crime, high mobility

2. a. Early involvement with drugs and alcohol.
   b. Easy access to weapons, especially handguns.
   c. Association with antisocial, deviant peer groups.
   d. Pervasive exposure to violence in the media.

3. a. Recommit to raising children safely and effectively.
   b. Make prevention a reality.
   c. Give more support to schools struggling to educate at-risk children.
   d. Forge effective partnerships among families, schools, social service systems, churches, and other agencies.

4. a. 1. Define what students want.
      2. Have students describe their feelings.
      3. Explain the reasons underlying their wants and feelings.
      4. Try to see the conflict from the other student's perspectives.
      5. Generate at least three optimal agreements that benefit both parties.
      6. Come to an agreement about the best course of action.

   b. 1. Stop the hostilities.
      2. Ensure that the parties are committed to the mediation.
      3. Facilitate negotiations between the disputing parties.
      4. Formalize the agreement.

Depression and Suicide
Guided Review

1. sadness
2. depression
3. lethargy/hopelessness
4. two
5. daily functioning
6. major depressive
7. black
8. poetry/morbid
9. music/depressive
10. sleep
11. conduct
12. substance
13. eating
14. females
15. males
16. depression
17. parent
18. unavailable
19. marital conflict
20. economic
21. drug
22. Elavil
23. psychotherapy
24. cognitive
25. suicide
26. proximal/immediate
27. distal/earlier
28. boyfriend/girlfriend
29. poor grades
30. unwanted
31. family
32. friendships
33. depression
34. hopelessness
35. self-esteem
36. self-blame

Depression and Suicide
Section Review

1. N   2. Y   3. N   4. Y   5. N   6. N   7. Y   8. Y   9. N

Eating Disorders, The Interrelationship of Problems, and Prevention/Intervention
Guided Review

1. negatively
2. two
3. physically
4. pubertal
5. obesity
6. anorexia nervosa
7. bulimia
8. Twenty-five
9. heredity/ environmental
10. 70
11. two
12. high
13. energy-saving
14. physical activity
15. anorexia nervosa
16. thinness
17. individuality
18. sexuality
19. overcontrolling
20. hypothalamus
21. binge-and-purge
22. two
23. control
24. bulimics
25. Depression
26. gastric/chemical
27. interrelated
28. more than one
29. 2/3
30. intensive, individualized
31. collaborative
32. identification/ intervention

Eating Disorders, The Interrelationship of Problems, and Prevention/Intervention
Section Review

Heavy substance abuse is related to early sexual activity, lower grades, dropping out of school, and delinquency. Early initiation of sexual activity is associated with using cigarettes, alcohol, marijuana, and other illicit drugs, lower grades, dropping out of school, and delinquency. Delinquency is related to early sexual activity, early pregnancy, substance abuse, and dropping out of school.

Stress and Coping
Guided Review

1. circumstances/events
2. threaten
3. tax
4. stress
5. multiple
6. physical
7. environmental
8. emotional/personality
9. sociocultural
10. intellectual
11. relationship/caring parent
12. attachments
13. resilient
14. cope
15. problem
16. face
17. solve
18. emotional
19. defensive
20. avoid
21. rationalize
22. deny
23. laugh
24. Close/positive
25. Mothers/peers/siblings
26. more than one

Stress and Coping
Section Review

Source	Characteristics
Individual	Good intellectual functioning; appealing, sociable, easygoing disposition; self-efficacy, self-confidence, high self-esteem; talents; faith.
Family	Close relationship to caring parent figure; authoritative parenting; socioeconomic advantages; connections to extended supportive family networks.
Extrafamilial context	Bonds to prosocial adults outside the family; connections to prosocial organizations; attending effective schools.

Explorations in Adolescence

Many seemed to be driven by feelings of powerlessness, and violence infused them with a sense of power. Some lived in poverty and lacked adequate parental involvement and supervision. Some were involved with aggressive cliques. Some had said that they were going to commit acts of violence.

Adventures for the Mind

1.   Individual activity. No answer provided.

2.   Individual activity. No answer provided.

Adolescence in Research

The research method was meta-analysis, a review of the research on resilience. The review concluded that a number of individual, family, and extrafamilial factors characterize resilient children.

Comprehensive Review

1. d	**5.** b	**9.** c	**13.** d	**17.** c
2. a	**6.** b	**10.** d	**14.** b	**18.** c
3. b	**7.** d	**11.** b	**15.** a	**19.** a
4. b	**8.** a	**12.** b	**16.** c	**20.** a

Cognitive Map Exercises

Chapter 1: Key Terms

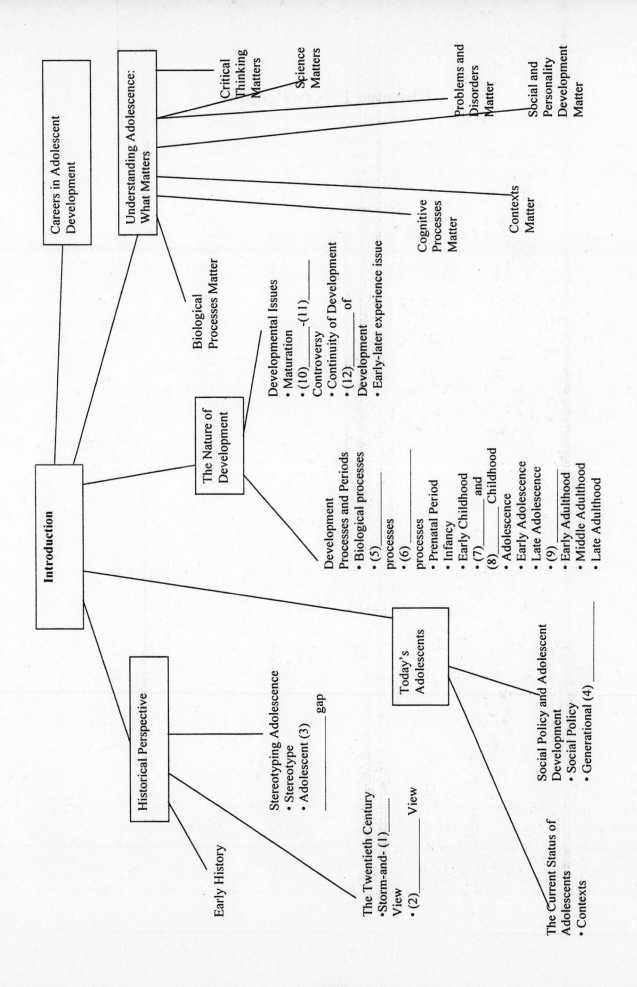

Careers in Adolescent Development

Understanding Adolescence: What Matters
- Critical Thinking Matters
- Science Matters
- Problems and Disorders Matter
- Social and Personality Development Matter
- Contexts Matter
- Cognitive Processes Matter
- Biological Processes Matter

Introduction

The Nature of Development

Developmental Issues
- Maturation
- (10) _____ -(11) _____ Controversy
- Continuity of Development
- (12) _____ of Development
- Early-later experience issue

Development Processes and Periods
- Biological processes
- (5) _____ processes
- (6) _____ processes
- Prenatal Period
- Infancy
- Early Childhood
- (7) _____ and _____ Childhood
- (8) _____ Adolescence
- Early Adolescence
- Late Adolescence
- (9) _____ Early Adulthood
- Middle Adulthood
- Late Adulthood

Historical Perspective

Stereotyping Adolescence
- Stereotype
- Adolescent (3) _____ gap

The Twentieth Century
- Storm-and- (1) _____ View
- (2) _____ View

Early History

Today's Adolescents

Social Policy and Adolescent Development
- Social Policy
- Generational (4) _____

The Current Status of Adolescents
- Contexts

269

Chapter 1: Key People

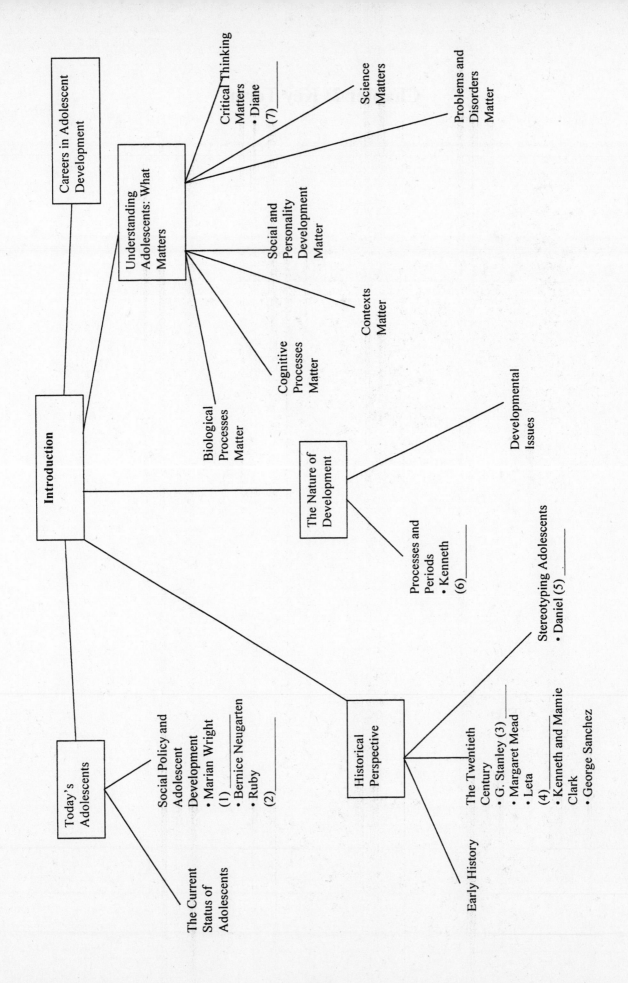

Careers in Adolescent Development

Introduction

Understanding Adolescents: What Matters

Critical Thinking Matters
• Diane ____ (7)

Science Matters

Problems and Disorders Matter

Social and Personality Development Matter

Contexts Matter

Cognitive Processes Matter

Biological Processes Matter

The Nature of Development

Developmental Issues

Processes and Periods
• Kenneth ____ (6)

Today's Adolescents

Social Policy and Adolescent Development
• Marian Wright ____ (1)
• Bernice Neugarten Ruby ____ (2)

The Current Status of Adolescents

Historical Perspective

Stereotyping Adolescents
• Daniel (5) ____

The Twentieth Century
• G. Stanley (3) ____
• Margaret Mead
• Leta ____ (4)
• Kenneth and Mamie Clark
• George Sanchez

Early History

271

Chapter 2: Key Terms

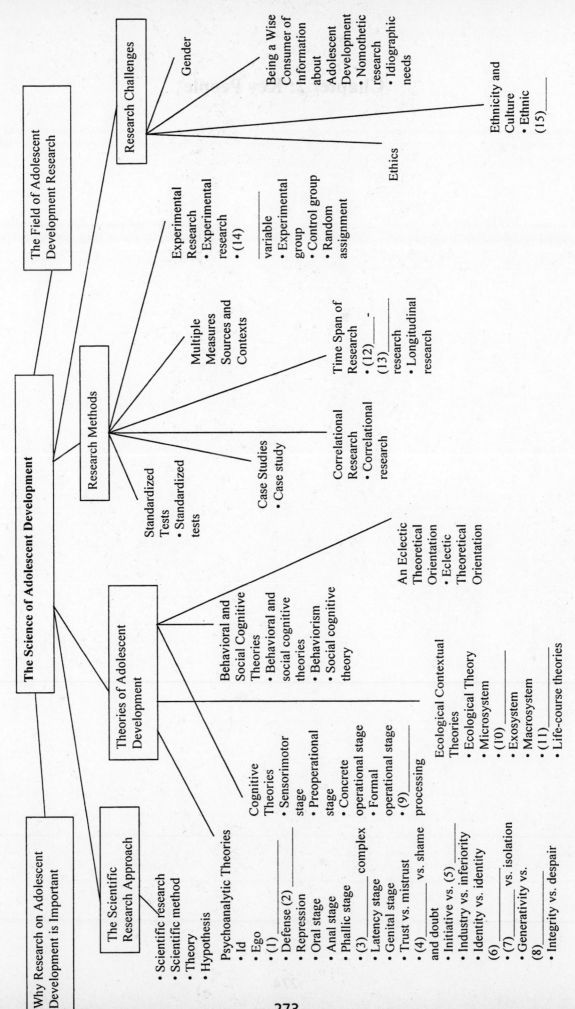

The Science of Adolescent Development

Why Research on Adolescent Development is Important

The Field of Adolescent Development Research

Research Challenges
• Gender
• Being a Wise Consumer of Information about Adolescent Development
• Nomothetic research
• Idiographic needs
Ethics
Ethnicity and Culture
• Ethnic _____ (15)

The Scientific Research Approach

Research Methods
Standardized Tests
• Standardized tests
Multiple Measures Sources and Contexts
Case Studies
• Case study
Correlational Research
• Correlational research
Time Span of Research
• (12) _____ - (13) _____ research
• Longitudinal research
Experimental Research
• Experimental research
• (14) _____ variable
• Experimental group
• Control group
• Random assignment

Theories of Adolescent Development

Behavioral and Social Cognitive Theories
• Behavioral and social cognitive theories
• Behaviorism
• Social cognitive theory
An Eclectic Theoretical Orientation
• Eclectic Theoretical Orientation

Cognitive Theories
• Sensorimotor stage
• Preoperational stage
• Concrete operational stage
• Formal operational stage
• _____ (9) processing

Ecological Contextual Theories
• Ecological Theory
• Microsystem
• _____ (10)
• Exosystem
• Macrosystem
• _____ (11)
• Life-course theories

Psychoanalytic Theories
• Id
• Ego
• (1) _____
• Defense (2) _____
• Repression
• Oral stage
• Anal stage
• Phallic stage
• _____ (3) complex
• Latency stage
• Genital stage
• Trust vs. mistrust
• _____ (4) vs. shame and doubt
• Initiative vs. (5) _____
• Industry vs. inferiority
• Identity vs. identity
(6) _____ vs. isolation
• (7) _____
• Generativity vs.
(8) _____
• Integrity vs. despair

Scientific research
• Scientific method
• Theory
• Hypothesis

273

Chapter 2: Key People

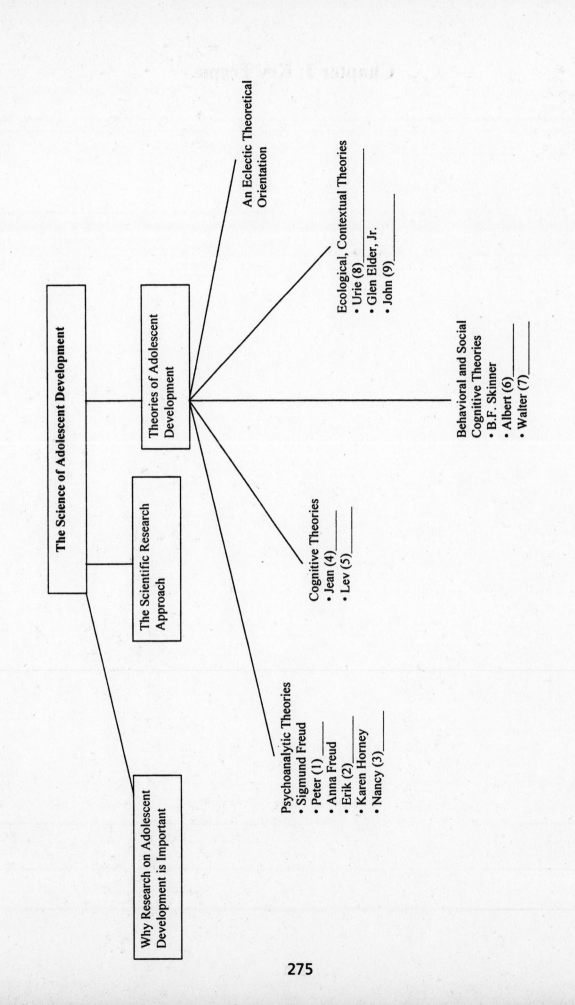

The Science of Adolescent Development

Why Research on Adolescent Development is Important

The Scientific Research Approach

Theories of Adolescent Development

An Eclectic Theoretical Orientation

Ecological, Contextual Theories
• Urie (8) _____
• Glen Elder, Jr. _____
• John (9) _____

Behavioral and Social Cognitive Theories
• B.F. Skinner
• Albert (6) _____
• Walter (7) _____

Cognitive Theories
• Jean (4) _____
• Lev (5) _____

Psychoanalytic Theories
• Sigmund Freud
• Peter (1) _____
• Anna Freud
• Erik (2) _____
• Karen Horney
• Nancy (3) _____

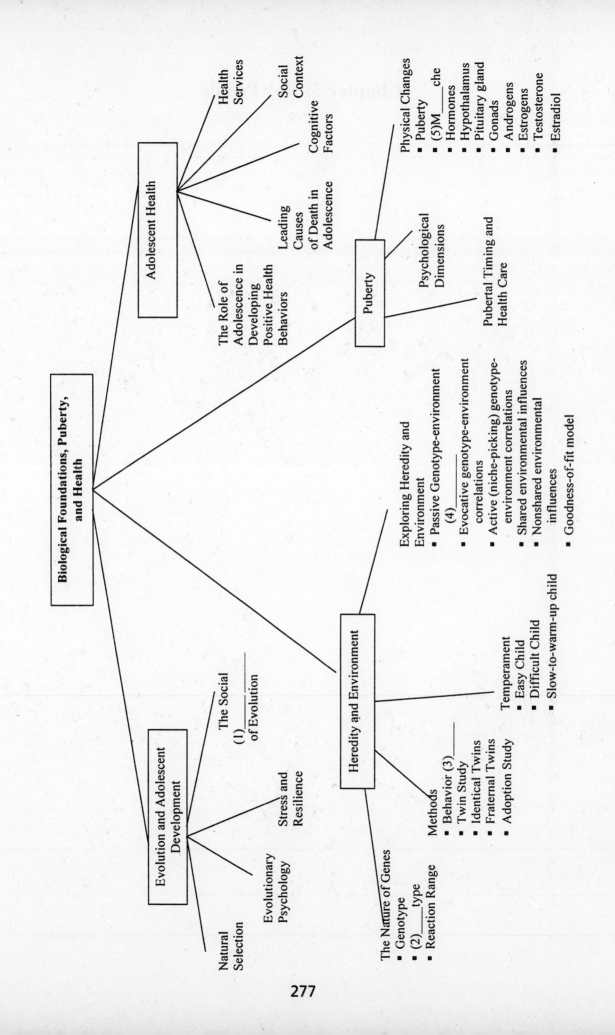

Biological Foundations, Puberty, and Health

Evolution and Adolescent Development

- Natural Selection
- Evolutionary Psychology
- Stress and Resilience
- The Social (1) _____ of Evolution

Heredity and Environment

The Nature of Genes
- Genotype
- (2) _____ type
- Reaction Range

Methods
- Behavior (3) _____
- Twin Study
- Identical Twins
- Fraternal Twins
- Adoption Study

Temperament
- Easy Child
- Difficult Child
- Slow-to-warm-up child

Exploring Heredity and Environment
- Passive Genotype-environment (4) _____
- Evocative genotype-environment correlations
- Active (niche-picking) genotype-environment correlations
- Shared environmental influences
- Nonshared environmental influences
- Goodness-of-fit model

Adolescent Health

- Health Services
- Social Context
- Cognitive Factors
- Leading Causes of Death in Adolescence
- The Role of Adolescence in Developing Positive Health Behaviors

Puberty

- Physical Changes
  - Puberty
  - (5)M_____che
  - Hormones
  - Hypothalamus
  - Pituitary gland
  - Gonads
  - Androgens
  - Estrogens
  - Testosterone
  - Estradiol
- Psychological Dimensions
- Pubertal Timing and Health Care

Chapter 3: Key People

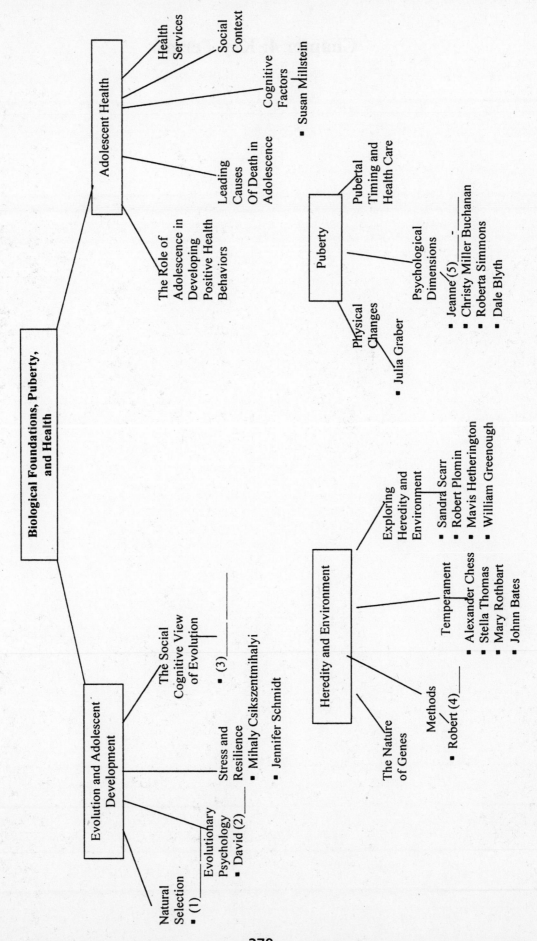

Biological Foundations, Puberty, and Health

Evolution and Adolescent Development

Natural Selection
- (1)

Evolutiohary Psychology
- David (2)

Stress and Resilience
- Mihaly Csikszentmihalyi
- Jennifer Schmidt

The Social Cognitive View of Evolution
- (3)

Adolescent Health

Health Services

Social Context

Cognitive Factors
- Susan Millstein

Leading Causes Of Death in Adolescence

The Role of Adolescence in Developing Positive Health Behaviors

Puberty

Pubertal Timing and Health Care

Physical Changes
- Julia Graber

Psychological Dimensions
- Jeanne (5)
- Christy Miller Buchanan
- Roberta Simmons
- Dale Blyth

Heredity and Environment

Exploring Heredity and Environment
- Sandra Scarr
- Robert Plomin
- Mavis Hetherington
- William Greenough

Temperament
- Alexander Chess
- Stella Thomas
- Mary Rothbart
- Johnn Bates

The Nature of Genes

Methods
- Robert (4)

279

Chapter 4: Key Terms

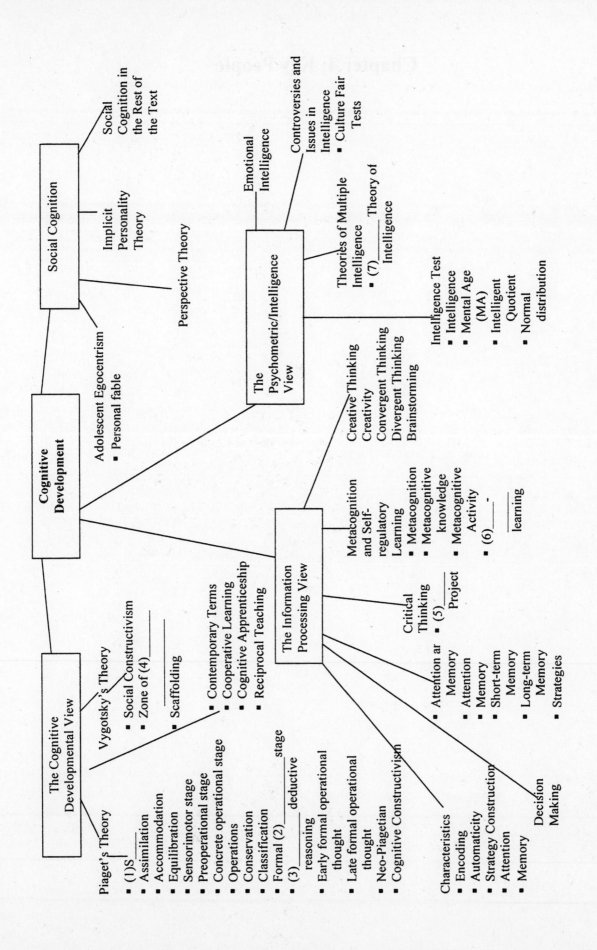

Social Cognition
- Social Cognition in the Rest of the Text
- Implicit Personality Theory
- Perspective Theory

Cognitive Development
- Adolescent Egocentrism
  - Personal fable

The Cognitive Developmental View

Piaget's Theory
- (1)S _____
- Assimilation
- Accommodation
- Equilibration
- Sensorimotor stage
- Preoperational stage
- Concrete operational stage
- Operations
- Conservation
- Classification
- Formal (2) _____ stage
- (3) _____ deductive reasoning
- Early formal operational thought
- Late formal operational thought
- Neo-Piagetian
- Cognitive Constructivism

Vygotsky's Theory
- Social Constructivism
- Zone of (4) _____
- Scaffolding

- Contemporary Terms
- Cooperative Learning
- Cognitive Apprenticeship
- Reciprocal Teaching

The Psychometric/Intelligence View
- Emotional Intelligence
- Controversies and Issues in Intelligence
  - Culture Fair Tests
- Theories of Multiple Intelligence
- (7) _____ Theory of Intelligence
- Intelligence Test
  - Intelligence
  - Mental Age (MA)
  - Intelligent Quotient
  - Normal distribution

The Information Processing View

Metacognition and Self-regulatory Learning
- Metacognition
- Metacognitive knowledge
- Metacognitive Activity
- (6) _____ learning

Creative Thinking
- Creativity
- Convergent Thinking
- Divergent Thinking
- Brainstorming

Critical Thinking
- (5) _____ Project

Attention ar Memory
- Attention
- Memory
- Short-term Memory
- Long-term Memory
- Strategies

Characteristics
- Encoding
- Automaticity
- Strategy Construction
- Attention
- Memory

Decision Making

281

Chapter 4: Key People

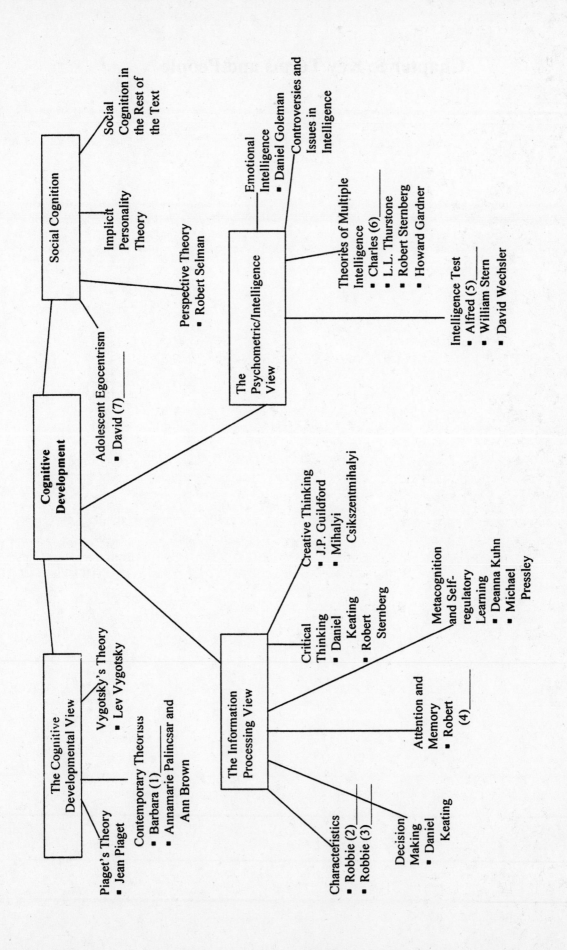

The Cognitive Developmental View

Piaget's Theory
■ Jean Piaget

Vygotsky's Theory
■ Lev Vygotsky

Contemporary Theorists
■ Barbara (1)
■ Annamarie Palincsar and Ann Brown

Cognitive Development

Adolescent Egocentrism
■ David (7)_____

Social Cognition

Implicit Personality Theory

Perspective Theory
■ Robert Selman

Social Cognition in the Rest of the Text

The Psychometric/Intelligence View

Emotional Intelligence
■ Daniel Goleman

Controversies and Issues in Intelligence

Theories of Multiple Intelligence
■ Charles (6)
■ L.L. Thurstone
■ Robert Sternberg
■ Howard Gardner

Intelligence Test
■ Alfred (5)
■ William Stern
■ David Wechsler

The Information Processing View

Creative Thinking
■ J.P. Guildford
■ Mihalyi Csikszentmihalyi

Critical Thinking
■ Daniel Keating
■ Robert Sternberg

Metacognition and Self-regulatory Learning
■ Deanna Kuhn
■ Michael Pressley

Attention and Memory
■ Robert (4)_____

Characteristics
■ Robbie (2)
■ Robbie (3)

Decision Making
■ Daniel Keating

Chapter 5: Key Terms and People

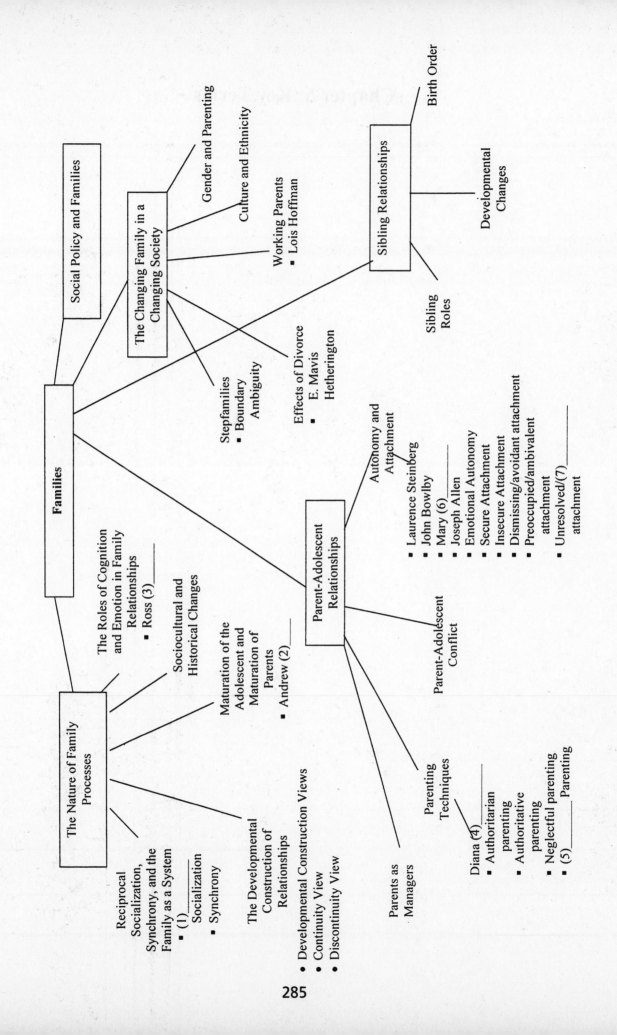

285

Chapter 6: Key Terms

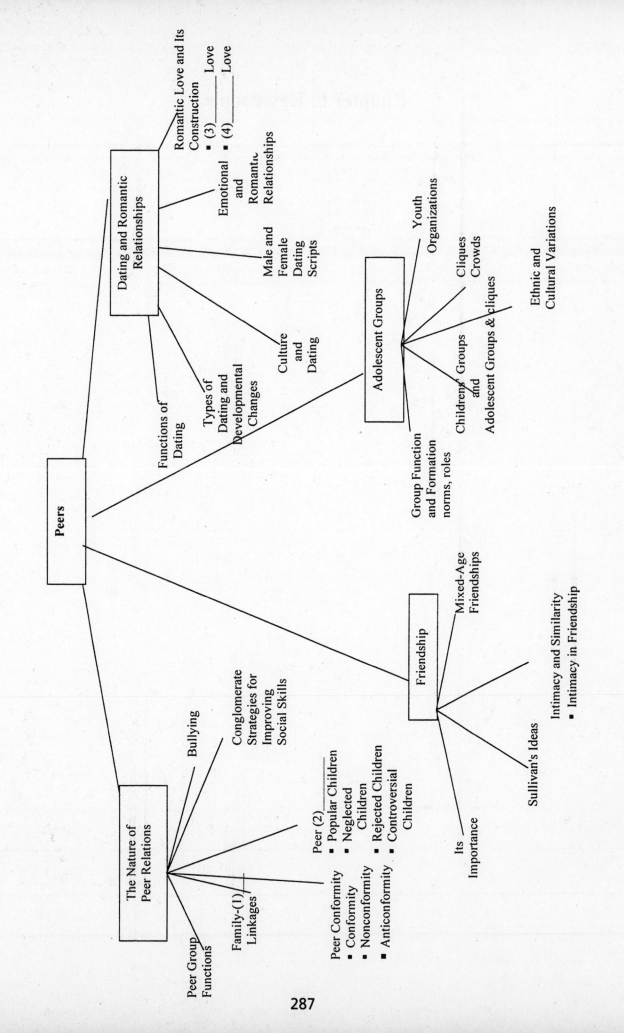

287

Chapter 6: Key People

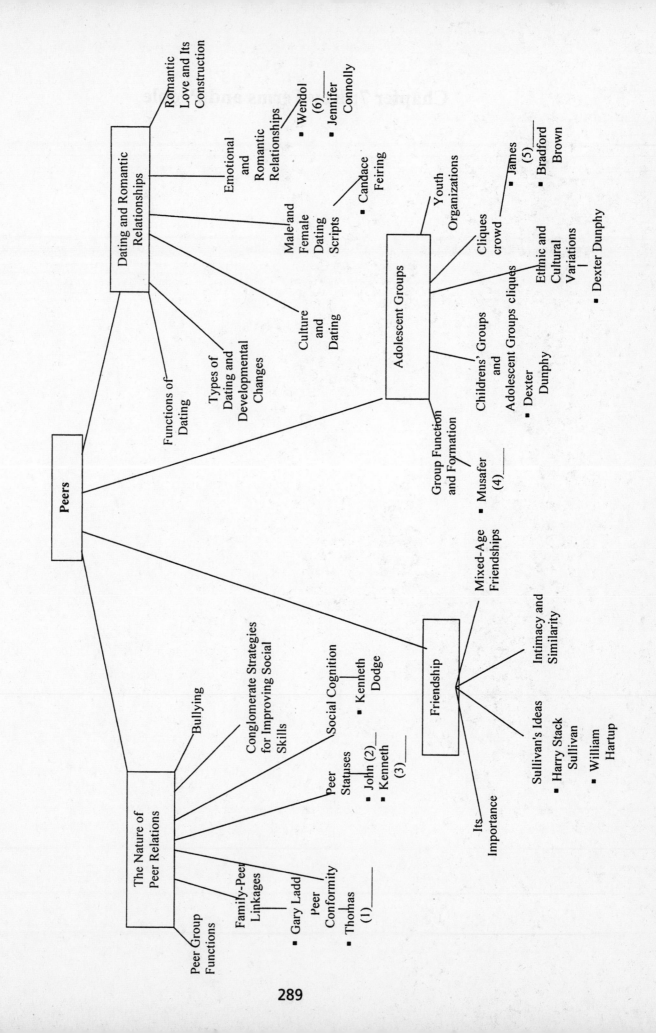

Chapter 7: Key Terms and People

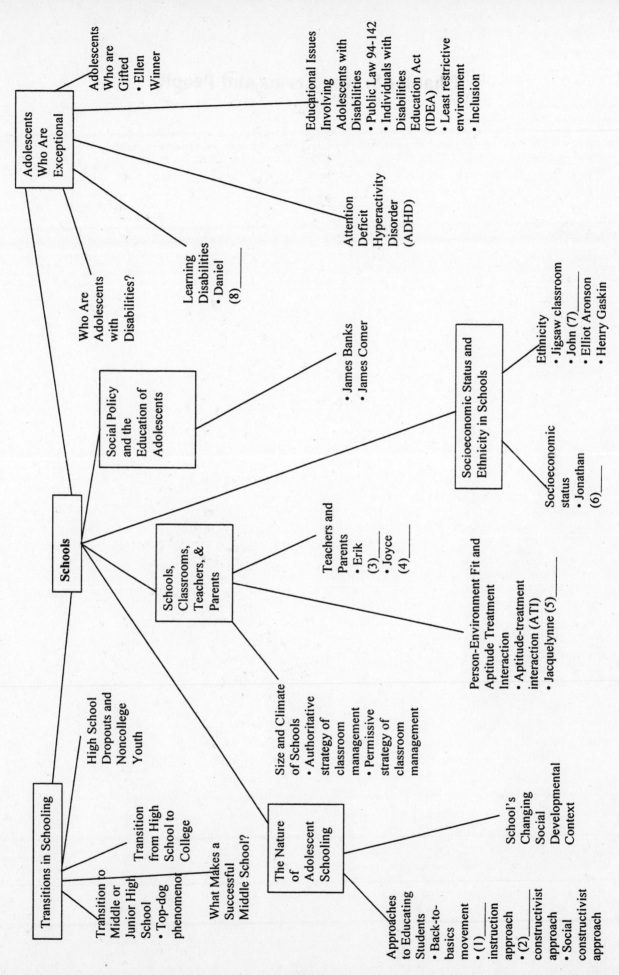

Transitions in Schooling

High School Dropouts and Noncollege Youth

Transition to Middle or Junior High School
• Top-dog phenomenon

Transition from High School to College

What Makes a Successful Middle School?

The Nature of Adolescent Schooling

Size and Climate of Schools
• Authoritative strategy of classroom management
• Permissive strategy of classroom management

School's Changing Social Developmental Context

Approaches to Educating Students
• (1) _____ instruction approach
• (2) _____ constructivist approach
• Social constructivist approach

Schools

Social Policy and the Education of Adolescents
• James Banks
• James Comer

Schools, Classrooms, Teachers, & Parents

Teachers and Parents
• Erik (3) _____
• Joyce (4) _____

Person-Environment Fit and Aptitude Treatment Interaction
• Aptitude-treatment interaction (ATI)
• Jacquelynne (5) _____

Socioeconomic Status and Ethnicity in Schools

Socioeconomic status
• Jonathan (6) _____

Ethnicity
• Jigsaw classroom
• John (7) _____
• Elliot Aronson
• Henry Gaskin

Adolescents Who Are Exceptional

Adolescents Who are Gifted
• Ellen Winner

Educational Issues Involving Adolescents with Disabilities
• Public Law 94-142
• Individuals with Disabilities Education Act (IDEA)
• Least restrictive environment
• Inclusion

Attention Deficit Hyperactivity Disorder (ADHD)

Who Are Adolescents with Disabilities?

Learning Disabilities
• Daniel (8) _____

291

Chapter 8: Key Terms and People

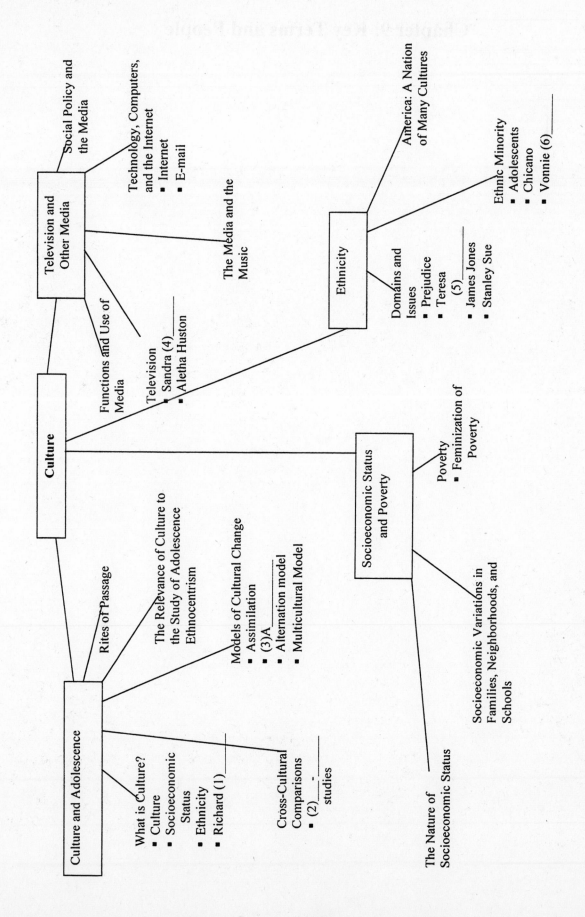

Culture

Culture and Adolescence

- Rites of Passage

- The Relevance of Culture to the Study of Adolescence
  - Ethnocentrism

- Models of Cultural Change
  - Assimilation
  - (3)A_____
  - Alternation model
  - Multicultural Model

What is Culture?
- Culture
- Socioeconomic Status
- Ethnicity
- Richard (1)_____

Cross-Cultural Comparisons
- (2)_____-studies

Television and Other Media

Social Policy and the Media

Technology, Computers, and the Internet
- Internet
- E-mail

The Media and the Music

Functions and Use of Media

Television
- Sandra (4)_____
- Aletha Huston

Socioeconomic Status and Poverty

The Nature of Socioeconomic Status

Socioeconomic Variations in Families, Neighborhoods, and Schools

Poverty
- Feminization of Poverty

Ethnicity

America: A Nation of Many Cultures

Domains and Issues
- Prejudice
- Teresa (5)_____
- James Jones
- Stanley Sue

Ethnic Minority
- Adolescents
- Chicano
- Vonnie (6)_____

Chapter 9: Key Terms and People

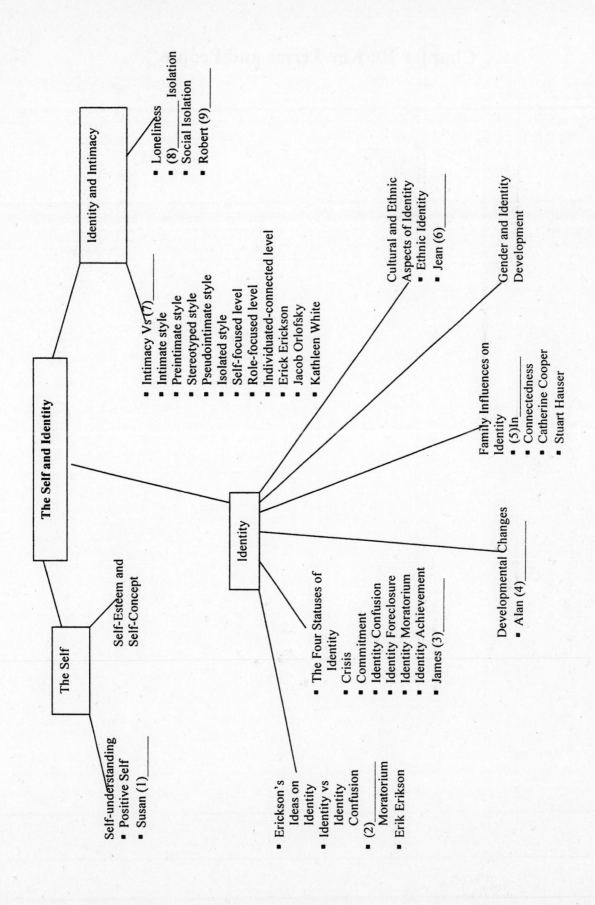

The Self and Identity

The Self
- Self-understanding
  - Positive Self
    - Susan (1) _____
- Self-Esteem and Self-Concept

Identity and Intimacy
- Intimacy Vs (7)
  - Intimate style
  - Preintimate style
  - Stereotyped style
  - Pseudointimate style
  - Isolated style
  - Self-focused level
  - Role-focused level
  - Individuated-connected level
  - Erick Erickson
  - Jacob Orlofsky
  - Kathleen White
- Loneliness
  - (8)
  - Social Isolation
    - Robert (9) _____
- Isolation

Identity
- Erickson's Ideas on Identity
  - Identity vs Identity Confusion
  - (2)
  - Moratorium
  - Erik Erikson
- The Four Statuses of Identity
  - Crisis
  - Commitment
  - Identity Confusion
  - Identity Foreclosure
  - Identity Moratorium
  - Identity Achievement
    - James (3) _____
- Developmental Changes
  - Alan (4) _____
- Family Influences on Identity
  - (5)In
  - Connectedness
  - Catherine Cooper
  - Stuart Hauser
- Cultural and Ethnic Aspects of Identity
  - Ethnic Identity
    - Jean (6) _____
- Gender and Identity Development

Chapter 10: Key Terms and People

296

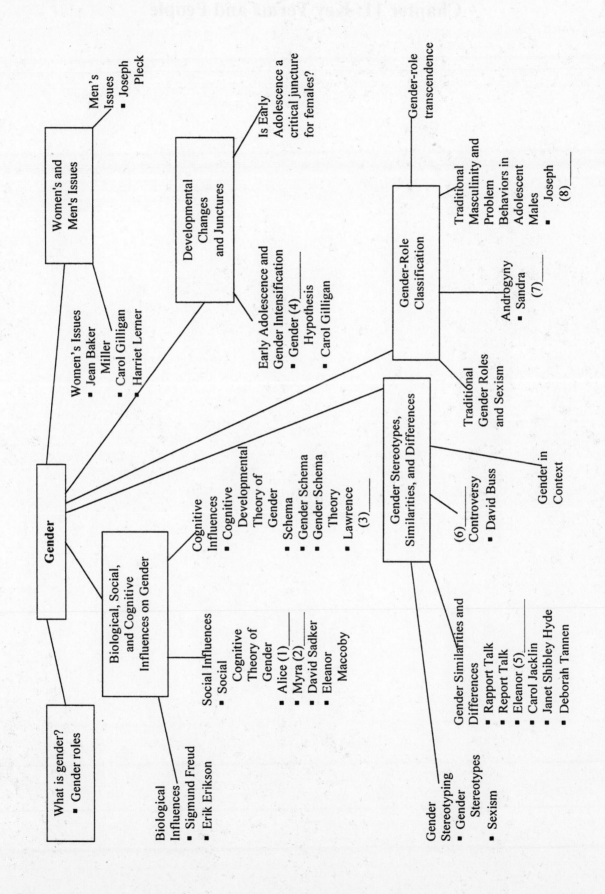

Gender

What is gender?
- Gender roles

Biological, Social, and Cognitive Influences on Gender

Biological Influences
- Sigmund Freud
- Erik Erikson

Social Influences
- Social Cognitive Theory of Gender
- Alice (1) ___
- Myra (2) ___
- David Sadker
- Eleanor Maccoby

Cognitive Influences
- Cognitive Developmental Theory of Gender
- Schema
- Gender Schema
- Gender Schema Theory
- Lawrence (3) ___

Women's and Men's Issues

Women's Issues
- Jean Baker Miller
- Carol Gilligan
- Harriet Lerner

Men's Issues
- Joseph Pleck

Developmental Changes and Junctures

Early Adolescence and Gender Intensification
- Gender (4) ___ Hypothesis
- Carol Gilligan

Is Early Adolescence a critical juncture for females?

Gender Stereotypes, Similarities, and Differences

Gender Stereotyping
- Gender Stereotypes
- Sexism

Gender Similarities and Differences
- Rapport Talk
- Report Talk
- Eleanor (5) ___
- Carol Jacklin
- Janet Shibley Hyde
- Deborah Tannen

(6) ___ Controversy
- David Buss

Gender in Context

Gender-Role Classification

Androgyny
- Sandra (7) ___

Traditional Masculinity and Problem Behaviors in Adolescent Males
- Joseph (8) ___

Gender-role transcendence

Traditional Gender Roles and Sexism

297

Chapter 11: Key Terms and People

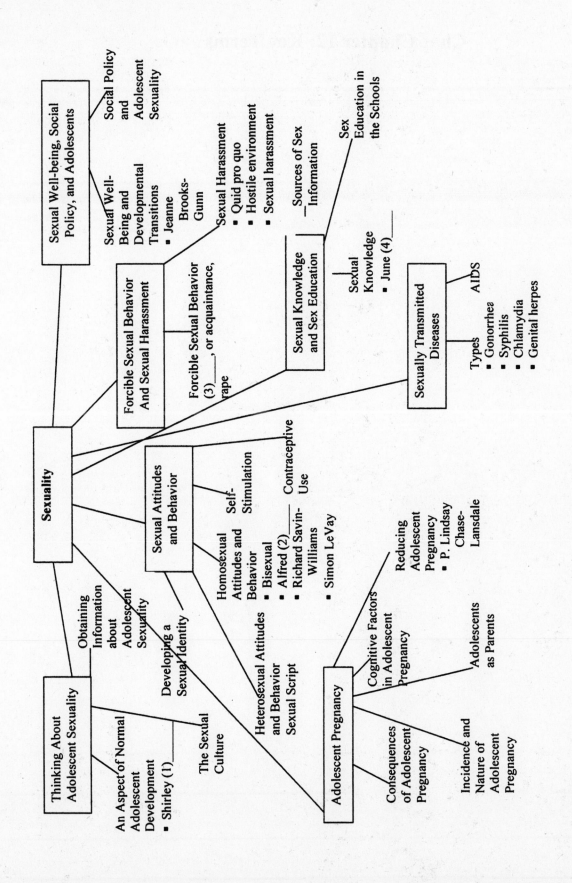

Sexuality

Thinking About Adolescent Sexuality
- An Aspect of Normal Adolescent Development
  - Shirley (1)
- The Sexual Culture
- Developing a Sexual Identity
- Obtaining Information about Adolescent Sexuality

Sexual Attitudes and Behavior
- Heterosexual Attitudes and Behavior Sexual Script
- Homosexual Attitudes and Behavior
  - Bisexual
  - Alfred (2)
  - Richard Savin-Williams
  - Simon LeVay
- Self-Stimulation
- Contraceptive Use

Forcible Sexual Behavior And Sexual Harassment
- Forcible Sexual Behavior
  - (3) , or acquaintance, rape
- Sexual Harassment
  - Quid pro quo
  - Hostile environment
  - Sexual harassment

Sexual Well-being, Social Policy, and Adolescents
- Sexual Well-Being and Developmental Transitions
  - Jeanne Brooks-Gunn
- Social Policy and Adolescent Sexuality

Sexual Knowledge and Sex Education
- Sexual Knowledge
  - June (4)
- Sources of Sex Information
- Sex Education in the Schools

Adolescent Pregnancy
- Incidence and Nature of Adolescent Pregnancy
- Consequences of Adolescent Pregnancy
- Cognitive Factors in Adolescent Pregnancy
- Reducing Adolescent Pregnancy
  - P. Lindsay Chase-Lansdale
- Adolescents as Parents

Sexually Transmitted Diseases
- Types
  - Gonorrhea
  - Syphilis
  - Chlamydia
  - Genital herpes
- AIDS

299

Chapter 12: Key Terms

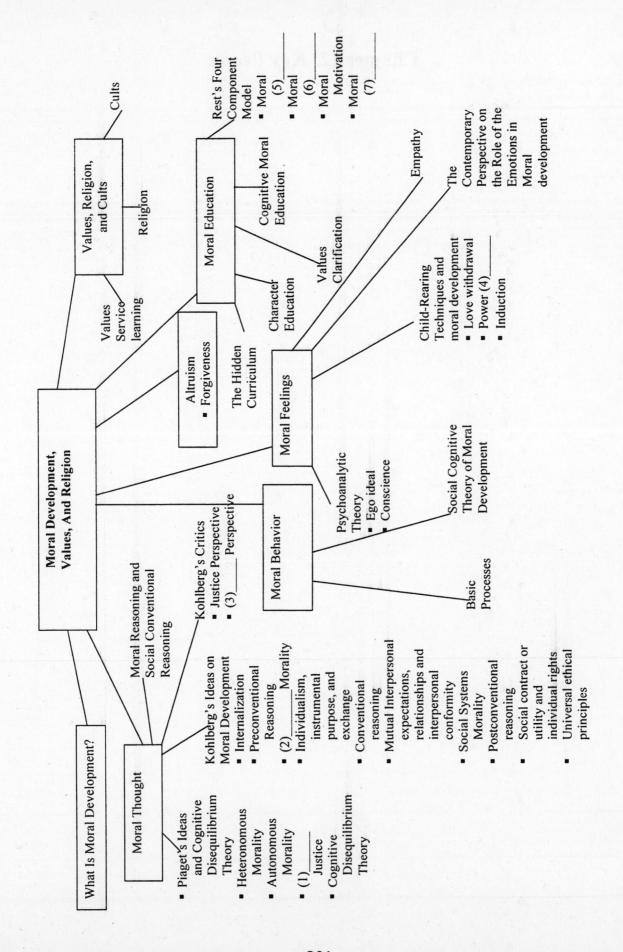

Moral Development, Values, And Religion

What Is Moral Development?

Moral Thought

Moral Reasoning and Social Conventional Reasoning

Piaget's Ideas and Cognitive Disequilibrium Theory
- Heteronomous Morality
- Autonomous Morality
- (1) _____ Justice
- Cognitive Disequilibrium Theory

Kohlberg's Ideas on Moral Development
- Internalization
- Preconventional Reasoning
- (2) _____ Morality
- Individualism, instrumental purpose, and exchange
- Conventional reasoning
- Mutual Interpersonal expectations, relationships and interpersonal conformity
- Social Systems Morality
- Postconventional reasoning
- Social contract or utility and individual rights
- Universal ethical principles

Kohlberg's Critics
- Justice Perspective
- (3) _____ Perspective

Moral Behavior

Basic Processes

Social Cognitive Theory of Moral Development

Psychoanalytic Theory
- Ego ideal
- Conscience

Moral Feelings

Child-Rearing Techniques and moral development
- Love withdrawal
- Power (4) _____
- Induction

Empathy

The Contemporary Perspective on the Role of the Emotions in Moral development

Values, Religion, and Cults

Cults

Religion

Values
Service learning

Altruism
- Forgiveness

The Hidden Curriculum

Moral Education

Cognitive Moral Education

Values Clarification

Character Education

Rest's Four Component Model
- Moral (5) _____
- Moral (6) _____
- Moral Motivation
- Moral (7) _____

301

Chapter 12: Key People

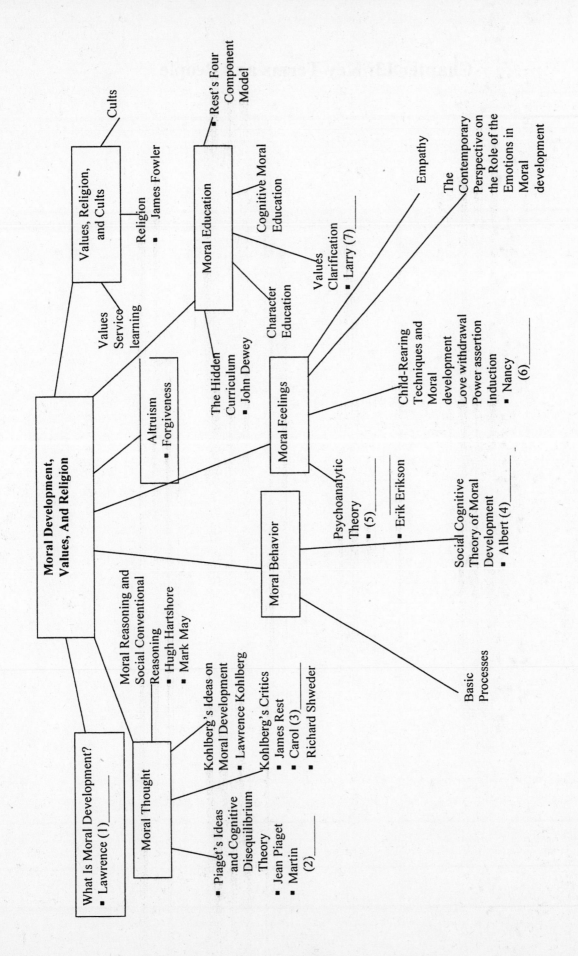

Moral Development, Values, And Religion

What Is Moral Development?
- Lawrence (1) _____

Moral Thought

Piaget's Ideas and Cognitive Disequilibrium Theory
- Jean Piaget
- Martin
- (2) _____

Moral Reasoning and Social Conventional Reasoning
- Hugh Hartshore
- Mark May

Kohlberg's Ideas on Moral Development
- Lawrence Kohlberg

Kohlberg's Critics
- James Rest
- Carol (3)
- Richard Shweder

Moral Behavior

Basic Processes

Social Cognitive Theory of Moral Development
- Albert (4) _____

Psychoanalytic Theory
- (5) _____
- Erik Erikson

Moral Feelings

Child-Rearing Techniques and Moral development
Love withdrawal
Power assertion
Induction
- Nancy _____
(6)

Empathy

The Contemporary Perspective on the Role of the Emotions in Moral development

Values, Religion, and Cults

Values
Service learning

Altruism
- Forgiveness

Religion
- James Fowler

Cults

Moral Education

The Hidden Curriculum
- John Dewey

Character Education

Cognitive Moral Education

Values Clarification
- Larry (7) _____

Rest's Four Component Model

Chapter 13: Key Terms and People

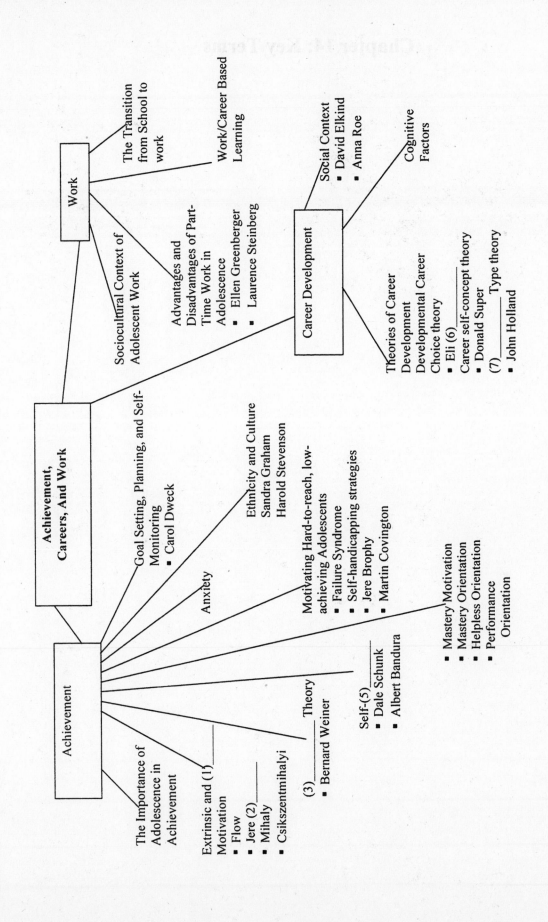

Achievement, Careers, And Work

Achievement

- The Importance of Adolescence in Achievement
- Extrinsic and (1) _____ Motivation
  - Flow
  - Jere (2) _____
  - Mihaly Csikszentmihalyi
- (3) _____ Theory
  - Bernard Weiner
- Self-(5) _____
  - Dale Schunk
  - Albert Bandura
  - Mastery Motivation
  - Mastery Orientation
  - Helpless Orientation
  - Performance Orientation
- Motivating Hard-to-reach, low-achieving Adolescents
  - Failure Syndrome
  - Self-handicapping strategies
  - Jere Brophy
  - Martin Covington
- Ethnicity and Culture
  - Sandra Graham
  - Harold Stevenson
- Anxiety
- Goal Setting, Planning, and Self-Monitoring
  - Carol Dweck

Work

- The Transition from School to work
- Work/Career Based Learning
- Sociocultural Context of Adolescent Work
- Advantages and Disadvantages of Part-Time Work in Adolescence
  - Ellen Greenberger
  - Laurence Steinberg

Career Development

- Social Context
  - David Elkind
  - Anna Roe
- Cognitive Factors
- Theories of Career Development
  Developmental Career Choice theory
  - Eli (6) _____
  - Career self-concept theory
  - Donald Super
  - (7) _____ Type theory
  - John Holland

305

Chapter 14: Key Terms

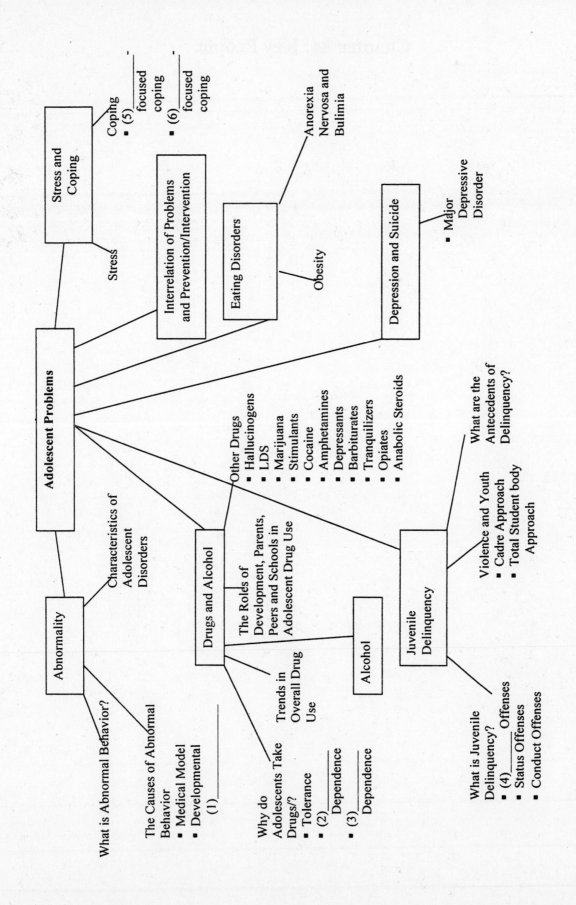

Chapter 14: Key People

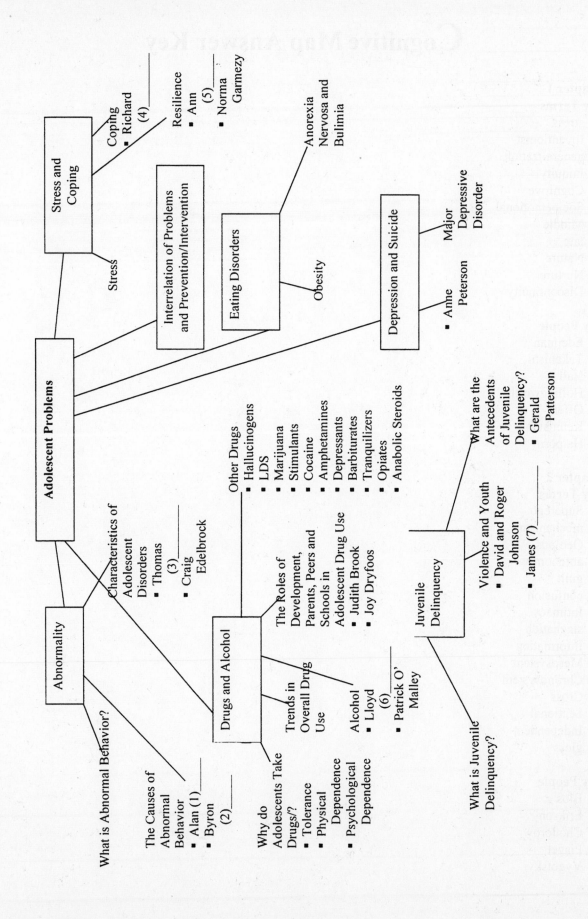

Adolescent Problems

Stress and Coping
- Stress
- Coping
  - Richard (4)
- Resilience
  - Ann (5)
  - Norma Garmezy

Interrelation of Problems and Prevention/Intervention

Eating Disorders
- Anorexia Nervosa and Bulimia
- Obesity

Depression and Suicide
- Major Depressive Disorder
- Anne Peterson

Abnormality
- What is Abnormal Behavior?
- The Causes of Abnormal Behavior
  - Alan (1) _____
  - Byron (2) _____
- Characteristics of Adolescent Disorders
  - Thomas (3)
  - Craig Edelbrock

Drugs and Alcohol
- Other Drugs
  - Hallucinogens
  - LDS
  - Marijuana
  - Stimulants
  - Cocaine
  - Amphetamines
  - Depressants
  - Barbiturates
  - Tranquilizers
  - Opiates
  - Anabolic Steroids
- The Roles of Development, Parents, Peers and Schools in Adolescent Drug Use
  - Judith Brook
  - Joy Dryfoos
- Why do Adolescents Take Drugs/?
  - Tolerance
  - Physical Dependence
  - Psychological Dependence
- Trends in Overall Drug Use
- Alcohol
  - Lloyd (6) _____
  - Patrick O' Malley

Juvenile Delinquency
- Violence and Youth
  - David and Roger Johnson
  - James (7) _____
- What are the Antecedents of Juvenile Delinquency?
  - Gerald Patterson
- What is Juvenile Delinquency?

Cognitive Map Answer Key

Chapter 1
Key Terms
1. stress
2. Inventionist
3. generalization
4. iniquity
5. Cognitive
6. Socioemotional
7. Middle
8. late
9. Nature
10. Nurture
11. Discontinuity

Key People
1. Edelman
2. Takanishi
3. Hall
4. Hollingworth
5. Offer
6. Kenniston
7. Halporn

Chapter 2
Key Terms
1. Superego
2. mechanism
3. Oedipus
4. autonomy
5. guilt
6. confusion
7. Intimacy
8. stagnation
9. Information
10. Mesosystem
11. Chronosystem
12. Cross
13. Sectional
14. Independent
15. gloss

Key People
1. Blos
2. Erikson
3. Chodorow
4. Piaget
5. Vygotsky

6. Bandura
7. Mischel
8. Brofenbrenner
9. Clausen

Chapter 3
Key Terms
1. Cognitive View
2. Phenotype
3. Genetics
4. interactions
5. Menarche

Key People
1. Charles Darwin
2. Buss
3. Albert Bandura
4. Plomin
5. Brooks-Gunn

Chapter 4
Key Terms
1. Schema
2. operational
3. Hypothetical
4. Proximal Development
5. Jasper
6. Self-regulatory
7. Triarchic

Key People
1. Rogoff
2. Siegler
3. Case
4. Sternberg
5. Binet
6. Spearman
7. Elkind

Chapter 5
Key Terms and People
1. Reciprocal
2. Collins
3. Parke
4. Baumrind
5. Indulgent
6. Ainsworth
7. Disorganized

Chapter 6
Key Terms
1. Peer
2. Statuses
3. Romantic
4. Affectionate

Key People
1. Berndt
2. Coie
3. Dodge
4. Sherif
5. Coleman
6. Furman

Chapter 7
Key Terms and People
1. Direct
2. Cognitive
3. Erikson
4. Epstein
5. Eccles
6. Kozol
7. Ogbu
8. Hallahan

Chapter 8
Key Terms and Key People
1. Brislin
2. Cross-cultural
3. Acculturation
4. Calvert
5. Lafromboise
6. McLoyd

Chapter 9
Key Terms and Key People
1. Harter
2. Psychosocial
3. Marcia
4. Waterman
5. Individuality
6. Phinney
7. Isolation
8. Emotional
9. Weiss

Chapter 10
Key Terms and Key People
1. Eagly
2. Sadker
3. Kohlberg
4. Identification
5. Maccoby
6. Gender
7. Benn
8. Pleck

Chapter 11
Key Terms and People
1. Feldman
2. Kinsey
3. Date
4. Reinisch

Chapter 12
Key Terms
1. Immanent
2. Heteronomous
3. Care
4. assertion
5. sensitivity
6. judgement
7. character

Key People
1. Walker
2. Hoffman
3. Gilligan
4. Bandura
5. Sigmund Freud
6. Eisenberg
7. Nucci

Chapter 13
Key Terms and People
1. Intrinsic
2. Brophy
3. Attribution
4. Graham
5. Efficacy
6. Ginzberg
7. Personality

Chapter 14
Key Terms
1. Psychopathology
2. Physical
3. Psychological
4. Index
5. Problem
6. Emotion

Key People
1. Sroufe
2. Egeland
3. Achenbach
4. Lazarus
5. Masten
6. Johnston
7. Garabino

Notes

Notes

Notes

Notes

Notes

Notes

Notes

Notes

Notes

Notes

Notes

<u>Notes</u>